The Future of the Past

The Future of the Past

Archaeology in the Twenty-first Century

Eberhard Zangger

Translated from the German edition by Storm Dunlop

Weidenfeld & Nicolson
LONDON

First published in Germany in 1998 by
Schneekluth Verlag GmbH, München

This revised edition published in 2001
By Weidenfeld & Nicolson

A CIP catalogue reference for this book
is available from the British Library

ISBN 0 29764389 4

Typeset by Selwood Systems, Midsomer Norton

Printed in Great Britain by
Butler & Tanner Ltd, Frome and London

Weidenfeld & Nicolson

The Orion Publishing Group Ltd
Orion House
5 Upper Saint Martin's Lane
London WC2H 9EA

Contents

Translator's Note ix
Introduction xiii
Notes on Some Conventions and on References xv

Part One The Doubtful Significance of Natural Catastrophes

1 The Eruption of Thera: An Unwanted Research Project 3
Life and Death on the Volcano 3
A Visit from a Mathematician 7
Excavations in the Library 9
How Archaeology and Geology Found Common Ground 14
Trends in the Spirit of the Age 15
The Eruption of Krakatau 18
In the Realm of King Minos 20
The Theories of Spyridon Marinatos 22
How Does One Start a Tsunami? 25
Outmoded Hypotheses or Unnecessary Hysteria? 28
The Remnants of Former Glory 29
Crete Goes for a Swim 34
But There It Is! 35
Where or What was the Collapse? 37
Irreconcilable Discrepancies 39
The Year of the Eruption 42

2 Earthquake: Was Civilisation Nature's Plaything? 47
The earth quakes in Heraklion 47
A 4000-year-old Town Straight from the Drawing Board 49
How the Sites Defied Earthquakes 53
The Secrets of the Amari Valley 57
Earthquakes Past and Present 62
What Causes Radical Cultural Change? 65

3 Climate: History Cutting Capers 69
Did Climate Change Cause the Upheaval about 1200 BC? 69
Discovery and Investigation of the 'Palace of Nestor' 72
Pollen and the History of Climate 73
The Pylos Regional Archaeology Project 75
Climate or Humans? 79

Part Two Archaeological Research in the Twenty-first Century

4 Techniques: Archaeology Past and Present 85
Aegean Prehistory in Former Times 88
Aspects of Modern Field Archaeology 90
Fieldwork in the Future 91
The Organisation and Requirements of Fieldwork 93
Archaeology Takes Off 98
Down to Earth 100
The Limits of Technology 103

5 Humans and the Environment: A Lost Paradise 107
Vanished Landmarks 107
The Exhaustion of Natural Resources 108
Challenges for Geoarchaeology 111
Existence in the Garden of Eden 113
The Move to Settlement 116
The Untouched World of Albania 121

6 Engineering Knowledge: The Control of Water and Town
Planning 125
Technical Reconstruction 125
Hydraulic Engineering in Mycenaean Times 126
A Granary Becomes a Desert 130
Of Ports and Men 132
Urban Development 135
Mysterious Labyrinths 136
A Magical Dance 139
Future Prospects 141

Part Three Great Riddles of Mediterranean Archaeology

7 Atlantis: The End of a Legend 145
A Gruesome Find 145
Lost in Space and Time 146

Plato's Most Ambitious Project 148
Plato's Role as a Disseminator of Ideas 150
Fiction or Fact? 151
Past and Present Explanations 157
Prehistoric Greece in Plato's Text 158
Critical Translation Errors 161
Features of Atlantis 168
An Independent Opinion 178

8 Troy: The Circle-girt City 181
Back into the Labyrinth 181
The Harbour at Troy 185
On Transporting Ships 188
'The Myth of Troy' 191

9 Western Asia Minor: The Gordian Knot 193
A Caravan Crosses Central Asia Minor 193
The Peculiarities of Asia Minor 195
Progress in the Stone Age 196
The Age of Metals and Fortifications 198
The Hittite Empire 201
World War Zero 205
Where is the Problem? 208

10 The Dark Age: Where the Bull Came from that Bore Europa Away 213
The States of Asia Minor 213
Developments in Phrygia and Lydia 216
Caria: A Rendezvous 218
The Situation in Greece 220
Influences from the East 221
The State of Science 224
The Rise of Etruscan Culture 226
Intermediaries in Time and Space 229

Part Four The Future of the Past

11 Archaeology Yesterday, Today and Tomorrow 237
The Philhellenes' View of the World 237
New Methods of Archaeological Research 244
What Does the Future Hold for Archaeology? 246
Adieu, Thera! 249

Bibliography 255
  The Eruption of Thera 255
  Earthquake 255
  Climate 256
  Techniques 256
  Humans and the Environment 256
  Engineering Knowledge 257
  Atlantis 257
  Troy 258
  Western Asia Minor 258
  The Dark Age 258
  Archaeology Yesterday, Today and Tomorrow 259

Translator's Note

There is considerable confusion in books about the Mediterranean and archaeology over the use of the names 'Thera', 'Santorin' or 'Santorini' for the island in the Cyclades that was once the site of major volcanic activity. Some earlier authors have even tried to use 'Santorin' or 'Santorini' for the pre-eruption island, and 'Thera' for the post-eruption island group. I have used 'Thera' throughout, except in direct quotations from other authors.

The word 'tsunami' is the proper term for the giant waves created by volcanic activity, earthquakes or landslides. They are also known to scientists as 'seismic sea waves', and this term is occasionally employed here. Many older works and modern popular books frequently use the term 'tidal waves', which is incorrect, because the waves have no connection with tides whatsoever. The term is not used here except, once again, in direct quotations.

As sources for the numerous quotations from ancient Greek texts, notably the *Iliad*, the *Odyssey*, together with Plato's *Critias*, *Timaeus*, and *Laws*, standard English-language translations by E.V. and D.C.H. Rieu, and by Benjamin Jowett have been used. In two cases (the paragraph in the *Timaeus* dealing with the location of Atlantis with respect to the Pillars of Heracles, and one in the *Critias* describing the inner city of Atlantis), there do appear to be some minor inconsistencies between the English and German translations from the original Greek text. Regrettably, I am unable to read ancient Greek, but an examination of the context suggests that the words used in the German versions are more appropriate. I have therefore modified the first quotation slightly from the passage in Jowett's version by substituting the word 'sea' for 'Atlantic' and 'bay' for 'harbour'. The second follows the German text, which appears to provide greater detail than Jowett's translation.

I should like to thank Margarita Reifer for her help on several passages, and Ray Perkins and Nicholas Griffin of the Bertrand Russell Internet discussion group for tracking down a quotation that had eluded me.

Storm Dunlop
Chichester

Greek Mainland	Crete	Asia Minor	Troy	
		Iron Age		
				Dark Ages
	1200			*Crisis Years*
Mycenaean Golden Age	1375	New Hittite Kingdom	Troy VIIa	*Knossos destroyed*
	1450	Arzawa		*Minoan Kingdom destroyed*
Rise of Mycenaean Culture	New Palace Period 1700	Old Hittite Kingdom	Troy VI	*Chariots*
Middle Helladic III	First Palace 1900	Assyrian trading states	Hiatus?	*Palaces, writing*
Middle Helladic I–II	Middle Minoan Ia	Early Bronze Age III	Troy IV, V 2100	
Early Helladic II (late)	Early Minoan III 2350	Crisis	Troy III	
Early Helladic II (early)	Early Minoan II	Early Bronze Age II	Hiatus?	
Early Helladic I	3000		Troy I	*Plough, bronze, sailing vessels*
		Late Stone Age		

Introduction

About one hundred years ago, archaeology saw its last great revolution. Previously it had been concerned almost exclusively with ancient Greece and Rome, but then the unexpected discovery of the palaces at Troy, Mycenae and Knossos showed that there were impressive cultures in the countries around the Aegean long before classical antiquity. This was how a new discipline, that of Aegean prehistory, was born. It lives on nowadays in our fascination with the heroic age of Homer, in the tales of Odysseus and the Trojan War, with the superb palaces on Crete and the Greek mainland, as well as with stories of the pioneers such as Heinrich Schliemann and Arthur Evans. These early excavation leaders – in black frock coat, with top hat and stick – directed a horde of assistants, whom they had shift as much earth as possible, in the hope of spectacular discoveries. The interpretation of the finds was also undertaken solely by the patriarchal head of the excavations. Because knowledge of prehistoric cultures was extremely limited, there was nothing else that these pioneers could do other than seek simple answers to their questions. So they put forward the assumption that the end of the palaces and of the 'Golden Age' had been caused by nationwide natural catastrophes. They proposed volcanic eruptions, seismic sea waves, earthquakes and droughts as the reasons for major interruptions in cultural history. In the first part of this book ('The Doubtful Significance of Natural Catastrophes') there is a critical stocktaking of such simple scenarios from the early days of Aegean prehistory, many of which are still widely recognised today. The pioneers' explanatory models also provide the starting point – the basic hypothesis – for further discussion.

The methods and knowledge of modern archaeological research provide an alternative view to these explanations that rely upon a single cause. They are discussed in the second part of this book ('Archaeological Research in the Twenty-first Century'). In many respects field research in Aegean prehistory appears quite different from what it was one hundred years ago. For example, the number of disciplines that take part in archaeological research has markedly increased, and with them the number of experts who contribute to an excavation, among which there are many scientists. In the fields of geology, anthropology, zoology, botany and physics there are now experts who are solely concerned with archaeological problems. Year by year, technical advances provide them with new methods, which give deeper insights into the lifestyle of our forebears. Individual finds – and the *artistic* achievements of past cultures – have thus gradually tended to be pushed into the background in favour of a more general picture. Nowadays, research increasingly attempts to understand societies as a whole, their *technical* achievements, and their relationships to their natural environment.

Following theory and counter-theory, we have an overall synthesis in the third part of this book ('Great Mysteries of Mediterranean Archaeology'). This broadening and greater depth in both overall perspectives and methods is gradually beginning to have an effect on the theories of archaeology itself. Meanwhile, the simple catastrophe theories of the pioneers appear extremely questionable – but not just these alone. Other fundamental concepts, which originated in the early years of archaeology, have also naturally gathered some dust. Instead of supporting these outmoded models longer than necessary, the increase in knowledge in the last few decades may now be used to provide plausible solutions to many archaeological mysteries. Examples of such questions in Mediterranean prehistory, which now appear to be soluble, are covered in the third part of this book.

The gradual opening of Aegean prehistory to other disciplines – in particular, to scientists – has thus ensured that Mediterranean archaeology must now change and find a new, comprehensive basis for research in the twenty-first century. Not just schools of thought, but also the methods, the organisation of projects, the questions posed, the goals that are set, and even training must be considered and brought up to date. These are subjects that are discussed in the final part of this book ('The Future of the Past').

The whole field of research into Aegean prehistory – yesterday, today and tomorrow – combines into a fascinating mixture in which, alongside the scientific method, pragmatism, wishful thinking, love of adventure, romance and changes in the spirit of the times, all get a look in. I shall be happy if I have succeeded in expressing these different aspects of our research.

Eberhard Zangger
Zürich

Notes on some conventions and on references

The terms 'Asia Minor' and 'Anatolia' are here employed interchangeably and should be taken to mean the Asian part of present-day Turkey. In this book, I have altered my approach from that in my earlier works with respect to references. The basic theories have been largely explained recently in specialised publications. Because of this, notes on sources may be omitted in the interests of legibility. The corresponding details are, in the main, to be found in the publications listed under 'Bibliography'.

Part One

The Doubtful Significance
of Natural Catastrophes

The Eruption of Thera:
An Unwanted Research Project

Tell me about the past,
and I will know the future.

CONFUCIUS

Life and Death on the Volcano

The busy town, whose name is unknown, lay on the southern coast of a small island in the warm, sunny Aegean Sea, slightly to the north of Crete. The unsuspecting inhabitants were going about their everyday tasks, and there was a lively bustle in the streets and markets. The fishermen had returned from their morning trip and were offering a plentiful catch of mackerel for sale. The stonemasons' workshops were full of hammers, anvils, mortars, lamps and cutting tools. Through the large windows alongside the doors in the lower storeys of the houses one could see women busy at their looms. In the town's smithy there were not only knives, sickles and saws for sale, but also pots, pans, cans and baking trays. In the upper storeys it was quieter – that was where the living and sleeping rooms were found. The wall-paintings depicted scenes from people's lives: there were shepherds tending their flocks of sheep and goats; and children holding fistfights. Panoramas of distant landscapes showed agile wild animals: deer fleeing for their lives from lions; swallows and wild duck flying over the marshes.

It was one of the inhabitants, who lived in a house on the mountainside high above the town, who first noticed the eruption. One morning he saw stones rolling down the slope and cracks in his house. Not long after, down in the port, a dull rumbling could be heard. At the same time, rocks started to fall from the cliffs. Boulders continually rolled down the slope, and the

3

din gradually increased. More and more cracks and gaps opened up in the earth and the houses. Bubbles of gas rose in the harbour, and the shore began to be affected by white, suffocating fumes from the agitated water. Slowly, at the edge of the harbour basin, it began to boil. The smell of sulphur, like rotten eggs, spread everywhere. The ground continually shook, and gradually collapsed. The restless sea turned red and became lukewarm; dead and half-dead fish were floating in the water. The birds had long since disappeared. Finally, red flames burst from the volcano, followed by black smoke. A gigantic pall of smoke darkened the fiery red sky over the Aegean.

People had been living for generations in this picturesque spot and they had become used to the mountain's moods. Now they were overwhelmed with anxiety. It is not easy for anyone to leave their home, but this time it was absolutely unavoidable. The clouds of smoke increased day by day, and the ceaseless trembling of the ground suggested that even worse was to follow. Common sense said that the town should be abandoned. Calmly, and without panic, the townspeople collected their most valuable portable goods, and arranged all the remaining objects in their houses, confident that they would soon be able to come back. They did not suspect that no one would ever be able to return. People, sheep and goats embarked and were taken to safety – to Mochlos on Crete, for example, or to Rhodes; places that were well-known to the traders. There they remained for some weeks, while back in the home town, more and more violent earthquakes caused stairways and, finally, whole houses to collapse.

Finally the volcano quietened down. Hoping that the worst was over, a few men returned to the island, aiming to start repairs as soon as possible. They carried debris from the streets to rubbish dumps, cleared out the entrances to the buildings, and mixed up mortar to mend the cracks. But the builders had underestimated the volcano. Suddenly, a hail of tiny pumice stones, like grains of rice, started to fall from the sky. They covered the whole island, centimetres thick. Now even the previously undaunted builders had to abandon the island. There was nothing more to rescue – the island would be uninhabitable for an unknown length of time.

An old man, who had spent his whole life in this rather special place, was of no mind to start again anywhere else. Nothing – not even an imminent volcanic eruption – would make him leave his home. If the mountain were starting an entirely new phase of its life, then he would do the same. So he became possibly the only eye-witness of what many scientists and laymen alike consider to have been the greatest natural catastrophe of all time. He did not, however, get the opportunity to tell the world about his impressions. A pyroclastic flow overwhelmed him – a glowing mixture of air and ash that burst out of the crater like a rocket and rushed down the mountainside. Moments later, ashes buried his body, and with him his house and the whole town to which his house belonged, as well as all the other towns on the island.

In the following days and weeks, the volcano spewed out millions of tonnes of molten droplets of magma. As soon as these neared the surface, the pressure on the molten rock decreased and the previously trapped gases escaped – in just the same way as when you open a bottle of lemonade. The degassed droplets of magma hardened in the air and fell from the sky as white ashes, pumice stone, or volcanic bombs. Fine particles were shot high into the stratosphere.

The small port, which had flourished in the second millennium BC on the island of Thera, about 120 kilometres north of Crete, disappeared under ash and pumice. Its buried remains are now known by the name of 'Akrotiri', after a nearby village. The early Akrotiri belonged to the high Minoan culture, the centre of which lay on the largest Aegean island of Crete. At that time, the Middle Bronze Age towns on Crete were graced by giant, multistoreyed palaces full of precious objects, and with overflowing storage rooms. This lasted for hundreds of years, until this advanced civilisation collapsed in the midst of its splendour.

Experts disagree about the effects of the eruption of Thera on the centres of Minoan culture – and on the rest of the world. According to the most widely accepted account, the volcano ejected so much ash that sunlight had difficulty in filtering through the clouds. Years without a summer followed, and even on a global scale, the climate became cooler. A rain of ash fell over Crete, burying the previously fertile fields and setting fire to the woods. Fire also consumed the towns, earthquakes shook building foundations and caused houses and settlements to collapse.

Many researchers assume that, before the eruption, Thera consisted of a circular mountain island that rose more than 1600 metres above the sea. After the volcano had erupted ashes for weeks on end, a gaping cavity was created beneath the surface. Then the roof of this now-emptied magma chamber gave way, and the volcano collapsed. Where a mountain had towered before, now a bottomless pit opened up into the Earth's interior. In an instant, seawater crashed into the cavity, filling it to the brim. This sudden rush of an inconceivably enormous mass of water set the whole Mediterranean surging to and fro. A gigantic wave, two hundred metres high, burst out of the collapsed volcano. With the speed of a rocket, it raged over the shores of the Aegean, towering ever higher as it did so. It broke upon Crete a few minutes later as a foaming white mountain, over three hundred metres high – higher than the tallest building in Europe. The water surged as many as fifty kilometres inland. The Minoan palaces, the product of hundreds of years of tradition and craftsmanship, were submerged by the flood in just a few seconds.

According to the American oceanographer James Mavor, the destructive power of the volcanic eruption was comparable with atomic warfare: 'Hundreds of thousands of people in the towns, ports and villages on the Aegean islands, and also on the Greek and Turkish mainlands, may have lost their lives.' According to the American palaeontologist Charles Pellegrino, the day of the eruption of Thera changed the course of world history. The whole of the eastern Mediterranean was in turmoil. The Minoan high culture was not the only one that fell; the Hittite empire in central Asia Minor also collapsed, and mass migrations of people ensued. Pellegrino even maintains that, if it were not for this volcanic eruption, the Minoan inhabitants of Crete would have sent expeditions to the Moon before the birth of Christ, and founded colonies on Alpha Centauri.

All that remains of Thera is a broken ring of islands about ten kilometres across, forming the southernmost group of islands in the Cyclades. On the inner side of the largest and sickle-shaped island, the cliffs rise almost vertically to a height of 250 metres above the sea. In antiquity, this group of islands was known, from its shape, as Strongyle ('round'); later Kalliste ('most beautiful') because of its appearance; then Thera by its settlers (after 'Theras' in Sparta); and finally it was given the name 'Santorini' by Venetian traders, from a chapel to Saint Irene to be found there, where the Italians blessed their ships.

All that remains today of the stupendous natural events are the legends – tales under various names that emerge in the earliest documents of human history and that all, basically, hark back to the same event: an inconceivable natural catastrophe in the second century before Christ. Many experts believe that the eruption of Thera is even to be found in the Bible, in connection with the plagues that affected the land of Egypt and caused the exodus of the Israelites; as well as in Greek mythology as Deucalion's flood; and in ancient literature as the fall of Atlantis. All these legends may thus describe one and the same event: the volcanic eruption of Thera around 1500 BC.

A Visit from a Mathematician

About 3500 years after this event, I received a letter from Melbourne: a professor of applied mathematics wanted me to become involved in a current research project. The aim of this research was to improve the accuracy of the calculation of the sizes of the waves that were created by the eruption of Thera. Joseph J. Monaghan – that was the researcher's name – had developed computer models that simulated the development of the waves produced by volcanic eruptions, taking into account the relief of the sea floor, the lie of the coastline, and also the topography of the affected land areas. The project had reached the stage in which geological and archaeological evidence of destruction by waves was required to calibrate and test the computer models. For this reason Professor Monaghan was looking for an expert in Aegean geological/archaeological research. He wanted to visit me and discuss details of the study in person.

A few weeks later we walked together along the promenade by Lake Zurich. It was May, and probably the most beautiful day of 1996. The mountain wind from the northern slopes of the Alps caused the mountains to seem near enough to touch. Rarely had there been such a crowd at the lake. Clowns, drummers, open-air entertainers and refreshment kiosks provided relaxation and sustenance.

Joe Monaghan was in his early fifties, tall and unusually athletic. He combined the contented, well-balanced lifestyle of many Australians with an extreme courtesy developed during many years of research in Cambridge. Athletic, uncomplicated, friendly and outstandingly intelligent – no one could wish for a better partner for a research project.

The main occupation of mathematicians is so demanding mentally that they are only able to carry out their investigations for a few hours a day. So they have a lot of time free to devote to other things: sport, for example, or politics. For this reason, I have always found mathematicians to be pleasant associates; like Lorenz Magaard from Honolulu, who spent two years on calculations of Rossby waves, only to discover that his problem was not mathematically soluble, and then met a colleague at a conference who told him that he himself had also struggled fruitlessly for two years on the same problem. Or Fritz Büsching, who, during our mutual taxi drive across Sinai, used the enforced emergency stop at El Aresh caused by forces beyond our control – namely a stone that shattered the windscreen – to stand for hours on the shore, observing the breaking waves, and repeatedly saying 'You see the small white caps on the waves? I can calculate their movement!' Or

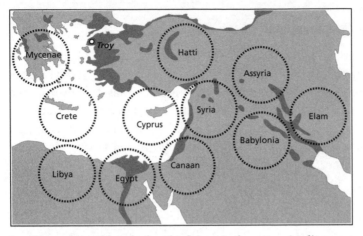

Late Bronze Age circles of cultural influence in the eastern Mediterranean; the dark shaded areas indicate fertile arable land

Malcolm Green, who punctuated his lectures in Cambridge, overburdened with mathematical formulae, with transparencies of giant waves, which he himself had 'ridden' on his surfboard.

Joe Monaghan was really keen for me to contribute to his project, but I was already involved in several research projects and had always kept well clear of Thera, both in the geographical and in the figurative sense. To my mind, so many scientists had already dabbled in investigating the volcanic eruption that it did not really seem capable of yielding any original results.

Naturally I described my thoughts to my visitor in detail. But his project was already in full swing; he desperately needed a scientist with experience in the field – and he wanted me. Why did he make it so difficult for me to say no? Why, indeed, had he come all the way from Australia to Zurich, even though his trip also involved a teaching commitment in Germany? If there had only been some way of setting him at fault! Like many scientists, I know when invisible lettering on something seems to advise: 'Just say: No!' But this time it was hopeless.

My personal criterion for becoming involved in a project – which I may best describe as a scientific commandment – was that I would not only undertake 'sure things', by which I mean projects the success of which is guaranteed in advance. After all, I am a researcher and not a politician – and certainly not a diplomat!

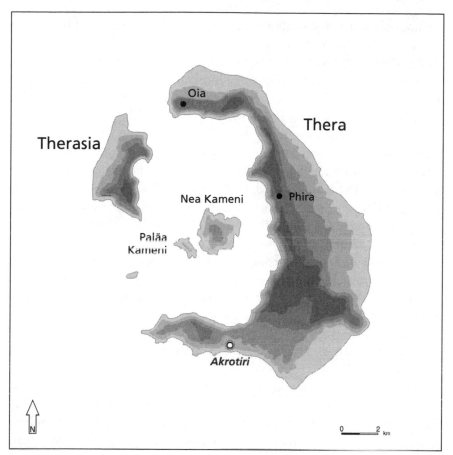

The Thera island group

Excavations in the Library

So I joined the large group of researchers who had become involved with the effects of what was apparently the greatest natural catastrophe in the history of humanity. But where does one start such an undertaking? At least Thera was such a well-known and clearly defined archaeological problem that publications dealing with the volcanic eruption and its effects had their own keyword in my bibliographic database. The computer threw up no less than 182 references in response to 'Thera'. But where should I go from there? Luckily, the references could be sorted by their year of publication and, suddenly, the very first had a name: 'Fouqué, Ferdinand (1879): *Santorin et ses éruptions*. G. Masson, Paris. 440 pages.' A moment later, my computer was informed by its big brother at the Swiss Technical College's computing centre that I could examine the book the next morning.

The next day I was standing on the uppermost floor of the old building of the University Library, in front of a twin-leafed wooden door carrying the inscription 'Old printed works'. I impatiently waited for my ring to be answered and to be let in. One of my favourite working places is hidden behind that door. Whoever goes there is treated with the same degree of respect as the precious volumes themselves. How many 'discoveries' had I already made in those rooms! In studying scientific publications from previous centuries I had gained the impression that the boundaries of our knowledge have hardly changed. Our contributions to knowledge roughly correspond to what becomes lost over the same period of time. How much may be learned today, simply by reading what had long been known in the nineteenth century!

The works of Monsieur Fouqué looked like being promising reading. Obviously only a few modern experts had read his book in the original. So I was eager to see what lay before me – and I was not disappointed. Fouqué's monograph turned out to be a masterpiece, a folio with wonderful hand-coloured illustrations. But the content was even better than the pre-sentation. It seemed as if I had found the best possible introduction to the material.

When the building work for the Suez Canal began in 1859, enormous amounts of hydraulic cement were required. For thousands of years it has been known that such a cement may be prepared from a mixture of lime and volcanic ash or pulverised pumice stone. As early as the time of the Roman Empire, volcanic pozzolano earth had been quarried to be used for the internal coating of cisterns and aqueducts. For the construction of the Suez Canal, they turned to the ash layers on Thera. They provided the right material, the so-called Santorin earth, in utterly inexhaustible quantities. In addition, Thera was cost-effectively reached by ship. To work the layers of ash and pumice stone, quarries were established at various points around the islands. These were mainly on the western and southern coast of the island of Therasia, and in a small bay on the main island. During the work on Therasia, completely unexpectedly, worked stone blocks were revealed under metre-thick layers of ash. It was immediately obvious to the workers that they were dealing with walls that had been laid by human hands. After this discovery, the owner of the quarry and a friend who was a doctor began to uncover the remains of the building.

On 26 January 1866, the Thera volcano once again began to spew forth fire – the detailed description of the earlier eruption given at the beginning of this chapter is drawn from eye-witness accounts of this later event. The promised eruption led to a great deal of interest in intellectual circles and a whole series of scientists – above all from Germany – made their way to the group of islands. One of them, Karl von Seebach, described the striking mood that prevailed when observing the eruption at night:

> The sight of the eruption's events at night is unceasingly superb. For hours on end one is held enthralled, half delighted, half trembling, surrendering oneself to the combined influence of the splendid fiery display and the rumbling thunder of the escaping gases.

Another, Karl Wilhelm von Fritsch, maintained that Thera had long been known as a geological curiosity:

> The name of the Greek island is, for natural scientists, inevitably linked with the idea of a mysterious elevation of the sea floor, for which Santorini has become a classical locality in almost all geological textbooks.

Many ancient authors, including Strabo, Seneca, Plutarch, Pausanias, Justin, Eusebius and Pliny, mention the island in their writings. Eruptions of the volcano since 197 BC have been recorded and described. Fouqué meticulously lists all these ancient sources. He was sent by the Paris Académie des Sciences to follow the course of the eruption in great detail. He wanted to obtain further data during this trip to support his theories about the course of volcanic eruptions. He held the view that the different stages of a volcanic eruption could be determined by the chemical analysis of the corresponding gases that escaped.

In reading Fouqué's work, I was particularly interested in when he first realised from the buried houses on the island that he was dealing with the remains of a prehistoric, and thus preclassical, settlement. Obviously what I wanted to know was who got the idea that the collapse of the volcanic cone at the end of the eruption took place during the Minoan age. After all, the waves produced by the collapse were central to our investigation.

With Ferdinand Fouqué I'd come to the right place. Although his speciality was volcanology, he also made expert observations in the fields of botany, zoology and anthropology, and also immediately undertook additional archaeological investigations. It was he who discovered the skeleton of the old man that had remained on the island. Because he found many remnants of olive wood in the prehistoric ruins on Therasia and at

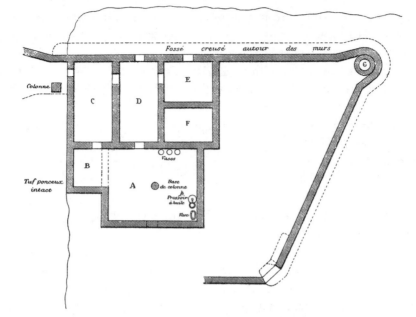

A house excavated by Fouqué at the southern point of Therasia

Akrotiri, he concluded that the islands were once wooded and that the inhabitants had practised agriculture and animal husbandry, and not wine-growing as nowadays. He noted timber pillars in the walls of the houses, which in his view were designed to alleviate the destructive effects of mild earthquakes. On the basis of the petrographic composition of the prehistoric pottery, which Fouqué ground so thinly that he could examine the mineral components through a transmission microscope, he determined that practically all of the pottery found in the excavations had been produced on Thera itself. This observation is still valid today. However, individual vases showed that Akrotiri had connections with Cyprus, and two small gold rings offered proof that there were trading relations with the nearby mainland – Fouqué suspected with Asia Minor, because certain of the rivers there were renowned in antiquity for being rich in gold.

The volcanologist determined that the vases, tools and buildings in the buried settlement were older than the remains from classical times that had also been found on Thera. The eruption must thus have been long before the oldest historically established eruption of 197 BC, and Fouqué concluded that the settlement dated back to the second millennium BC, that the enormous eruption must have taken place around 1500 BC, and that, at that time, people had lived on the island for hundreds of years. All these

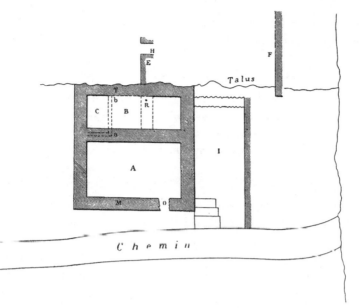

Remains of a building discovered in an eroded gully in Akrotiri

conclusions are still valid today. The pioneering contribution of Fouqué was immense. He was able to determine that some thousand years before classical antiquity 'a civilised population with many artistic skills existed on the island, and who were eyewitnesses and victims of the natural disaster'.

Of course, not all his theories got to the heart of the matter. His main concern, that of being able to predict the course of a volcanic eruption from the chemical composition of the gases that were released, brought him nothing but scorn and derision. Based on his analysis, he officially predicted the end of the eruptions far too early and, naturally, all the newspapers were only too ready to announce the expected end of the danger. When the strength of the eruptions increased – and indeed continued for yet another year – public confidence in the accuracy of scientific forecasts was badly shaken.

Another of Fouqué's conclusions has had more disastrous consequences and repercussions – even down to the present day. Because the geological layers on Thera, including the pumice deposits from the prehistoric eruption, are exposed on the inner side of the island in a vertical section, the geologist concluded that before the Minoan eruption a volcanic cone existed in the centre of the island, and that the modern bowl-shaped hollow – the so-called 'caldera' – was created either by the disruption or by the collapse of this volcanic cone. He supported the view that the collapse

of the caldera must have been a natural catastrophe of enormous proportions, and have occurred shortly after the eruption around 1500 BC:

> But it is extremely probable that both events [eruption and collapse] –
> between which no other geological events can be established – followed
> closely upon one another, which means that it is difficult, if not impossible,
> to understand how two such enormously powerful phenomena could have
> occurred at the same place independently of one another.

Fouqué began his investigations on Thera at about the same time as the
excavations at Pompeii – which were the first systematic excavations in the
history of archaeology. Pompeii, the Roman port on the Bay of Naples, was
also the victim of a volcanic eruption. The catastrophe of 24 August 79 AD
killed 18,000 people. Nowadays, Pompeii and Thera are among the most
famous, best preserved, and most visited excavations in the world. When
one thinks of their significance for the history of research into antiquity, it
is not surprising that archaeologists have referred to natural disasters as
important triggers for breaks in the history of culture.

This important question of how far natural catastrophes, as we understand them today, could actually be the causes of fundamental breaks in
cultural history lies at the very centre of my interest. It cannot be denied
that whole towns have been the victims of volcanic eruptions and earthquakes, but have such sudden natural events also influenced the course of
human cultures to such an extent that, as people have maintained about
the Thera eruption, it was: 'the day that changed the course of world
history'?

How Archaeology and Geology Found Common Ground

While Fouqué was measuring water temperatures and determining gas
compositions on Thera, a German/Russian/American businessman and
multimillionaire, who, in a sort of mid-life crisis, was seeking a new aim in
life, happened to be travelling through Greece. The man's name was Heinrich Schliemann and, on the eastern shores of the Aegean, on an incon-
spicuous hill a long way from any large town, he found what he was seeking.

Schliemann was searching for ancient Troy. He not only found the ruins
of this legendary city but, at the same time, discovered many forgotten
civilisations, and thus, in the twinkling of an eye, he established the basis
for a new research discipline: that of Aegean prehistory. I can still remember

being taught in school how Schliemann had expressed his intention of discovering Troy as early as the age of seven; how he had subsequently learned two dozen languages and acquired a fortune solely to be able to make his childhood dream eventually come true; how he then searched for Troy at a spot where no one suspected it might lie and how, after he had found and excavated the city, he was drawn to Greece, where he uncovered the Lion Gate at Mycenae – by far his greatest discovery according to our teacher at the time. As a schoolboy, those achievements made a deep impression on me. In particular, I admired Schliemann for suspecting that the legendary city of Troy lay where no one else had expected it to be. How had he done that?

When I later became familiar scientifically with Schliemann's work, I realised that what we had been taught in school was a modern-day myth. Schliemann certainly did not, as a child, decide to search for Troy. There is not a single indication that he was the slightest bit concerned with antiquity before he was 47 years old. And even then his interest in archaeology arose rather from a general fashion: during the years of Germany's rapid industrial expansion it was a sign of good taste among the educated classes to be interested in antiquity.

In any case, Schliemann did not discover the Lion Gate, because it had been known for a long time and was exposed when he first visited Mycenae. He did not discover Troy either. During his visit to the region, he did search for the remains of the ancient city, but in the wrong place; in fact, precisely where the majority of people at that time expected Troy to be. Schliemann was about to leave the area empty-handed, but he missed his steamer. While he was waiting, he met the British consul for the area, Frank Calvert. Calvert told him about the theory of a Scottish geologist called Charles MacLaren, who maintained that Troy lay on a hill called Hisarlik. Calvert, who, by chance, happened to own part of this hill, had already asked the Royal Society in London some years before for support in mounting an archaeological excavation – unfortunately with no success. After talking to Calvert, Schliemann left the Troas without, apparently, even having seen the Hisarlik mound and the possible site of Troy. But he had found his new aim in life.

Trends in the Spirit of the Age

In the eighteenth century some scholars searched for a model and an identity for the Europe that was then forming and, in doing so, turned to classical Greece and ancient Rome. Henceforward, these epochs, two thousand years in the past, would come to serve more and more as the core of a role model for modern European society. The goal of this pre-occupation with the history of art and philology was the discovery of the roots of western culture and the establishing of bridges between antiquity and modern times. An important part of this view of the world was the school of thought that western civilisation sprang from a cradle in ancient Greece. This dogma was based on the medieval interpretation of the origin of the world and mankind, which had its origins in a literal interpretation of the history of creation found in the Old Testament. God had created the world, and mankind in less than a week. The Anglo-Irish Archbishop James Ussher, for example, believed that the exact date of Creation could be determined, and in 1654 he calculated that God had created the Earth on 26 October 4004 BC. A later Father of the church even refined this date, in that he specified the exact time: it must have been nine o'clock in the morning. 'An appropriate time', as my tutor Professor Tjeerd H. van Andel used to say. Some few thousands of years later, European high culture must have appeared in classical Greece, just as suddenly as the Earth came into existence.

Only a few years after Archbishop Ussher, natural scientists recognised that geological strata reflected developments over time. In 1669, the Roman Catholic bishop Nicholaus Steno – later to be beatified – articulated the fundamental law of stratigraphical geology and archaeology, whereby younger deposits always lie above older ones. Finally, the French naturalist Georges-Louis Leclerc, Comte de Buffon, first formulated the concept that the laws of physics, chemistry and biology observed today must also have applied to processes in the past, and that the geological sequence is the result of such processes: 'To determine what happened in the past or will happen in the future, we only need to study the present.' This 'uni-formitarianism' was subsequently extended by the Scottish geologist James Hutton. He recognised that geology depends upon basic physical laws, and he thus elevated it to the status of a science. His groundwork eventually led to an understanding of human evolution and the history of culture.

Between 1822 and 1841, the German geologist Karl Ernst Adolf von Hoff published a five-volume work *Geschichte der durch Überlieferung nach-gewiesen natürlichen Veränderungen der Erdoberfläche* (*History of Natural Changes of the Earth's Surface as Indicated by Tradition*), in which, by means of historical sources from the previous two thousand years, he reconstructed the slow, but continual development of the landscape. In this work, von Hoff laid the foundation for more geoarchaeology. The Scottish geologist Charles Lyell finally combined the disciplines of geology and archaeology in his book *The Antiquity of Man* (1863). Similar works followed, including *Man and Nature, or Physical Geography as Modified by Human Action* by G.P. Marsh in 1864.

The interest in the mutual relationship between ancient civilisations and their environment also sprang initially from geology. Classically trained archaeologists specialised in the cultural achievements of the past. They saw the landscape as a sort of background – like the gaudy backdrop for a play in which ancient heroes contemplated or achieved tremendous feats 'in quiet simplicity and noble greatness'.

Around 1870, there was a general upheaval in politics, industry and commerce, art, and science, which indeed also encouraged the achievements of Fouqué and Schliemann. The industrial revolution had overtaken Central Europe, and Germany had changed from an agrarian to an industrial state. In France the Third Republic had been established, and the New Reich in Germany. Dostoyevski wrote *The Idiot*, Tolstoy *War and Peace*, Jules Verne *Around the World in Eighty Days*, Karl Marx *Das Kapital*, Charles Darwin *The Descent of Man*, and Richard Wagner composed *Die Meistersinger von Nürnberg*. In art, Impressionism, Naturalism, Realism and Art Nouveau were soon on an equal footing. In France alone, artists such as Auguste Rodin, Edgar Degas, Claude Monet, Auguste Renoir, Édouard Manet, Paul Cézanne and Honoré Daumier were at the peak of their careers.

In 1869, on his way to the festivities for the opening of the Suez Canal, the German Crown Prince Friedrich visited the Greek King George in Athens. The later German Kaiser Friedrich III – who had the historian and archaeologist Ernst Curtius as his tutor – travelled to Athens again to suggest to the Greek government that, together, they should revive the spirit of antiquity, in the form of excavations at Olympia. A few years later, the Greek government gave its approval of this plan. Ernst Curtius was appointed as the first director of the excavations. His work at Olympia was, after that at Pompeii, the second, systematically undertaken, field study in the history of archaeology.

The waves that had been created by Darwin's book *On the Origin of Species*, eventually caused a final breach with creation mythology, as far as the sciences were concerned. The study of antiquity went through a similar process almost at the same time. After Schliemann's excavations at Troy, Mycenae, Tiryns and Orchomenos, the school of thought that held that western culture arose in Greek antiquity could no longer be supported.

Researchers discovered more and more remains of much older cultures in the lands around the Aegean. This opened up several thousand years of cultural history, which meant that scientific study was essential. These newly discovered epochs included periods in which writing was unknown, artistic objects were rare and architecture was largely unspectacular. The classical disciplines in the study of antiquity (philology, art history and architecture) no longer sufficed for research into prehistoric cultures.

Archaeology was thus forced to expand its methodology. Instead of exclusively searching for documents, art objects and the remains of buildings, archaeologists developed an interest in the everyday objects of earlier, simpler cultures. The branch of science dealing with pre- and early history was born. Research into prehistory and early historical times is primarily concerned with the broad span of time between the production of the first stone tools, some 2.5 million years ago, and the beginning of classical antiquity. Within the framework of this research, an institutional basis was found for the investigation that was already being carried out into the mutual relationship between humans and the landscape.

The Eruption of Krakatau

Just seven years after the appearance of Fouqué's monograph on Thera, the greatest volcanic catastrophe of modern times occurred, the effects of which were the first to be captured by scientific observations and to be disseminated worldwide by modern communications. After a two-hundred-year period of repose, the 2000-metre-high volcano of Krakatau in the Sunda Strait between Java and Sumatra erupted again. It produced numerous enormous explosions, the strongest of which were audible in Singapore and northern Australia. The climax of the eruptive activity came on 26 August 1883. What exactly occurred that day is still a subject of controversy between experts. For two-and-a-half days complete darkness reigned over an area of eighty kilometres in radius. Subsequently the volcano became dormant, but it had been reduced to less than half its earlier height and less than one-third of its previous area. In total, it had blasted eighteen cubic kilometres of ash into the air, reaching heights of thirty kilometres. The ash in the atmosphere spread across the whole world, and caused spectacular twilight effects. These could still be seen some three years later.

Although the island of Krakatau itself was uninhabited, the event claimed more than 36,000 lives. During the eruption, immense waves, known as 'tsunamis', were repeatedly created, the largest of which reached a height of thirty to forty metres. These surges devastated 165 coastal settlements in Java and Sumatra. A gunboat belonging to the Dutch navy was carried almost three kilometres inland.

The name 'tsunami' comes from the Japanese, and means 'harbour wave'. Tsunamis are waves that have been caused by the movement of large masses of submarine material, as a result of earthquakes, landslides or volcanic eruptions. Their velocity amounts to several hundred kilometres per hour. In the Pacific (where most of them occur), they reach, on average, 700 kilometres per hour. However, because the distance between two wave crests may be a few hundred kilometres, and the wave height in the open sea is just a few decimetres, tsunamis frequently go unnoticed on board ships. It is only when the surges encounter the continental shelf that they begin to mount up. Frequently the arrival of the wave is preceded by a retreat of the sea, lasting several minutes. The seafloor along the coast is suddenly dry. Fish flap in the mud, and ships are stranded. In many cases this extraordinary sight has attracted sightseers, who have then paid for their curiosity with their lives. In Hawaii, where tsunamis occur relatively frequently, the rule is that whenever there is an unnatural withdrawal of the water, you flee as fast as possible towards high land.

Eye-witnesses tell that the arrival of each tsunami is accompanied by a rumbling sound, which has been compared with the noise of countless goods trains. The noise is caused by the boulders that the wave drags across the sea floor. An individual tsunami may smash into the shore as a wall of water, but more frequently it occurs as a simple increase in the height of the sea. As far as its destructive power is concerned, the shape of the wave is immaterial. The devastation mainly occurs when the water drains back. These water movements literally appear to ignore the laws of physics: the sea actually boils. The turmoil causes a degree of destruction that resembles the power of an atomic bomb. Even the height of a tsunami is irrelevant as far as its destructive power is concerned. A two-metre-high wave causes comparable destruction in the affected area to that caused by a much larger tsunami, although higher waves naturally damage larger swathes of the coast. The area affected at any one time remains sharply defined. If anyone finds themselves only slightly above the wave's high-water mark, they remain unharmed. Generally, several tsunamis occur rapidly one after the other, and the first is not always the largest. Between the wave-crests the water drains back well below the normal level of the sea.

Tsunamis caused by volcanic eruptions are generally less frequent and, as a rule, not as great as the waves caused by earthquakes and submarine landslides. In the Mediterranean, only two per cent of historically established tsunamis were caused by volcanic eruptions. Probably the most important mechanism that operates during volcanic eruptions is the impact of masses of ejected volcanic material on the water. The result is that tsunamis occur not once – as would happen with the collapse of a caldera – but may, as in the eruption of Krakatau, extend over several days and, in doing so, reach very differing heights.

After the catastrophe at Krakatau, in 1885, the French scholar Auguste Nicaise used Plato's account of Atlantis by way of comparison and drew parallels between the natural disaster described there and the events on the islands of Krakatau and Thera. Because at that time there had been no excavations on Crete, the advanced Minoan civilisation was still unknown. Despite this, Nicaise was perfectly familiar with the level of culture of the Minoans through the work of Fouqué. He referred to their highly developed agriculture, and described the cultivation of pulses, rye and barley; their pastoral agriculture with the herding of sheep and goats; and their handicrafts, including the working of gold, wall-painting and wheel pottery. Finally, he came to the conclusion that natural catastrophes might be responsible for the declines that repeatedly occurred throughout the history of human culture. Since then, Thera has been regarded as proof that natural disasters may lead to the collapse of whole cultures.

In the Realm of King Minos

Shortly after Nicaise had published these ideas, Aegean prehistory entered its golden age. After the end of the Turkish occupation of Crete in 1898, many excavations were started at various points on the island. Arthur Evans directed the project at the palace of Knossos, Italian archaeologists dug at the palace of Phaistos on the southern coast, Greek and French researchers exposed the palace at Malia, and American scientists investigated the settlements at Gournia, Vassiliki, Pseira and Mochlos. Simultaneously, archaeologists took over the excavations that Schliemann had begun at Troy and Mycenae.

Arthur Evans began his excavations at Knossos in 1900. Five years later he introduced the chronological system for Aegean prehistory that remains in use today. In this, the Bronze Age (c. 300–1200 BC) is divided into three main phases: Early, Middle, and Late. These three periods of time are again each split into three subdivisions, which are differentiated by the Roman numerals I–III. In devising this chronology, Evans followed the customary practice for Egypt of dividing the periods into Old, Middle, and Late Kingdoms. He called the prehistoric culture on Crete 'Minoan', after the legendary King Minos, who was mentioned by the Greek historian Herodotus. Evans assumed that, beginning about 3000 BC, this civilisation had gradually developed to a much higher degree of complexity.

For travellers who visit the ruins on Crete, the chronology introduced by Evans is not very helpful – many experts also feel that it could be improved. The Greek archaeologist Nikolas Platon therefore proposed another system, various versions of which are used nowadays. According to this, the Bronze Age in Crete is divided into the Pre-Palace Period (3000–2000 BC), the First Palace Period (2000–1700 BC), the New Palace Period (1700–1450 BC), and the Post-Palace Period (1450–1050 BC). During the Pre-Palace Period the prehistoric culture on Crete did not fulfil the criteria that we generally associate with the concept of 'civilisation'. There was, as yet, no significantly structured society, no division between urban centres and an agrarian population, and no knowledge of writing. The cultural level on Crete corresponded with that found in other regions of the eastern Mediterranean.

Between the third and second millennia BC, Cretan society underwent fundamental political and economic changes; palace administration was introduced. The many storage vessels in the palaces show how great an economic importance this central administration had assumed. Olive oil, wine, barley and figs from the whole of the region were transported to the palace, where they were kept in the storehouses. In return, the palace provided the agricultural and craft population with protection and earnings. Apart from these economic and political activities, the palaces also served religious functions. The aristocracy probably increased their reputation and authority not only by exerting control over politics and trade, but also by assuming responsibility for religion.

In the First Palace Period, Crete was obviously divided into many small units or city-states, which had hardly any contact with one another. Possibly the individual city-states on Crete had closer relations with sister states on the surrounding mainland than with their immediate neighbours.

Around 1700 BC, most of the Cretan cities were destroyed by fire. Following this destruction, the island saw a new political organisation. In the subsequent, New Palace Period, between 1700 and 1450 BC, Knossos appears to have exerted centralised power over the kingdom. This was the time of the greatest flowering of Minoan culture, and also the time in which the palaces were established, the ruins of which may still be seen on Crete. Because the excavations show no distinct indications of a military nature in Minoan society – as are characteristically found in Mycenaean Greece in the form of daggers, swords, helmets, shields and, above all, as massive fortifications – Evans described the Minoan culture as 'peace-loving'. This is, however, in contrast to the historical tradition, because Herodotus (1.171) stated that King Minos 'was a great conqueror and prospered in his wars'.

The peak of Minoan culture ended around 1450 BC (with the 'Late Minoan Period IB' or 'LM IB'). Most of the centres in Crete, including the palaces at Malia, Phaistos and Knossos, went up in flames and were eventually abandoned. Only Knossos was exempt for a while. Around 1375 BC, however, this centre was also destroyed. Because many of the settlements showed signs of violence, the excavators unanimously came to the conclusion that the destruction was caused by enemy attacks, and since Crete was eventually strongly exposed to the influence of Mycenaean Greece, the natural assumption was that the assailants had come from there.

The Theories of Spyridon Marinatos

Although at the time of Fouqué's work, geology and archaeology were still closely related, at the end of the 19th century and the beginning of the 20th, the two disciplines became estranged. Individual specialised fields developed in the sciences and quantitative measurements came to the fore. Geology was no longer regarded as a philosophically motivated enquiry into the history of the Earth, but as an instrument for prospecting mineral deposits, which meant it lost its high scientific status. The newly born study of prehistory developed in the opposite direction: in English-speaking countries archaeology as a whole became part of social anthropology; in Europe it became annexed to classical archaeology. Henceforward, anyone who studied prehistory had to be concerned, as in classical archaeology, with Latin, ancient Greek and the history of art.

When Thera erupted again between 1925 and 1928, a comprehensive interdisciplinary scientific account, such as Fouqué had furnished, was hardly conceivable. This time a German team of experts, led by the Berlin geologist Hans Reck, conducted the research on the spot. Reck's three-volume publication of the investigations carried out on Thera is highly specialised, and only understandable and readable to geological scientists. Yet it is also of value as a pioneering scientific work. Reck was particularly interested in the mechanisms of caldera formation, which is still the subject of controversy among experts today.

Whereas Fouqué had assumed that calderas were created through the explosion of volcanoes, the German geologists insisted that what was involved was 'an area of collapse of the roof of an exhausted [magma] chamber'. They agreed, however, with Fouqué, in that, in the middle of the second millennium BC, a 'paroxysmal eruption' occurred after a long, volcanically quiet phase. Finally, the caldera collapse took place.

The collapse of the caldera must inevitably have been accompanied by major tremors and earth movements, yet signs of such effects are completely absent for the eruption in Minoan times. Reck noted that in the Minoan eruption 'neither the pumice explosion nor the formation of the caldera was accompanied by powerful ground tremors'. This should have led him to the conclusion that the caldera could not have been formed after the Minoan eruption, because then the deposited layers of pumice would have been disturbed. But they have not been. They lie like icing sugar over the range of hills. In addition, most of the prehistoric buildings have remained unscathed and, where there is evidence of earthquake activity, the damage occurred during the early phase of the Minoan eruption – yet a caldera collapse could only have occurred at the end of the eruption.

The fact that Reck and his colleagues did not interpret these phenomena correctly is probably because of the specialised orientation of their work. Because the geologists were, above all, directing their attention to the mechanisms of caldera formation, they appear to have had little interest in historical and archaeological questions. Archaeological aspects were, however, soon to play a central part in the discussion.

Reck's report appeared in 1936. In the following year, the Dutch geologist Jan Schoo published a comprehensive article in the historical journal *Mnemosyne*, in which he, first, linked the eruption of Thera with that of Krakatau; second, assumed that during the Minoan eruption giant waves caused a 'terrible disaster'; and, third, suggested that these contributed to the collapse of Minoan culture:

> If the catastrophe occurred at the peak of the Minoan culture, then we need to consider to what extent traces of this disaster have been revealed on Crete itself by the comprehensive excavations carried out there.

At the time, the director of the largest archaeological museum in Crete, and the head of various excavations, was Spyridon Marinatos. Immediately after Schoo's articles appeared, he began to give lectures on the fall of Minoan culture as the result of the Bronze Age eruption of Thera. As early as 1937, he spoke on this topic at a history congress in Istanbul and, eventually, in 1938, at Reck's own university in Berlin. Subsequently, Marinatos spent three months at the universities of Utrecht and Leyden, where he devoted his attention to the effects of the eruption of Krakatau.

In the following year, his significant article 'The Volcanic Destruction of Minoan Crete' appeared in the English journal *Antiquity*. In it, Marinatos took up the ideas of Nicaise and Schoo – without, however, mentioning either of these experts – and also adopted Fouqué's theory in which the eruption in Minoan times had 'blown away' the centre of the island. After what was, in his opinion, 'the greatest [eruption] that can be proved historically', all that remained, according to Marinatos, was 'the greatest and most imposing caldera in the world'. In his view, tsunamis – as in the Krakatau eruption – as well as 'a series of violent earthquakes' accompanied the volcanic eruption and the caldera collapse.

Marinatos assumed that the catastrophe around 1450 BC (at the end of LM IB) affected the whole of Crete at the same time. He remarked 'Nor can we believe in an invasion from abroad' and therefore concluded that the only possible explanation remaining was a natural disaster. Arthur Evans had argued similarly, and had later suggested earthquakes as the cause of the collapse. Marinatos, on the other hand, pointed out that earthquakes on Crete cause only local effects, because there is no extensive fault zone on the island. The collapse of Minoan culture must therefore be ascribed to some other cause. Because the eruption of Thera was regarded as clearly the greatest historically known natural event, the obvious suggestion was that this natural catastrophe should be seen as the trigger for the collapse of the Minoan kingdom.

Marinatos made the comparison with the eruption of Krakatau and maintained that because the Thera island group was about four times as large in area (83 km^2) as the Krakatau group (22.8 km^2), the explosion of Thera and the tsunamis that it created must have been correspondingly larger. In the Krakatau eruption, the destruction extended for a radius of 100 to 150 km. On Crete, 120 km to the south of Thera, similar or even worse devastation must have occurred. Marinatos maintained that all the settlements on the coast must have been destroyed by tsunamis. These are supposed to have displaced massive stone foundations and buried a rectangular pit under pumice stone at Amnisos, the harbour for Knossos, as well as leaving dozens of votive tables piled on top of one another at

Niru Chani, the nearby residence of a Minoan noble family. According to Marinatos the Minoan palace at Malia 'was almost certainly destroyed by the waves'. In his view, the volcanic eruption must have caused strong earthquakes, which destroyed the palaces at Knossos and Phaistos that lay on higher ground.

According to Marinatos, these natural catastrophes dealt a blow to the Minoan civilisation from which it never recovered. The major part of the population fled in fear from the island, which sank into insignificance. Finally, the Mycenean people from the Greek mainland fell upon a weakened Crete.

The editors of *Antiquity* added a postscript to Marinatos' article, in which they pointed out that, in their opinion, this theory needed to be supported by further excavations. The article appeared in December 1939, immediately after the outbreak of the Second World War. Because of the political situation, many libraries never received a copy of this edition of the journal. Even after the war, for a long time no one was interested in the catastrophe scenario. At that point no one suspected that three international conferences and innumerable scientific investigations would be dedicated to reinforcing Marinatos' suggestions.

How Does One Start a Tsunami?

All the preparations had been made. On 12 August 1996 at half-past-six in the morning, my jeep rolled off the ferry at the port of Heraklion. Joe Monaghan had reserved accommodation for us at Agios Nikolaos – that is, immediately opposite Thera. From this central point we could conveniently locate sites that had been destroyed by tsunamis in daily excursions. Our planned working area stretched from Heraklion on the northern coast along to the easternmost point of Crete.

For me, the trip to Agios Nikolaos was also a trip into the unknown. Rarely had I been so uncertain at the beginning of a project as to what to expect in the next two weeks. Joe had arranged for help from a doctoral student by the name of Andrew Kos from Australia; he himself would join us in the second week.

Generally I am invited to participate in archaeological projects to reconstruct the former landscape in the surroundings. In doing so I have encountered all the common forms of excavation accommodation and lodgings, so there are rarely any surprises concerning logistics, equipment, clothing or the experience of the experts involved – everything seems familiar, even when I join a project in an area that I do not know. The landscape and the history of a settlement, on the other hand, often hide surprises, which is why every new project is fascinating and a challenge. But with this tsunami project, everything was different. There was no sharply defined research area – the whole of the north coast of Crete was of interest to us. Anywhere along this stretch, which takes five hours to cover in a car, evidence of tsunamis from the Minoan volcanic eruption might be hidden. There was also no clearly defined methodology. A generally valid technique for detecting prehistoric tsunamis has yet to be found.

During the drive to Agios Nikolaos, I thought yet again about the methods of proceeding with the fieldwork. First and foremost, of course, we would need to visit all excavations of Minoan settlements to check the visible excavation results for signs of tsunamis. At many sites, excavation takes place in the summer, and I knew we would be able to speak to the experts involved there and obtain important information from them. Other excavations have since become tourist sights; that means that the arch-aeological remains are exposed and preserved in the best possible manner. Archaeological work has finished there and more detailed information has to be gained from the scientific publications. Yet other sites have been left to themselves. Many are protected by barbed wire, and often not even that. Overall, however, the initial requirements as far as archaeological finds were concerned, were fully satisfied. We had every chance of unearthing some discovery.

The second in my list of possible methods involved the geological effects of tsunamis. When these waves destroyed houses, they must also have removed any deposits of loose material. In many places, erosion marks should show how high or how far inland the waves had reached. From my earlier work in Crete I knew areas where waves – which, at the very least, had the destructive power of several atomic bombs – would have left visible traces of erosion.

But the waves not only drag material away, they also deposit material. In the eruption of Krakatau, the tsunamis threw six-hundred-tonne blocks of coral on to the shore. And on the Pacific coast of Australia, people had found eighty- to ninety-tonne giant boulders as much as 32 metres above sea level. Their orientation, and arrangement like roofing tiles, indicates that they were laid down by flowing water. I thought of sections of the coast of Crete where the limestone mountains gently slope down into the sea. These flat surfaces would be splendid ramps for all sorts of material that the tsunamis might have dragged with them. We would keep a lookout for giant boulders there.

Finally, there was yet a third question of how we could search for traces of giant waves. Tsunamis stir up a lot of fine material from the sea floor, carry it far inland and deposit it in valleys. Such deposits may be recognised in borings by looking for the shells of microscopically small mussels, gastropods (such as whelks), crabs, and single-celled organisms that live in salt water and at considerable depths. If one finds the remains of such organisms in a core – and if, in addition, the shells are damaged – then one is probably dealing with a tsunami deposit.

It would not be easy to find suitable localities for bores. On the Greek mainland there are many extensive coastal plains, in which metre-thick deposits from recent geological periods have been preserved – but not on Crete. The island's relief is so steep that heavy flash floods, which occur every couple of hundred years, are likely to sweep away all the sediments that have accumulated in the interim.

When I reached Agios Nikolaos, I was pleasantly surprised to find that particularly comfortable accommodation had been reserved for us. It was on the uppermost floor of a modern apartment hotel – right in the middle of the town but still with a small beach directly in front of the door. My new colleague was the second pleasant surprise. I took Andrew Kos for a pleasant mathematician and, in unpacking, pressed a GPS satellite navigation receiver into his hand, so that he could become familiar with its operation. The equipment would help us to determine accurately how far apart our search locations were. Andrew looked at the GPS with an air of interested scepticism, and soon explained that he was no mathematician but a geologist. Joe had recruited him from another institute as a scientist from a complementary discipline. Our collaboration became far easier, because there is a form of solidarity among geologists that transcends country boundaries. This probably arises because the laws of geology are valid everywhere and we all have to work with the forces of nature, or perhaps because our job often takes us far from home and is not always completely free from danger. Whatever the case, geologists always seem to welcome being together. I remember a half-day stopover in the mining town of Mt Isa in the Australian outback, where the young woman at the hotel reception asked me what I was studying. When I said 'geology', a car was immediately sent from the mine. The chief geologist and his team welcomed me personally, and I was allowed to take part in an unforgettable underground excursion, and also to acquire numerous rock samples as souvenirs. Lead-zinc ore – Lufthansa took a lot of pleasure in that! And this is just one of many similar experiences. When Andrew and I realised we were both geologists, we were straightaway on familiar terms: compass, geological hammer, loupe, notebook and walking boots – even our equipment was identical! The next morning we would start.

Outmoded Hypotheses or Unnecessary Hysteria?

K.T. Frost's theory that Plato's Atlantis corresponded to Minoan Crete struck such a chord that, even before 1920, a considerable series of publications, including whole books, had appeared on the subject. In addition, the Greek archaeologist Nikolas Platon, the excavator of the palace at Zakros, gave two lectures in 1945 on that theme. A few years later (in 1949), an article by Robert Scranton appeared in the American popular-science journal *Archaeology*. In it he described a Bronze Age irrigation and drainage system in central Greece and compared it with Plato's tale of sunken Atlantis, which had similar installations under its control.

Marinatos, whose theory of the destruction of Minoan culture through seismic sea waves had failed to arouse any attention during the confusion of the Second World War and the subsequent civil war in Greece, reacted to Scranton's publication in a letter in Greek that was published in *Cretica Chronica* in 1950, and in which he somewhat disparagingly spoke of a 'bold hypothesis'. Marinatos claimed that his own theory of 1939 agreed better with Plato's account. The tale of the collapse of legendary Atlantis could, he argued, reflect the same natural catastrophe that had struck Crete around 1450 BC, there destroying almost all the towns, their monumental buildings and two of the three palaces. Because the Atlantis saga originated from Egypt, the pharaohs (according to Marinatos) must have found out about how the island of Thera was overwhelmed: an island, moreover, with which they were probably not acquainted from their own experience. The catastrophe must thus have affected the whole of Crete, 'an island that was so severely affected that all contact with it was suddenly broken off'.

The Greek geophysicist Angelos Galanopoulos subsequently took up this idea, and tried to underpin it with scientific arguments. He even supported the view that traces of the artificial channels and port of Atlantis were still visible today at the bottom of the caldera. At the end of the 1960s, the American oceanographer James Mavor, and the expert on early linguistics from Dublin, John Victor Luce, endorsed the Thera theory. So, the supporters of this theory could rely upon mutually supporting arguments from archaeology (Marinatos), ancient linguistics (Luce), geophysics (Galanopoulos) and oceanography (Mavor). All four researchers published popular books on the subject in the 1960s, some of which became international best-sellers. Following this, the idea that the saga of Atlantis might be concealed behind the collapse of the Minoan culture was something that could no longer be avoided. Year after year, innumerable sightseers at Knossos and Akrotiri were introduced to the idea by eloquent tour guides.

The coup by the military junta in Greece in 1967, seems to have been a political change that did no harm – at least as far as Spyridon Marinatos was concerned. The generals appointed him general inspector of the archaeological service. As such, he was able to fulfil his life's dream: in the same year he began excavations on Thera. Two years after beginning the excavations, he organised the first International Thera Conference. Two others followed in August 1978 and September 1989. These conferences supported the catastrophe theory, even though Spyridon Marinatos did not live to see them.

On 1 October 1974, a few weeks after the military regime was overthrown, he fell to his death at his excavation in Akrotiri. There, in one of the Minoan houses, he is buried.

At the end of the first Thera Conference he had once again summed up the core of his theory. His words sound like a legacy:

> I thought then, and still think now, that it is impossible that the explosion of Santorini and the formation of the caldera could have occurred without the creation of seismic sea waves. It is just as impossible to imagine that Crete could have avoided heavy destruction caused by the waves. In my view these are solid facts, as absolute as the laws of nature.

The Remnants of Former Glory

We began our tour of inspection outside Heraklion, still in sight of the airport. There lies the significant Minoan site of Amnisos, which Marinatos himself began to excavate in 1932 and which was a key locality for his catastrophe theory. Homer described Amnisos as the 'difficult' harbour of Knossos. The ruins of the Minoan buildings still visible today lie right on the beach, about one to four metres above sea level. Parts of the remains of these buildings stretch out under water. In Amnisos, Marinatos had discovered foundations that originally consisted of eight ashlar blocks. Of these, two are missing and another is slightly tilted outwards. In a preliminary excavation report of 1932, the excavator described this displacement as earthquake damage. Later he found the 'true explanation': the whole building, including the two stone blocks must have been washed away by the waves, while the third stone was merely shifted. Also at Amnisos, Marinatos found a rectangular pit that was full of pumice stone. Initially, he interpreted this find as a merchant's collection of raw material. Later, he came to the conclusion that the ruins of the buildings in Amnisos must have been buried under deposits of pumice stone from the Minoan eruption.

Between 1983 and 1985, new excavations took place at Amnisos, this time under the direction of the Heidelberg archaeologist Jörg Schäfer. This team was able to understand Marinatos' conclusions only with difficulty, because the latter proved to have been careless in the scientific evaluation of his finds. Marinatos had neither published the results of the excavation, nor saved enough pottery objects for dating of the settlement horizons to be possible. As far as his tilted foundation stone is concerned, Jörg Schäfer maintains that it is 'highly unlikely' that a wave altered its original position. The underlying settlement layers were completely intact and, on the inside of the building, the remains of the wall plaster with its colourful paintings lay intact on the ground. It is practically impossible for giant waves to have washed away the two missing blocks and left the plaster fragments behind. Furthermore Amnisos was, without question, destroyed by fire, which is a finding that hardly chimes with destruction by masses of water. If the fire occurred before the tsunami, then the wave – quite apart from the fact that it is no longer required to account for the destruction – would have washed the burnt remains of the buildings into indiscriminate heaps, which is obviously not the case. But the fire would not have occurred after the wave, when it would have found nothing to destroy, because greater devastation than that caused by a tsunami is hard to imagine.

The pumice-stone 'deposits' mentioned are certainly not of natural origin. They lie in a storage chamber, which is accessible only through a small, high opening. Obviously the pumice stone was stored here after the eruption of Thera, and before Amnisos was destroyed by fire. This is a further indication of the fact that the town's collapse could hardly have occurred in connection with the eruption of Thera.

All in all, the archaeological findings at Amnisos argue for it being regarded as the key locality *against* the tsunami theory. The sole apparent effect of eruption of Thera on the inhabitants of Amnisos is that they were able to pick up pumice stone from the beach.

Charles Pellegrino, in his book *Unearthing Atlantis*, speaks of 300-metre-

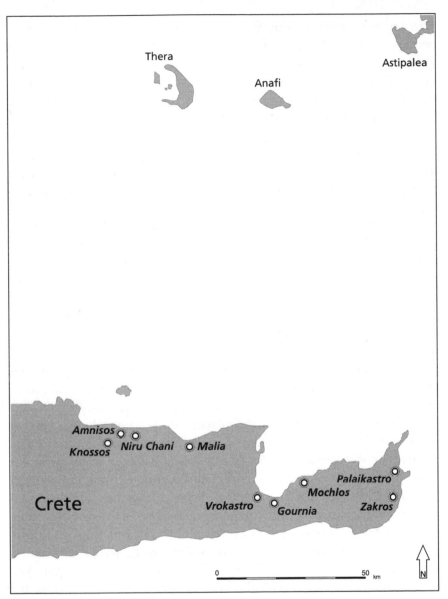

Known Minoan sites of the northeastern coast of Crete

high waves that overwhelmed Crete, and washed away the Minoan culture. When the book appeared in 1991, it was already perfectly well known that in the last 3500 years Amnisos could never have been affected by even a three-metre wave. The British prehistorian Denys Page, the American geologist Dorothy Vitaliano, the Mannheim archaeologist Wolfgang

Schering, the Tübingen mineralogist Hans Pichler, and many others, have pointed out that the state of preservation of the buildings at Amnisos cannot be reconciled with destruction by waves. Despite this, they, like nearly all other experts, continue to maintain that the eruption of Thera was of an extraordinary size, and therefore must undoubtedly have had lasting effects on the Minoan population.

Andrew and I drove in the Jeep a few kilometres eastwards along the coast. The next Minoan site awaited us just one bay farther on. This settlement is called Niru Chani. Here we are obviously dealing with the remains of the residence of some Minoan nobleman, which Marinatos had also excavated. Today this is accessible to anyone interested, and is an archaeological site that is wonderfully preserved by the staff. The foundations of the buildings lie approximately eight metres above sea level.

The villa at Niru Chani fell victim, at about the same time as Amnisos, to fire. Here, Marinatos found bronze votive tables piled on top of one another, and concluded that the waves must have stacked them in this way. Are there really waves that are as powerful as atomic bombs and can stack tiny three-legged tables on top of one another? Either way, there are walls of dried mud brick preserved at Niru Chani that consist of a single leaf only about fifteen centimetres thick. If Niru Chani had been subsequently hit by tsunamis, these walls would no longer exist today. So here again there are no indications of destruction by waves. Quite the contrary!

Half an hour later we reached the palace at Malia, where, despite arriving without prior notice, we received an extremely friendly welcome from Silvie Müller. For some years, this Swiss archaeologist has been carrying out research in the area around the palace. Malia, uniquely among the great Minoan palaces, lies directly on the sea. Marinatos was therefore convinced that Malia was 'with probability verging on certainty' destroyed by seismic sea waves. But, on the spot, no one believes in this theory. We were told by Silvie Müller that both the buildings from the First Palace Period, around 1700 BC, and from the New Palace Period, around 1450 BC, were destroyed by conflagrations. Not one of the experts who have taken part in the excavations at Malia over the last eighty years has ever claimed that the palace suffered any damage from tsunamis or earthquakes.

Our activities were to take us frequently to Malia. During this first visit, we therefore straightaway bought a brochure published by the Greek Ministry of Culture with a description of the archaeological sites. This stated that 'war was the most likely explanation for the collapse of the palaces' at the end of the Minoan heyday.

The following morning we left Aiglos Nikolaos heading east, into an area with which I was familiar from earlier projects. The first great Minoan settlement east of Aiglos Nikolaos is Gournia, a site that, at the moment, is being investigated by the American archaeologist Vance Watrous from State University in Buffalo. As part of his project, I am responsible for research into the early landscape. Gournia counts as the sole fully excavated Minoan town, but Vance Watrous is of the opinion that, so far, only twenty to fifty per cent of the buildings have been uncovered.

Because Gournia lies in the funnel-shaped Mirabello Bay, the tsunamis must have reached particularly gigantic proportions. But here again, we found no signs of any destruction by waves. The findings are the same as at the other sites: Gournia perished in flames. Directly on the shore there are even the undisturbed foundations of two large Minoan buildings, which probably served as boathouses. A tsunami would have left nothing of these boathouses remaining.

Somewhat farther to the east, we came to Mochlos, a sleepy little place far from the nearest main road. This Minoan site must have been swamped, because it lies on a small island in front of the modern village. Jeffrey Soles, another American prehistorian and director of the excavations, patiently answered our questions. Here again, the remains of the Minoan settlement stretch out under the water. Here again there are no signs whatsoever of devastation from waves. All the same, at one point, for a length of about ten metres, a layer of Thera ash, the thickness of a hand, has been preserved.

However, the volcanic eruption was obviously not without effects on Mochlos. Quite the contrary. Immediately after the event the population even rose. Jeffrey Soles interprets this as a possible sign of an influx of previous inhabitants of Thera. After the towns on the island devastated by the volcano became uninhabitable, the population must have sought new places to settle. Mochlos would have been a good choice. Before we left Mochlos, Jeffrey Soles told us how the old fishermen in the village described how, on one occasion in the 1950s, extraordinarily high waves crashed against the seaward side of the small island.

We continued with our excursions. For several days we drove along the coast from site to site – always with the same result. The Minoan settlements at Palaikastro and Zakros also went up in flames. Only Nikolas Platon, the excavator at Zakros, steadfastly believed that his site actually fell victim to waves. Mind you, Zakros lies in a bay in eastern Crete that is not even facing Thera. And there again, there are no indications whatsoever of destruction corresponding to powerful effects caused by water. The inhabitants had left the town before the fire. They had carried gold and jewellery away with them, preferring to leave behind heavy objects like double axes and stone vases. The excavators found votive offerings in a spring. This suggests that, at the last moment, priests prayed to the gods of the underworld to protect their town from the disaster. The inhabitants obviously knew that the end was approaching.

After we had visited all known Minoan sites on the north coast of Crete, Andrew and I began to search for giant boulders that had been thrown ashore by tsunamis. We were hardly surprised when we were unable to find a single example of such a large rock. Yet there are many plateaux that might hold such deposits; east of Malia, for example.

East of Gournia, on one of the world's most dramatic tectonic faults, the Trifti Mountains rise nearly vertically for several hundred metres. At the bottom of this steep slope, piles of rubble have collected, some of which reach the sea. Any tsunami, even if it were only a few metres high, would have dragged away the bottom of the detritus fan and left highly visible erosion marks. Nothing of the sort is to be seen. The fans of rubble are completely regular, and the desert varnish – a sort of patina that forms over hundreds of years – on the individual stones shows the great age of many of the fans. The geological findings thus do not reveal the slightest indication of any tsunamis. On the contrary, the lack of any erosion marks makes it clear that this area has not been affected by metre-high tsunamis for thousands of years. The preliminary result of our work during this first season in the field was unambiguous: there are no indications on Crete that the Minoan eruption of Thera produced destructive seismic sea waves.

Crete Goes for a Swim

In the 1970s, together with two colleagues at Cambridge, Joe Monaghan developed the so-called Small Particle Hydrodynamics (SPH) technique. In this mathematical model, a wave is regarded as consisting of innumerable solid particles. The advantage of SPH is that it allows the path of each individual particle to be followed, even when one is dealing with the mixing of two different fluids. SPH enjoys great popularity among astrophysicists, who are able to use it to model exploding supernovae.

The formation and development of tsunamis also involves exceptionally complicated mathematical processes. In particular, SPH allows one to determine the properties of nuées ardentes (known to specialists as pyroclastic flows) as they encounter the surface of the water, and, subsequently, to calculate how the waves develop in relation to the depth of the water, the profile of the sea bed and the trend of the coastline. Such calculations show that the formation and type of tsunamis strongly depend on the density of the mixture of ash and gas. If this is less than that of water, the pyroclastic flows will simply slide across the surface of the sea, and gradually peter out. If they are denser than sea water, they crash into the water like a piston. The force of the impact produces a sudden displacement of huge masses of water, and a tsunami is born.

Joe and his team have simulated these mathematical models in laboratory experiments. To do this they set up a volume of water comprising two layers, in a flow channel with transparent glass sides. The upper layer consisted of fresh water, and simulated the atmosphere. The lower layer represented the sea; it contained a lot of salt and was thus denser. The boundary between the two represented the sea surface. The scientists then released coloured salt water at an angle down a slope on to the contact surface between the two layers of water, to simulate the impact of pyroclastic flows. High-speed cameras filmed the development of the waves to document their progress. In another experiment, the researchers constructed a model of the coast of Crete on a reduced scale in a large tank 25 by 25 metres in size. There were even small houses as models of the Minoan coastal settlements. Large moveable surfaces set the water in the tank into sudden movement, allowing the course of the waves relative to the coastline to be studied. The model houses on the shore in the model did not withstand this experiment.

But There It Is!

Thirty-five years ago, Nicholas Ambraseys, Professor of Civil Engineering at London University, and a former pupil of Galanopoulos, compiled a list of tsunamis that had struck Crete over the last 3500 years. He came to the conclusion that only one, namely the wave of 8 November 1612, caused notable damage at many places on Crete. The maximum height that it reached was between three and four metres.

It was to look for evidence of this or other tsunamis that we returned to Crete, a year after our initial inspection, with a larger team and heavy equipment. The Greek geological authority had given us permission to carry out boring in our search area to look for signs of possible tsunami sediments. We had located a suitable area for such deposits in the form of an isolated swamp behind the tourist beach at Malia. The ground surface there is 1.4 metres above sea level – any wave more than one metre in height would have reached this spot.

Since his last field trip, Joe Monaghan had contacted a young English scientist, who, for his doctorate, was investigating evidence for tsunamis on Crete and other Aegean islands. So our team was increased by Dale Dominey-Howes. For Dale, even restrained statements about tsunami events in the Aegean are unjustified exaggerations. Dale had not even been able to confirm the wave in 1612 mentioned by Ambraseys. He found out that only the greatest Aegean seaquake in the twentieth century, on 9 July 1956, had produced a notable tsunami, which at a point on the island of Astipalea, about fifty kilometres east of Thera, had created deposits at a height of 2.15 metres above sea level. This was presumably the event that the old fishermen at Mochlos could remember.

But Dale had not yet succeeded in obtaining bores on Crete that went deeper than two metres, because suitable layers were extremely hard to find on the north coast. Together, however, after a week of work, we were finally able to sink a continuous bore with an overall length of 9.3 metres. From this we took three samples every five centimetres. A full set went to Dale. He would determine from the microfossils whether the core contained tsunami deposits or not. The second set went to Groningen, where the samples would be examined for plant remains, from which the history of the vegetation in the last few thousand years could be reconstructed. The last set was stored as an archive.

Just a few weeks after the field studies had finished, we had a letter from Dale, who had studied all the samples in the meantime. In it he stated that by far the majority of the sediments had originated under conditions that corresponded to those found today: in a freshwater marsh. Only at a depth of 4.60 metres was there a thin layer of marine deposits that could be attributed to a tsunami. The position could correspond to a Bronze Age layer, but to be able to actually ascribe the thin layer to the eruption of Thera further detailed studies are required. But at least this much was already certain: if waves were actually produced during the eruption of Thera, their maximum effect was restricted to depositing a thin layer of sand, of just about one centimetre in thickness, at a depth of 3.2 metres *below* the present-day sea level.

Crete is a geologically active region, in that elevation and depression of the land – and thus, also, shifts in the coastline – occur repeatedly. As far as the area around Malia is concerned, archaeologists assume that the sea level in Minoan times was about two to three metres lower than at the present day. This means that, relative to modern conditions, settlement stretched farther out to sea. Our small tsunami deposit would thus have been produced at about the sea level that prevailed at the time.

Where or What was the Collapse?

Studies, like those that we performed on Crete, have naturally been tackled to a far greater extent on Thera. These have shown that the claim, originally made by Fouqué, that the caldera was formed immediately after the Minoan eruption, is not correct. Marinatos, Galanopoulos and the other advocates of the catastrophe theory always assumed that, in the Bronze Age, the island consisted of a volcanic cone more than 1600 metres high, which was initially blasted away in the Minoan eruption, creating the ring of islands with the water-filled basin in the centre. Since then, however, geologists have found petrified blue-green algae, which must have lived inside the caldera, below sea level, more than 10,000 years ago. So there was no mountain at all in the Minoan period, but a caldera instead, just like the one today. This is also shown by erosion gullies in the Minoan surface layers, which slope in the direction of the current caldera. In addition, layers of pumice stone from the Minoan eruption may be found on the inner, steep coast of the island, and the deposits at these sites imply that the caldera already existed. Archaeologists have discovered both Minoan buildings and graves right on the edge of the caldera, and not one of these remains show any signs of movement.

Thera did not, therefore, possess a large volcanic cone, at least not immediately before the eruption in the Minoan period. The caldera was formed much earlier, possibly during the last great eruption, 23,000 years ago. As far as may be determined nowadays, during the Bronze Age the group of islands appeared very similar to the way it does today. Certainly no great tectonic movements have occurred, and definitely not of the size of a caldera collapse – otherwise the Minoan buildings and the pumice layers would have been far more strongly disturbed.

The whole tsunami theory rests on the assumption, however, that the caldera collapsed in the Minoan period, and thus inevitably created giant waves. If, however, no tectonic disturbances occurred, how could the creation of tsunamis have occurred? By ash-flows that crashed on to the surface of the water, as appears to have been the case in the Krakatau eruption? But that is hardly conceivable, because pumice stone is known to be so full of gas bubbles that it is lighter than water. It would hardly give rise to a great displacement of water.

The comparison with Krakatau fundamentally undermines the theory that tsunami-induced catastrophes cause major cultural collapse. Because, despite the enormous death toll, life on Sumatra and Java continued without a break after the eruption. The destruction was, in any case, confined to a small stretch of the coast, and the height of the waves, when they reached the capital, Batavia (modern-day Djakarta), were only in the centimetre range. But if no tsunamis were produced, then the eruption of Thera could hardly have caused destruction across the region. There might still have been the ash, of course!

The British prehistorian Denys Page had already recognised many faults with the tsunami theory, and remarked: 'The ruins show no signs of destruction by tidal waves.' Despite this he felt that Marinatos' theory was more plausible than any other and was convinced that the eruption of Thera had some fundamental relationship with the collapse of the Minoan culture. The only conceivable possibility that remained by which the eruption could have had an effect across the region was through ash-fall. According to him, there could be no doubt 'that such heavy layers of ash fell on central and eastern Crete that life became impossible'.

Promptly, researchers set out to search for pumice stone and ash from Thera, and they did indeed eventually find them, although generally only as extremely thin deposits. The distribution of the ash shows that the wind was blowing towards the southeast, and thus towards the open sea, when the volcano erupted. On Crete, there is evidence for ash from Thera only on the eastern end of the island. These layers are a maximum of five millimetres thick, and occur only on flat land below 1000 metres altitude. Ejected ashes from Thera many centimetres thick have been found here and there in excavations, mainly on the island of Rhodes in the east; at one spot they were as much as sixty centimetres thick. But, even on Rhodes, the settlement layers immediately above the ashes show that life continued apparently unchanged after the eruption.

One might object that even a few millimetres of red-hot ashes would adversely affect life on the ground. But the ashes cool during the time that they spend in the air, however long or short that may be. Otherwise they are a valuable fertilizer for the ground. Research carried out after the eruption of Mt St Helens showed that centimetre- or even decimetre-thick layers of ash have a positive effect on the growth of plants. All in all, the

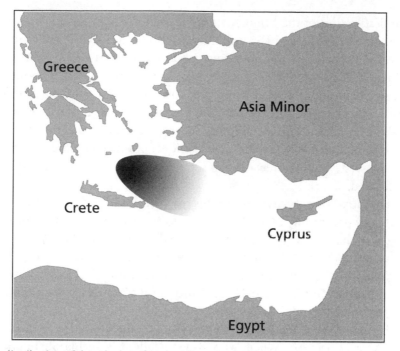

The distribution of the ash ejected in the Minoan eruption

effect of ash-fall on plant life is negligible in comparison with those caused by natural climatic changes.

But how much ash did Thera actually eject overall? Estimates vary between 13 and 39 cubic kilometres, tending towards the lower figure. An eruption of this magnitude would, without question, have produced an impressive natural spectacle. Its magnitude is comparable with that of Mount Katmai in Alaska in 1912. On that occasion about 15 cubic kilometres of ash were produced in just twenty hours. The eruption of Tambora on the Indonesian island of Sumbawa in 1815 was nevertheless far greater. At 100 cubic kilometres of ash, this volcano shot about four times as much material into the stratosphere as Thera. And a late Ice Age eruption of a volcano on Sumatra was over seventy times as great as the Thera eruption, producing some 2000 cubic kilometres of ash!

Irreconcilable Discrepancies

The ideas of Marinatos would have been justified as working hypotheses if the collapse of the Minoan high culture and the eruption of Thera had occurred at about the same point in time. This is not the case, however.

The destruction of the Minoan cities by fire took place at the end of the Late Minoan phase (LM IB), and thus about 1450 BC. The Thera eruption, however, occurred in the preceding ceramic period, the Late Minoan IA (LM IA). The exact date is controversial. Many experts set it at about 1630 BC; others at about 1530 BC. In either case, the event took place at least eighty, and possibly even one hundred and eighty, years before the collapse of the Minoan culture. Attempting to see a causal connection between fundamentally different events – a volcanic eruption and political collapse – that are separated by three, or even six, generations, must inevitably seem far-fetched.

Marinatos knew this as well. For this reason he tried at the time to explain pottery of phases LM IA and LM IB as local variants. In other words, he suggested that jars with the typical marine decorative motifs of LM IB had been developed in Crete, while pottery on Thera remained unchanged and decorated in the floral LM IA style. This attempt foundered, however, because all the imports into Thera – and not just pottery – were from the earlier period.

The gap in time between the eruption and the collapse can never be satisfactorily bridged. When, as a young student, Cynthia Shelmerdine, currently Professor of Aegean Prehistory at the University of Texas, asked Marinatos at the end of a lecture on the subject whether the discrepancy in dates could be explained, he only said 'How should I know? I had not been born then.' A reply that also illustrates the male chauvinist attitude of that academic generation.

To bridge the time span of at least fifty years, Denys Page proposed that the conflagrations in the Minoan settlements could have arisen at the end of the LM IB period through earthquakes, which occurred some decades after the eruption, but which, despite this, were still connected to the event. There are many arguments against this theory as well:

- Volcanic earthquakes lie close to the surface. The tremors that they produce are relatively weak and restricted to a small region.
- Not one of the Minoan houses at Akrotiri shows significant earthquake damage.
- The LM IB buildings on Crete show absolutely no signs of damage from earth tremors.
- A causal link between conflagrations and earthquakes was unknown until the twentieth century (see page 62).
- Earthquake damage, especially on Crete, is always restricted in area.

Sober consideration shows that there is no reason to view the eruption of Thera as fundamentally related to the collapse of Minoan culture. It is also quite incomprehensible why so many other phenomena should have been linked to the eruption. Many scientists wanted to use Thera as an explanation for events that occurred fully five hundred years later. Charles Pellegrino linked the collapse of the Hittite empire around 1190 BC with the eruption of Thera, which he set in the year 1628 BC – the intervening time span corresponds to that between Columbus' expedition to America and the landing on the Moon! Many other ideas about the possible effects of the eruption of Thera appear to us nowadays as utterly comical.

- The American historian J.G. Bennett linked the eruption of Thera with the ten plagues of Egypt, including those of frogs, maggots, flies and locusts.
- The Greek geophysicist Angelos Galanopoulos saw a possible effect of the Thera tsunami in the parting of the Red Sea that allowed the Israelites to pass. Remember though: the Red Sea and the Mediterranean are not connected!
- The Swedish archaeologist Arne Furumark maintained: 'What we understand by European civilization would certainly never have occurred, if Thera had remained dormant – or had not even existed.'
- An American amateur archaeologist called Leon Pomerance was of the opinion that the waves created by Thera washed away a million inhabitants, killed thousands of herds of sheep, goats and cattle, destroyed fields, woods, roads and water-sources, impregnated the ground with salt for decades, and destroyed hundreds of settlements on a thousand kilometres of coast. Because this sort of nearly global devastation corresponded better with the political and cultural hiatus at the end of the Bronze Age and the beginning of the Iron Age, Pomerance proposed shifting the time of the eruption from around 1600 BC to about 1200 BC.

Even when, during the respective Thera Conferences, individual scientists had pointed out that the magnitude and significance of the Thera eruption must be estimated as less than previously thought, the conferences acted to strengthen the original hypothesis. The individual experts believed that the arguments advanced by their colleagues were sound, and that the facts of a natural catastrophe were not in doubt.

Even scientists were not immune to the excitement. Many even looked out old fieldnotes to reinterpret them – but as additional support for the catastrophe theory. The conviction evinced by the tsunami theory appears to have arisen primarily from the sensational preservation of the site at Akrotiri. The unimpeachable position of Spyridon Marinatos may also have added extra weight. In addition, a deep-rooted human fascination with natural catastrophes may have played a part. All three factors reflect a fantasy world rather than cool detachment, which is why it is so difficult to refute the theory with rational arguments.

The Year of the Eruption

The present confusion that prevails over assessing the eruption of Thera is nowhere as significant as over the dating of the event. In the German *Brockhaus* encyclopaedia, for example, under the term 'Minoan culture' we find the remark 'according to the most recent research a major volcanic eruption occurred in 1645 BC'. Under the term 'Thera' we find, on the other hand, the date of 1628 BC given for the eruption. In the *Alte Kulturen* (*Old Cultures*) dictionary, published at the same time and by the same publisher, under the same term, it is stated that the eruption occurred around '1500 BC'. How has such confusion come about?

The eruption occurred in the second half of the Late Minoan IA phase. Given that this period has traditionally been dated, using pottery types, to between approximately 1600 and 1480 BC, the eruption must have taken place between 1540 and 1480 BC. Austrian archaeologists in their excavations at Auaris on the Nile Delta have actually found a large quantity of pumice stone, which undoubtedly came from Thera. The stratification of the layers in which the pumice stone was found, indicates a time around 1500 BC, between the reign-periods of the pharaohs Ahmose and Thutmosis III.

Naturally scientists were, and still are, anxious to determine the date of the eruption as accurately as possible. For this reason they have dated numerous organic remains from the excavations and pumice layers on Thera, using the radiocarbon method. The dates determined ranged across a wide spectrum. After a time, however, a concentration of dates around 1630 BC indicated statistically that this is the most likely date. Most Aegean prehistorians, however, reject this early date, objecting that radiocarbon dates from plants in volcanic areas, where carbon dioxide is escaping frequently, give unusable results. In other words, the plants on Thera could have assimilated 'old' carbon dioxide that had seeped unnoticed from the volcano before the eruption. Under such circumstances, the radiocarbon method would fail.

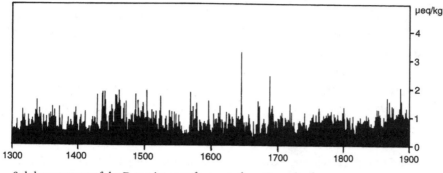

Sulphur content of the Dye-3 ice core from southern Greenland

Because the production of radioactive carbon does not always occur at the same rate, radiocarbon measurements must be calibrated. While the calibration curve used since 1986 implies that a date of around 1630 BC is more probable than one around 1530 BC, the newest curve (1993) is flat for the period of the 17th and 16th centuries BC. Measurements that fall within this period cannot be assigned exact absolute ages.

Further sources of accurate chronological data is ice cores from Greenland. Powerful volcanic eruptions enrich the atmosphere with sulphuric acid. Precipitation thus contains increased amounts of acid – even the snow that settles over Greenland. Over the course of the years, successive deposits of snow compress the lower layers into ice. The chemical composition of the gases contained within this ice enables scientists accurately to reconstruct the climate over the past 200,000 years. From the analysis of ice in the Camp Century core from northern Greenland, researchers first discovered a high acid content for 1390 BC, and they thus proposed that year as the date of the Thera eruption. Nevertheless, a few years later, this so-called acid peak could not even be found in the Dye-3 core from southern Greenland. It must, therefore, have been the signature of a volcanic eruption at high northern latitudes. Despite this setback, the geophysicists discovered a new peak. In the Dye-3 core, the year 1644 BC (± 7 years) stands out as having experienced particularly acid precipitation. From this it was concluded that the Thera eruption occurred in the previous summer; that is, in 1645 BC.

It seems remarkable that a volcanic eruption that did not even spread ash over neighbouring Crete above an altitude of 1000 metres should have had such a drastic effect on the ice in Greenland. It was not very long before it was realised that the sulphuric-acid production during the Thera

43

eruption was too small, by a factor of at least ten to twenty, to have caused the high acid content over Greenland. The exceptional peak of 1644 BC must, therefore, have been caused by a volcanic eruption on neighbouring Iceland, or through the combined effects of several volcanic eruptions.

A third way of precisely dating events thousands of years in the past is to use the growth rings of trees. Around 1628–1626 BC, trees in the American South-West exhibited greatly reduced growth rates for a number of years, which two American dendrochronologists, in an influential article that appeared in 1984, attributed to extraordinarily low temperatures. A volcanic eruption could perfectly well cause such a cooling, because the ash particles in the atmosphere weaken the solar radiation and thus lead to a slight dimming of sunlight. So, without further ado, the growth anomalies from the period 1628–1626 BC were assigned to the Thera eruption. Subsequently, dendrochronologists discovered similar growth differences in Ireland, like-wise around 1628 BC. Today, experts can point to comparable observations from three different continents. The question remains, however: do these really reflect the eruption of Thera?

Every year, around fifty volcanic eruptions occur around the world. In total, 1350 different volcanoes have been active during the past 10,000 years. If we assume that current volcanic activity is approximately the same as that in the 17th and 16th centuries BC, then, in those two centuries alone, about 10,000 volcanic eruptions must have occurred. We now know that, among others, Etna, Vesuvius and Mount St Helens also erupted during those centuries. Because the Thera eruption was not, as previously thought, of a particularly great magnitude, it will be difficult, if not impossible, to differentiate the effects that it caused from those of the many thousand other eruptions. According to three English archaeologists, who have carried out scientific dating together, the current state of knowledge means that neither ice cores nor tree rings are able to provide a satisfactory date for the eruption of Thera.

Just because two or more events occur at approximately the same time, they should not be taken as having some causal relationship. For any one of the phenomena put forward – whether it involves the unusual composition of the atmosphere or variations in the growth rate of trees – it must first be shown that they are *fundamentally* linked with the eruption of Thera.

In popular-science books the question is often asked what conclusions future archaeology might reach when our material remains are unearthed. The analogy is such a perennial one that Wolf Schneider, the former head of the School of Journalism in Hamburg, once remarked that he hoped never to hear it again. But let's pose it just once more! Imagine that, in the distant future, archaeologists are investigating the rise and fall of the Soviet Union. In doing so, they determine that in April 1986 the nuclear reactor at Chernobyl exploded and that a few years later the Soviet Union disintegrated. Must they assume that the Chernobyl catastrophe was the trigger for the political collapse? They might also explain the current economic problems of countries in southeast Asia with the eruption of Mt Pinatubo, the recurrent governmental crises in Italy as being linked with the eruptions of Vesuvius, and the Iran–Contra affair in the USA as a result of the eruption of Mount St Helens.

To say it once again: The bare fact that two events occur more or less at the same time does not allow one to conclude that they are causally related. After seventy years of research there is still no firm evidence – indeed, not even any indications – that point to the collapse of the Minoan high culture as having been initiated by the eruption of Thera. This idea may indeed sound exciting, but probably no one would have attached any importance to it if it had been expressed by a less influential archaeologist. Even Marinatos' original publication in *Antiquity* is full of contradictions and inconsistencies. Nowadays, an article of this sort and in such a journal is inconceivable. Subsequent research has even further weakened his theory. Despite this, it has taken root in encyclopaedias and textbooks.

The eruption of Thera may have been an impressive natural event, but other processes must have been responsible for the collapse of the Minoan culture. As we shall see in the next chapter, there has been no lack of attempts at an alternative explanation.

Chapter 2

Earthquake:
Was Civilisation Nature's Plaything?

... if you have a good scientific imagination you can think of all sorts of things that might be true, and that's the essence of science. You first think of something that might be true – then you look to see if it is, and generally it isn't.

BERTRAND RUSSELL (in *'Bertrand Russell Speaks His Mind'* – BBC TV *Interviews with Woodrow Wyatt*, Cleveland and New York: World Publishing Company, 1960, p. 13)

The earth quakes in Heraklion

The day of 26 June, 1926 had been calm and warm at Heraklion, which was then still called Candia. The excavator of the palace of Knossos had retired to his private room on the ground floor of the Villa Ariadne. It was 21:45. Sir Arthur Evans was then seventy-five years old. For twenty-six years he had been excavating at Knossos, at his own expense, and, as an appropriate setting for his life's work, had the Villa Ariadne built as his headquarters. He was lying on his bed, reading, when suddenly the building began to creak and groan. The whole house lifted and started to sway, so that Evans felt as if he were on a ship and was overcome with nausea, like seasickness. Small objects fell out of the cupboards, and a bucket full of water slopped over, spilling most of its contents. The earth gave out a dull moaning noise, like the distant bellowing of an angry bull. The only bell in the whole building rang, and Evans could hear the church bells of Candia away in the distance. People were shouting in the courtyard, and a couple of children were crying. Guests fled from the upper storey of the villa, staggered down the stairs and then outside between the trees, which were swaying so violently that it seemed that they were about to crash to the ground. The roofs of two small neighbouring houses fell in, and a sudden gust of wind raised a pall of dust that almost completely blotted out the Full Moon. One minute later, all the excitement was over. Luckily, there were no victims to be mourned.

The strongest earthquake to hit Heraklion in the twentieth century was not unexpected for Evans. On the contrary, for a long time he had counted on such an event occurring, ever since he had discovered various indications of earthquake damage during his excavations at Knossos. He found, for example, that at one point on the palace wall, giant blocks had broken loose and had fallen on to a small, adjacent building. On the basis of such observations, he had, for some time, been looking into descriptions of natural catastrophes. From a report by a French geologist he knew that hardly any other region of the Earth is as prone to earthquakes as Crete. The last great tremor in Heraklion, in 1856, had shown how human achievements are subject to the whims of nature. Of the 3620 houses in the town, after that earthquake 3602 were damaged or lay in ruins, and 538 people had lost their lives. In addition, the destruction observed at the Minoan palace was, in Evans' view, far too great to have been caused by human intervention. It seemed far more likely that natural forces had caused the damage.

In the course of his research into earlier earthquakes on Crete, Evans came across a letter, written in Latin, from the Venetian governor of the island, Girolamo Donato, in which he described his personal experiences during the earthquake of 29 May 1508: The houses, he wrote, waved 'like ships in a storm. They did not just move from side to side, but also up and down.' A 'horrible bellowing' came from the earth, together with a banging like the clash of weapons, while all around, buildings collapsed. The inhabitants of Candia fought their way out of the town. Priests held holy images up to Heaven, and administered the Host by the glow of lanterns. The governor himself ran barefoot, his youngest child in his arms, together with the rest of his family, to the administrative wing of the palace, where he discovered the reception hall was nothing but ruins. Although the passage through the courtyard was extremely dangerous, because of the surrounding high buildings, the noble family managed to escape. They ran through the narrow alleyways 'between walls leaning towards one another' until they reached an open space, where they spent the night. Nearly three hundred people lost their lives that night, but the town walls withstood the tremors.

In his study of the history of earthquakes on Crete, Evans found that the area around Heraklion was affected, on average, by major earthquakes twice a century. Because the last great earthquake took place in 1856, by the middle of the 1920s a second was long overdue. In addition, the excavator established that in the six hundred years between 1246 and 1856, central

Crete had been struck by nine particularly destructive earthquakes. The Minoan Palace Period lasted for a comparable period of time, long before our own era – from about 2000 to around 1375 BC. These parallels led Evans to the idea that the breaks in the history of Minoan settlement might have been caused by earthquakes. In the period between 2100 and 1400 BC, seven such interruptions of varying importance had occurred, which Evans subsequently put down to earthquakes. He even went so far as to suggest that the earthquakes gave the Minoan population a sense of insecurity, and that they thus saw themselves forced to seek new places to settle outside Crete; giving rise to 'a widespread colonisation of the Greek mainland by people of Minoan origin'.

Evans' ideas about the disastrous effects of earthquakes on the Minoan civilisation established yardsticks that are still, at least in part, current today. In searching for explanations for the three far-reaching cultural disruptions in the second millennium BC, many archaeologists have ascribed them to disastrous earthquakes. These disruptions include, among others, those at the end of the Old Palace Period around 1700 BC, the end of the New Palace Period around 1450 BC, and the end of the Late Bronze Age at about 1200 BC. With respect to the end of the Old Palace Period about 1700 BC, in particular, experts on Crete almost unanimously favour the idea that the disruption could have been caused only by powerful earthquakes. The alternative explanation – destruction by enemy attacks – finds little acceptance, especially because it is impossible to identify any opponents, at that early period, who may have been strong enough to cause such devastation: the Mycenaean culture did not yet exist, and most scholars assume that other well-organised states, such as Assyria and Egypt, were too far away.

A 4000-year-old Town Straight from the Drawing Board

In the summer of 1996 an inquiry reached me from the University of Crete. Athanasia Kanta, the Professor of Aegean Prehistory, who, for a long time, has been excavating the Minoan settlement of Monastiriki in the Amari Valley between Rethimnon and Phaistos, was anxious to enlist scientists for the excavation. She had already recruited archaeobotanists and archaeozoologists. Now she asked me to visit the site, so that I might later advise her how the development of the landscape in this region could be reconstructed.

I didn't hesitate a moment when I received this invitation. A visit to Monastiriki offered a unique opportunity to see a whole town from the

Old Palace Period. Monastiriki was founded around 2000 BC, and existed for three hundred years, until the town was destroyed during the devastation that accompanied the end of the Old Palace Period around 1700 BC. Because the site subsequently remained unoccupied, the foundations of the prehistoric buildings lie directly beneath the modern-day surface. In other excavation sites on Crete these older horizons are largely overlain by later settlement layers, and are thus exposed only here and there. During fifteen years of fieldwork, Athanasia Kanta had exposed the horizon from around 1700 BC, when the destruction occurred, over a large area. Monastiriki is thus the ideal place to compare Evans' earthquake scenario for the collapse of the Old Palace Period with the archaeological findings.

Because a trip to Monastiriki could be combined with another of my projects without any problem, I was all the more grateful for the opportunity to be able to reconnoitre the west of the island for a change. Most of the projects on Crete in which I had been involved had been directed by scientists from the USA – and for a hundred years their research interests had been concentrated in the east of the island.

My first meeting with Athanasia Kanta took place in a beach café in Rethimnon. During the subsequent chat, it became immediately obvious that in many respects we were on the same wavelength. Cooperation across the boundaries of countries, languages, climatic zones and scientific disciplines is generally far simpler than one might think – and actually always worthwhile – but in its initial phases it is by no means always free of prejudice. This becomes particularly understandable if one looks more closely at the history of the Monastiriki excavation site. During the Second World War, the German Army mercilessly terrorised the local population on Crete. After the island fell under the control of German soldiers – who chose Evans' Villa Ariadne as their headquarters – archaeologists from the Third Reich arrived to excavate the Greek sites. Included among these sites was Monastiriki, which had been found originally by John Pendlebury, the then curator of the Knossos excavations. But Pendlebury was killed, at the age of 36, in the first hours of the assault on Crete. To give the German experts full credit, they carried out their work carefully and judiciously, and finally published their results both rapidly and comprehensively. It is to the Greek experts' credit that they impartially include German specialists in their projects today.

From Rethimnon, we drove south into the mountains, into an area in which even the locals run the danger of losing their way. As a geographical feature, the Amari valley, in which Monastiriki lies, forms one of the deepest gorges in Crete's central mountain range, thus affording a natural link between the northern and southern coasts. Nowadays, however, practically no one uses this pass. The little-frequented road, which today runs through the valley in the direction of Phaistos, is recent, and the main link between the tourist centres of Rethimnon and Agia Galini bypasses the Amari valley farther to the west.

The landscape around Monastiriki is dominated by the 2500-metre peaks of the Psiloritis Massif, the slopes of which rise steeply to the west. The Minoan town, on the other hand, lies only about 320 metres above sea level, and right in the centre of the Amari valley on a cliff-like rise alongside the Genianos river. Whoever built the town, they chose its site with masterly skill. The bottom of the valley consists almost exclusively of flysch, a sedimentary rock that weathers easily and which is therefore utterly unsuitable as a foundation. Only in a few places do limestone outcrops occur in the flysch. The Minoans built Monastiriki right on one of these limestone hills and, in fact, on the one that stretches the farthest into the valley. So the spot lies directly on the river and fertile meadows, but at the same time is slightly higher. A further advantage of this position is the fact that the slab-like limestone is extremely suitable as a building material. No long journeys were required to transport material to the site – the town and quarry merge into one another.

The settlement is gigantic; its buildings not only stretch across the plateau, but also along the slopes of the hill. Impressive walls have been constructed there in the form of terraces. Without expert guidance, the exposed wall foundations say very little – in Athanasia Kanta's company, however, hours pass like minutes, there is so much to find out about the site.

At Monastiriki, it is primarily the basements of the former houses that have been preserved. The upper storeys have either been destroyed or have succumbed to later erosion. Giant storage jars fill the cellars. From the plant and animal remains still left in them, botanists and zoologists have established that the agricultural practices in this region four thousand years ago were similar to those found today. The farmers planted cereals and vines, and raised goats and sheep. Almost all the construction timber came from olive trees. The shape and size of the settlement, the terraced walls of cyclopean stone, and the enormous storage jars in between them – all this reminds me of the northern edge of the town of Mycenae. Yet the settlement at Monastiriki is seven hundred years older than the now exposed palace at Mycenae.

Why did Monastiriki come to an end around 1700 BC, and what caused the contemporary collapse of the Old Palace culture? Here, as there, it was fire that caused the actual destruction. Archaeologists nevertheless suspect that *earthquakes* kindled these fires; as in San Francisco, which, in April 1906, was less severely damaged by the earthquake itself – despite it having reached 8.3 on the Richter Scale – than by the subsequent fires.

But the population of Monastiriki escaped the disaster. There are no victims of the catastrophe in the ruins and, in addition, no valuable portable objects such as jewellery, bronze or seals are present. Immediately before the catastrophe, however, the population was making sacrifices to the gods. The findings from the excavation of the destruction layer are thus similar to those at the end of the New Palace Period around 1450 BC, as known at Zakros and the other Minoan towns along the northern coast.

Athanasia Kanta and her excavation team have neatly and tidily exposed many of the foundations. The walls mainly consist of unworked natural stones, a few decimetres across, piled on top of one another. Because no mortar is used in the construction, this is known as rubble wall masonry. Nowadays a heavy tread is enough to cause one of these walls to collapse. One of them even leans downslope slightly. But does that suffice as proof that Monastiriki was destroyed by earthquake? If the normally firm ground becomes fluid, with the subsoil taking on the consistency of jelly, wouldn't we expect to find hardly a single stone resting on another? In Monastiriki there are no signs of any such tremors. How could a site be the victim of an earthquake and yet still remain in such good condition?

During our visit, we were scorched by the midday sun for two hours and, naturally, our thoughts turned to cool refreshment, but the nearest taverna was almost an hour's drive away. So we strolled across to the family house where the members of the archaeological project were accommodated during the excavation campaign, hoping – even though unannounced – to get something to eat and drink. My thoughts were primarily on the latter. From data tables and our own experience we knew that when carrying out physical work in the summer in many hot countries, one needs to drink as much as nine litres of water a day. A lady archaeozoologist, who was accompanying us, tactfully prepared me for a simple lunch – as if I expected a five-star restaurant!

I was familiar with the living conditions of the Greek rural population, but in the Cretan mountains they are really less altered than elsewhere. As we subsequently sat in the living room of the mud-brick house, swapping various pieces of news, I looked at the simple house and wondered how far it differed from a Neolithic farmhouse of some seven thousand years earlier. The differences are definitely not very great. Well over two thousand years ago fired roof tiles became a fundamental building material. More recently, there is the unavoidable television set, but otherwise, not much seems to have changed. The method of construction, the furnishings, the food – all these have been essential parts of Greek rural life for thousands of years. The images on the holy icons may indeed have changed two thousand years ago, but their significance must still correspond to that of prehistoric times.

The farmer's wife made us heartily welcome and promised spinach for lunch. By way of welcome, she produced a clear litre bottle without a label, and poured an equally colourless liquid into small schnapps glasses. It was raki, grape spirit, approximately eighty per cent alcohol and the Cretan national drink. I provisionally deferred a request for water, so as not to upset our hostess. As my concentration was soon likely to waver, considering the type and quantity of the drink, I hastily tried to devise a plan of how I could investigate the area around Monastiriki.

There in the interior, the history of settlement is primarily determined by the agricultural potential, which means that the quality of the soil must also be determined. Even more important, however, is the regional water balance. In Greece, *what* grows *where* is mainly determined by the amount of water that is available. How large are the average rainfall rates, and how is rainfall distributed throughout the year? I discussed my plans with the excavation leader, and we decided that I would return a few months later to reconnoitre the surrounding area on my own. After the major projects in recent years, this task was an appealing change.

Half an hour later, the farmer's wife casually, and still deep in conversation, set down large water glasses for us. Secretly, I was eternally grateful to her. Then she served us from a two-litre bottle of *red wine*!

How the Sites Defied Earthquakes

Once Arthur Evans had put forward his catastrophe theory, it was not long before archaeologists discovered signs of destructive earthquakes at other sites. As already mentioned, many scientists tried, in particular, to ascribe the upheavals that occurred at the transition from the Bronze Age to the Iron Age at around 1200 BC to cataclysmic natural disasters. At that time, there was a radical cultural change that affected the whole of the eastern Mediterranean, the causes of which are still not satisfactorily explained. In the most commonly used three-period system, which divides the cultural history of the ancient world into the Stone Age, the Bronze Age and the Iron Age, the radical break around 1200 BC marks the second and last major advance, the progression from the Bronze Age to the Iron Age. From our present point of view it is hard to comprehend that this radical cultural change involved what was virtually a global upheaval affecting almost the whole of the then known world, occurred in a short period of time and destroyed many towns at the height of their glory. Failure to understand this cultural change led many to conclude that, here again, a widespread natural catastrophe might well have been the trigger.

Carl Blegen, the then excavator of Troy, was the first such person. He discovered deep cracks at a few points in the legendary fortress in the northwest of Turkey. In addition, a portion of the defensive wall had shifted slightly and was leaning towards the north. From this Blegen concluded that Late Bronze Age Troy also succumbed to a natural catastrophe, and was substantially destroyed. Blegen also discovered that part of the defensive walls was built on old settlement layers. He inferred from this that the intervening layers of compacted earth must have served as a sort of shock-absorber for earthquake waves. But this conclusion is false. The alleged 'buffer layer' would, in fact, have intensified the effects of the shocks from an earthquake. For buildings to be safe from earthquakes it is always advisable to base the foundations directly on bedrock. The fact that this was not taken seriously at Troy indicates that earthquake prevention was not of great significance in town planning. And all the cracks observed by Blegen occur in an area of the city that in any case slopes down into depressions. They can therefore be explained by perfectly ordinary soil creep. The signs of earthquake damage in Troy VIIa are thus rather doubtful. Furthermore, this city also succumbed not to earth tremors but to fire.

Soon after publication of the alleged earthquake damage at Troy, the Strasbourg archaeologist Claude Schaeffer, who excavated the Late Bronze Age port of Ugarit in Syria, concluded that this important trade centre fell victim around 1200 BC, not – as had long been thought – to enemy attack but to destruction caused by earthquakes. This was despite the fact that Egyptian temple inscriptions stated that Ugarit was destroyed after an attack by 'Sea People'. These so-called 'Sea People' were a group of well-organised and well-equipped forces who made the coasts of the eastern Mediterranean unsafe around 1200 BC. Written documents found in Ugarit confirm the threat from enemy ships. The last king begged his allies for support because an attack was imminent; half-a-dozen enemy ships had arrived shortly before and had caused a great deal of destruction. But the collapse came so swiftly that the cry for help did not even leave the city. At any rate, Schaeffer found no sensible explanation of why the attackers should have reduced a flourishing trading centre to rubble and ashes instead of using the buildings for their own purposes. He therefore subscribed to the view that an earthquake was the most likely cause for the destruction of Ugarit. Shortly afterwards, he suggested that the same natural event had affected other towns in Syria and Asia Minor. Subsequent excavations at Ugarit have, however, refuted Schaeffer's interpretation. The current view is that there is no cause to doubt that an enemy attack was responsible for the destruction of Ugarit.

Earthquakes, it is suggested, might have contributed to the destruction of another important palace of the Late Bronze Age, that at Mycenae. Spyridon Iakovides, one of the excavators, is convinced that earthquakes are the only possible satisfactory explanation for the fall of the kingdom. Shortly after the middle of the 13th century BC, and again around 1200 BC, fires obviously occurred in various parts of the citadel, houses collapsed, and at least one inhabitant was buried beneath the ruins. Nevertheless, there remain buildings in Mycenae that are extremely prone to collapse, which existed at the time of these events but which did not suffer any damage. Neither the cyclopean fortifications nor the precisely laid stones in the entrance to the Treasury of Atreus show any movement. The same applies to Mycenae as to all the other sites: destruction occurred through fire, not through earth tremors.

Very close to Mycenae lies Tiryns, another Late Bronze Age citadel. Its excavator, Klaus Kilian, actually identified three earthquakes, which, in his view, affected both Mycenae and Tiryns. In his investigations, he also made another surprising discovery. He noticed that the settlement outside the citadel was larger after the destruction of the palace than it was before – during the period when the Mycenaean culture was at its peak. He concluded from this that in the period of crisis at the beginning of the 12th century BC, Tiryns acted as a sort of general sanctuary for survivors from across the whole region. After Kilian had discovered signs of earthquakes in Tiryns, he collected evidence for natural catastrophes from other major excavation sites, and became convinced that not just Mycenae and Tiryns, but also Pylos in the western Peloponnese, Kastanas in northern Greece, Troy in western Asia Minor, Hattusa in central Asia Minor, and Alalach in Syria all came to an end through natural catastrophes. However, the arguments that suggest earthquake-related findings at Tiryns – at least those published so far in the excavation reports – are not accepted as such by everyone. In addition, the conclusion that the lower town grew after the decline of the palace proves to be a false assumption. What's more, no indications of earth tremors have been found at many of the sites named by Kilian, but there are obvious traces of enemy attacks.

Midea, a citadel that lies between Tiryns and Mycenae, and which has been investigated by Swedish archaeologists, is also supposed to have been destroyed by an earthquake. At least, that is what the excavator, Paul Åström, maintains. The epicentre of the earthquake could, therefore, have lain close to Mycenae, Tiryns and Midea. Recently, an earthquake has been posited as the cause of the destruction of the far more distant Thebes, around 1200 BC. The most recent excavations in the palace workshops there have revealed that, during the city's fall, a two-storey building collapsed, and that a woman was buried under the falling masonry.

In the eyes of the excavators mentioned, the evidence indicating that earthquakes played a part in the cultural collapse around 1200 BC is overwhelming. Seven of the most important sites in the eastern Mediterranean: Knossos, Troy, Ugarit, Mycenae, Tiryns, Midea and Thebes were, according to these prehistorians, destroyed by earthquakes. The archaeologists who subscribe to the earthquake theory include some of the most famous scientists in this field, and they found not just one or two tentative indications of earthquakes, but, as Spyridon Iakovides emphasised 'rock-solid and irrefutable excavation findings'. In addition, most of these sites do actually lie in earthquake-prone regions. Historical records confirm, for example, that in the northern Troas alone, in the last two thousand years there have been at least six earthquakes of magnitude 6 or more on the Richter scale. In the opinion of the earthquake supporters, cultural history as well as Earth history may, at least in part, be determined by natural events. If it was external forces – in the form of a comet – that caused the end of the dinosaurs, it was forces from the Earth's interior that affected the Late Bronze Age kingdoms.

Nevertheless, apart from the factors already mentioned, there are further numerous objections to the earthquake theory. Many documents from the period around 1200 BC describe imminent danger from attacking hordes, and the damage in the purported earthquake-affected excavation sites resembles the destruction found at dozens of other places that also came to an end in the crisis years around 1200 BC but which show no recognisable signs of earthquakes. All the affected cities went up in flames. In none of them are there any indications of measurable movements of the surface. At none of the places mentioned have archaeologists found a large number of people buried under the rubble. In the few individual cases where there were victims, these could have been people who had been injured before the building collapsed, or who had died from smoke inhalation.

For these reasons, among the often numerous excavators at each of the sites just mentioned, only one supports or has supported the idea that earthquakes brought about the collapse of the palaces. At most sites there have been a large number of excavation campaigns over many decades, which have brought numerous experts into contact with each site. They have all come to a completely different conclusion than the supporters of the earthquake theory.

The Secrets of the Amari Valley

For my fortnight-long investigation of Monastiriki and its surroundings, I had chosen my accommodation so that I stayed for the first week on the southern coast of Crete, and for the second on the northern coast. In driving to the area, I tried a new route almost every day, so that I could best determine how favourably placed the town was with respect to the passes and trade routes. Although Monastiriki lies a few kilometres south of the actual watershed, it is easier to reach from the north. To the south, it is impossible to travel through the middle of the valley alongside the river Platis. The Platis has cut deeply into the soft rocks, and the mountains prevent any attempt to establish a path around the rockfalls in the gorge. Because of this, the connecting road to the south winds around the mountain slope, so that it takes almost an hour to reach Agia Galini with a car, even though the distance is only about fifteen kilometres as the crow flies. So the Amari valley is not a convenient north–south link – to me Monastiriki's position seems rather isolated. Nevertheless, from the site, both approaches to the Amari valley from the north may be controlled with no problems.

In general, the sites from the Old Palace Period agree only in their essential architectural features; as far as the manufacture of particular goods is concerned, they appear to have been independent. At Monastiriki, however, this rule does not apply, because objects recovered during the excavations correspond in all respects to the artefacts found at Phaistos. There can be no doubt that Monastiriki belonged politically, economically and administratively to the palace at Phaistos. The imprint of a personal seal has even been found that was used both at Monastiriki and at Phaistos.

What is particularly fascinating about Monastiriki is that it is a sort of planned town, which was established as a result of a centralised decision, and at the very beginning of the Old Palace Period. For whatever reason, it must have been sensible to settle not just a few people but a very large number up in the mountains. The question of what motives may have lain behind this new settlement preoccupied me for a long time. For centuries both before and after the foundation of Monastiriki, the region seems to have been extraordinarily poor.

My first thought was that Monastiriki might have been a centre for domestic trade. But, first of all, during the Old Palace Period there was hardly any domestic trade on Crete and, second, the town was not so ideally placed as it might at first seem. In addition, archaeologists have found none of the uncommon objects that are often discovered at trade centres. Moreover, the stored goods were sealed and difficult to access, which implies that they were reserves, not intended for trade.

Monastiriki might, nevertheless, have been founded to make agricultural use of the fertile land in the surrounding area, or to centrally administer already existing agricultural holdings. In that case, the farmers would have delivered their harvest to the local leaders in Monastiriki, where it would have been stored in safe keeping and administered. This type of change from the Early Bronze Age farmsteads to centralised palace administration marks the start of the true Minoan civilisation.

There is, however, yet a third possibility that might explain the purpose of this artificially planned town: we could be dealing with a self-sufficient garrison. It is quite possible that the king of Phaistos ordered this outpost on the border to be established so that the northern approaches to his kingdom might be better supervised and guarded. Because of the long access routes, they tried to find a site that allowed the inhabitants to feed themselves by means of their own agricultural activity, independent of outside sources. An argument for this interpretation is the fact that people appear to have lived only inside the town itself. At all events, the remains of no Middle Bronze Age buildings have yet been found in the unprotected countryside. If such an interpretation is true, then it will have a lasting effect on our understanding of the Old Palace Period. The immense terraces at Monastiriki would then not be just retaining walls, but would form part of a defensive installation. But then the Minoan civilisation would not have been nearly so peace-loving as Arthur Evans wanted to believe.

Geoarchaeologists' practical fieldwork includes spending a lot of time sitting on high viewpoints, looking at the landscape, and pondering about what they see. During my two weeks in the Amari valley, this was not only an appealing task, thanks to the beauty of the landscape, but also one that produced a whole series of surprises. One of these related to the distribution of the settlements. The few modern villages lie noticeably high up on the slopes of the valley. On the one hand, the landscape in general appears extraordinarily green and fertile but, on the other hand, it is extremely thinly settled. In recent decades, migration to the towns has even further depopulated the area. In many villages the population has decreased by two-thirds in the last thirty years. During the third millennium BC – that is, before the Minoan settlement was established – the countryside was unusually poor and thinly settled. Only twice in the whole of history has it been intensively used: in the Old Palace Period and in the Graeco-Roman period. How could this valley support just a small number of people for thousands of years, and then suddenly feed a large population?

The key to answering this question probably lies in water management. Although the valley is covered with thick vegetation, enjoys considerable rainfall (about 1000 mm per year), has dozens of bubbling springs, and the river Genianos (which flows past Monastiriki carrying 6.5 million cubic metres of water a year), there's a lack of water! Because of the rugged karst terrain, the water table is more than three hundred metres deep, so groundwater is ruled out for agriculture. In addition, the steep relief, the complicated topography and the high rainfall produce high erosion rates. The weathered rock surfaces are able to retain enough moisture for shrubs, but to carry out cultivation additional water is required. This can be obtained from the numerous springs. They occur on the boundary between the limestone and the flysch, and because this geological seam lies far up the slopes, this is where the modern villages are sited. The additional spring water even enables the farmers to grow fruit – although only within an area of a few hundred metres. Of the remaining ground, only part can usefully be cultivated, and that is principally given over to olive trees.

The meadowland alongside the Minoan settlement currently belongs to an agricultural research institute, which, however, uses only a quarter of the area for cultivation. The rest lies fallow, for lack of water. Of what use is meadow soil if it cannot be tilled for lack of water? Because no ground-water is accessible, yet all useful plants except olives require irrigation during the four or five rain-free summer months, feeding a greater population in this area presumably demands irrigation works. This may well be the reason why the valley was densely settled only in Minoan and Roman times, because it was only during those periods – and also today, of course – that the knowledge of water management was widespread.

At present a dam is under construction on the northern slope of the pass, towards Rethimnon, while on the southern side, towards Phaistos, an artificial catchment basin has already been completed near the village of Vizari. So I met mayors, hydrologists and geologists to discuss details of local water management. The new basin contains 550,000 cubic metres of water, less than one-tenth of the total outflow. This quantity is sufficient to enable year-round cultivation of an area six times that of the Genianos meadows below Monastiriki. Similarly, in Minoan times it was presumably only by the use of water storage that it was possible to bridge the dry summer months, and thus feed a whole town full of people.

Monastiriki lies at the narrowest part of the valley. If one looks out from the Minoan settlement towards the opposite river bank, one can see a small hill. A visit to the other side of the valley shows that the surface there is covered in pottery fragments. Even remnants of walls are still preserved in many places. Looking back towards Monastiriki from this hill, I noticed a slight rise in the ground that stretched straight across the valley towards the Minoan site. This slight rise forces the Genianos towards the western side of the valley, so that it flows along directly below the Minoan town. A river like the Genianos that carries a lot of water ought to have removed such a ridge of land. In valley defiles, the contours never run at right-angles to the river – so someone must therefore have artificially intervened in the landscape. In which case, the noticeable rise might well be the remains of a dam. In searching for further evidence, I discovered various blocks of stone, several metres across, in the almost completely overgrown bed of the river. Even the remnants of a sort of embankment capping are still visible. If there actually were hydraulic works of this magnitude in Minoan Crete, it would be a great surprise.

During my exploratory trips through the Amari valley, I also visited the Minoan site at Apodoulou, which Marinatos first excavated, and which since 1985 is again being investigated by a Greek and Italian archaeological team. Apodoulou lies halfway between Phaistos and Monastiriki, also dates from the Old Palace Period, and is, on the basis of the artefacts, essentially identical to Monastiriki. Although Apodoulou lies on an extremely steep slope, there are no cyclopean terrace walls. This might be an additional indication that the walls at Monastiriki, which lay on the border of the kingdom, served primarily for defence, whereas Apodoulou, which lay in the centre of the kingdom of Phaistos, did not need any fortifications. Louis Godart from the University of Naples, who is excavating at Apodoulou, assumes that Phaistos, Monastiriki and Apodoulou fell victim to the same earthquake around 1700 BC, and that this was finally followed by a con-flagration. In Apodoulou, however, the dry-stone walls have been preserved intact to a height of 2.5 metres. Tremors, such as those caused by a strong earthquake, would have turned this settlement into a heap of rubble in just a few seconds.

Finds in the destruction layer of 1700 BC are similar in Phaistos, Mon-astiriki, Apodoulou and other Minoan settlements: The actual destruction occurred through fire – victims and valuable objects are absent. From this, the excavators conclude that the earthquake gave 'forewarning' – in other words, foreshocks indicated that an even stronger event was about to occur – and thus gave the inhabitants the chance to rescue their valuable goods and chattels. But such a conclusion contradicts both the basic char-acteristics of earthquakes and also the normal behaviour of people who are affected. Earthquakes are sudden releases of tension, in which the first shock is almost always the most powerful. The seismic waves with the greatest amplitude occur right at the beginning, and subsequently decrease in strength almost exponentially. Earthquakes basically occur unannounced, which is why they are so dangerous. They affect all forms of life and objects equally: kings, soldiers, craftsmen, farmers' wives, children and pets, and the whole inventory of buildings are shaken. Even jewels, therefore, remain in their original place. From this point of view, the Old Palace Period's destruction horizon does not display any of the char-acteristics resulting from an earthquake.

The behaviour of the inhabitants also seems abnormal. I remember an evening in a café in Olympia; I was sitting on one of those garden chairs that have frames of bent metal tubing, and suddenly it rocked from side to side. I simply thought that whatever it was – too much work, beer, sun, or an earthquake – it would soon stop. And it did. I reacted in exactly the same way, when the house in which we were living in California, directly over the San Andreas Fault, was hit by an earthquake of magnitude 5.6. After a short interruption, I simply went back to sleep. The next day, the earthquake was naturally the main topic of conversation at the Institute. As it turned out, all my colleagues and friends had reacted similarly. Arthur Evans, too, did not feel obliged to leave his room in the Villa Ariadne during the earthquake of 1926, which was nevertheless the strongest of the century in an extremely earthquake-prone region. Instead, he went to the window to get a better view of the event!

It is assumed, however, that the Minoan population behaved quite differently. Without exception, all the settlements on Crete must have been warned that a catastrophic earthquake would shortly occur. Although no house had collapsed and no wall had been shifted, people foresaw that the end was nigh. The whole population reacted in exactly the same way, despite the fact that all the towns were affected simultaneously and had no means of exchanging information. The inhabitants packed their things and vanished, never to be seen again.

Finally, the ground actually began to tremble, but not so strongly that, as is usual in earthquakes, there was a momentary liquefaction of the ground. The shaking was not even strong enough to cause walls or buildings to collapse. It only sufficed to overturn oil lamps. Once again, without prior consultation, people at all the different places, independently, and for reasons that are quite incomprehensible to us, must have had the idea of leaving their oil lamps burning in the houses when they left the town. The weak tremors, which were insufficient to cause lasting damage of any sort, merely ensured that the oil lamps fell over, and thus initiated a veritable inferno. And because this attack of stupidity furnished irrefutable proof that the flourishing administrative structure (which had been built up over centuries) was generally useless, in the aftermath of the catastrophic fires the rulers decided to reorganise the whole nature of the state, of trade, of the administration, and of the overall community.

Presumably, the widespread idea that in prehistoric times earthquakes could initiate conflagrations goes back to Arthur Evans. Before the introduction on a massive scale of wooden houses and gas lamps at the end of the nineteenth and the beginning of the twentieth centuries, no one had ever thought to consider earthquakes and fire as having any sort of connection. The Roman writer and natural historian, Pliny the Elder, described the effects of earthquakes in his *Natural History*, but does not mention fire at all. The same applies to Aristotle, who wrote a whole treatise on earthquakes. To date, there are no indications whatsoever from either historical, modern or experimental examples that burning oil lamps were generally capable of starting a fire in a collapsing mud-brick house. It is far more likely that the dust that was raised would immediately smother any fire.

Earthquakes Past and Present

Naturally, catastrophic earthquakes did indeed occur in prehistoric times. A particularly striking example is the event that occurred in 373 BC, when the town of Helike on the Gulf of Corinth vanished in less than a minute, as if swallowed up by the earthquake. Nevertheless, even in this catastrophe, the houses in the neighbouring town of Aigion, just a few kilometres away, were unscathed. The destruction of Helike was thus a localised, narrowly confined event.

Another example of a historically and archaeologically verified earthquake is the event of 21 July 365 BC at Kourion on Cyprus. Under the rubble, the archaeologists found, among other things, the skeletons of a complete family and a young girl, together with a mule. But Kourion was just one of the thousands of Greek villages on Cyprus. This earthquake, too, did not cause more than local destruction.

To cause political effects, an earthquake must, at the very least, affect a wide area. This presupposes the existence of extensive tectonic faults, such as those found in Asia Minor. There, the active fault zone of the Anatolian Plate runs parallel to the northern coast of the subcontinent. An earthquake occurred in August 1688 on this crack, along a six-hundred-kilometre fracture zone. With a surface magnitude of 8, this was one of the strongest in Asia Minor in the last thousand years. Over forty-seven days, more than two hundred shocks shook the ground. Despite this, no more than 8000 people lost their lives – too many, of course, but not so many for the event to have caused a radical cultural change. And the damage to the buildings was largely repaired within a year.

In contrast to Asia Minor, most of the faults in Greece and on Crete are short; that is, less than twenty kilometres long. Earthquakes of magnitude 7 or more, however, require movement along a fault that is at least forty kilometres long. Such strong earthquakes cannot therefore occur in Greece. Of the more than eighty notable earthquakes that have occurred in Central Greece in the last 2300 years, not one was of abnormal strength. The Parthenon on the Acropolis in Athens has, for example, patiently withstood earth tremors for over two thousand years. Serious damage occurred to it only with a shot from a Venetian gunner during the second Ottoman–Venetian war in 1697. The Turkish troops had stored their munitions on the Acropolis, so the direct hit caused an enormous explosion, which reduced the Parthenon to the state in which we see it today.

The earthquakes in recent centuries that were catalogued by Evans all had merely local effects – none of them precipitated a cultural upheaval. Evans was also struck by the fact that the west of Crete behaved differently from the central region. Because many buildings from the Venetian period survived in the west, Evans assumed that tremors were rarer there than in Heraklion. In fact, the greatest earthquakes occurred in western Crete at different times (1646, 1805, 1910, 1923) from those in central Crete (1508, 1547, 1612, 1655, 1810, 1856, 1926).

All the fundamental cultural and political changes on Crete in the last three thousand years took place with no contribution from natural events. It was rather the nations on the surrounding mainland that determined the island's fate. In 67 BC, Crete was captured by the Romans. Later, around 395 AD, the island fell to the Byzantine Empire. Arab sovereignty of parts of the island began in 824 AD. In 1204, it fell to the Venetians, and in 1669 Turkish forces captured Candia. Their rule ended in 1898, and shortly afterwards (1912), Crete was finally politically united with the Greek mainland. Each one of these radical changes determined the political fate of the inhabitants for a long time, but none of them were at all related to any form of natural catastrophe. Why should the island's fate since the beginning of recorded history be moulded exclusively by its neighbouring states, whereas previously it was exclusively determined by earthquakes?

Our knowledge of the effects of earthquakes in *historical* times was summarised, just over a quarter of a century ago, by Nicholas Ambraseys, as follows:

> Earthquakes in the past twenty-four centuries have had little, if any, serious influence on historical developments in the Middle and Near East. They did often account for the premature decline of a local economy or for a crisis in local human affairs. But they have never caused the ruin of a culturally advanced state, far less the end of a civilization. In contrast with wars, epidemics and other long-lasting calamities, which have serious and prolonged effects, earthquakes and volcanic eruptions, no matter how large, seem to have had little or no long-term impact on Man.

This statement is equally valid for present-day natural catastrophes. Year after year, a few hundred such disasters occur, in which, worldwide, some 40,000 people lose their lives. The probability that an individual will die as a result of a natural catastrophe thus amounts to just 0.01 per cent. To put it another way: Out of every 10,000 people, on average just one dies in a natural disaster. Traffic accidents claim six times as many victims, and malarial diseases as many as 25 or even 50 times as many as natural disasters. Every day, approximately as many children die, worldwide, as people die in a whole year through natural catastrophes.

Although the destruction from an earthquake may be devastating, the basic requirements of the population remain unchanged. The land is fertile, and the sea full of food. The majority of the population survives, their settlements lie, as before, on geographically suitable sites, and trade relations are untouched. Unlike wars or epidemics, natural disasters are thus obviously easier to cope with, because the whole destructive potential is released all at once, and subsequently reconstruction can take place unhindered. The many hundreds of historically recorded earthquakes have also almost always produced the same reaction in the survivors: the dead are buried, the houses are rebuilt, and the town continues to exist.

What Causes Radical Cultural Change?

If the cultural upheavals around 1700, 1450 and 1200 BC were not produced by natural disasters, there remains only one possible cause: they must have arisen through deliberate, malicious intent. Nevertheless, this possibility was not popular with prehistorians. On this point, Arthur Evans simply said that 'it would have been difficult for the destruction to be caused by human hands'. Marinatos similarly said 'Nor can we believe in an invasion from abroad.' Denys Page held the view that it would have been completely senseless to destroy all these wonderful buildings, instead of sensibly making use of them. He expressed the view of his generation of researchers in the following words:

> ... are we to believe that they [the Mycenaeans] systematically destroyed all the other palaces, the towns in the far east of Crete, the great mansions and harbour-towns in the neighbourhood of Knossos itself? Doro Levi calls such a theory 'an absurdity needing no further discussion'; the best that can be said about it is that it is very improbable ... If this were the best we can do, it would be better to do something else.

Many experts referred to the fact that, even with the current state of weaponry, it would not be easy to conquer an island like Crete. Admittedly, no one maintained that it would ever have been easy, but it would not have been impossible. After all, sovereignty of Crete has changed hands frequently enough in historical times.

Even at the time of the first Thera Conference, the British prehistorian Sinclair Hood had argued that the Minoan culture came to an end through war. At Pyrgos on the south coast, the erection of massive walls, a watchtower, and large cisterns indicated that the population was prepared for their town to be besieged. At Knossos, Gournia, Mochlos and Malia, the inhabitants quickly hid valuable bronze vessels – just as if the threat were the danger of a raid. Repeated signs of vandalism were discovered: smashed vases, cult objects and storage vessels are known from Malia, Myrtos, Zakros, Palaikastro, and other sites. At Myrtos and Petras, moreover, the destruction is primarily concentrated on the ruler's mansion. All the indications are that the population evacuated the town in the face of imminent danger from a raid – rather like the planned withdrawal of the inhabitants of Moscow in 1812.

Colin Macdonald, the then curator of the Knossos excavations, and the Belgian prehistorian Jan Driessen, emphasised the fact that setting the Minoan cities on fire was not an easy task, and could hardly have occurred by chance. On the contrary, it required careful preparations: doors had to be broken down to provide a draught, and probably piles of brushwood had to be brought in to feed the fire. The thick layers of ash in many of the destruction layers may be signs of this. So the whole concept of the peace-loving Minoan civilisation becomes completely untenable. Both the beginning and the end of the period when it was at its height (1700–1450 BC) appear to have been marked by destruction that razed everything to the ground.

In future, prehistorians will probably more frequently than heretofore view the evolution of the Minoan culture in connection with events in other regions around the eastern Mediterranean. It was not just Crete that experienced major disruptions in its cultural history. In the 20th century BC, when the early palaces on Crete first originated, many cities in neighbouring Asia Minor were also founded, including the sixth and most important phase of the city of Troy. At the same time, foreign trade between Mediterranean kingdoms increased considerably. The 15th century BC did not just see the end of the New Palace Period on Crete – the Old Hittite kingdom in central Asia Minor also collapsed around this time. In addition, the beginning and end of the Early Palace Period constitute chronological markers in the development of Mycenaean Greece. There, an independent culture first became established after 1700 BC, and a palace culture from about 1450 BC. The breaks on Crete therefore have parallels in the nearly simultaneous and similarly far-reaching discontinuities on the neighbouring mainland.

Because islands are so well-defined geographically, there is a tendency to regard them as also being politically (and archaeologically) homogeneous units. At any rate, they appear to exhibit an isolation that does not, in reality, exist. The Israeli archaeologist Avner Raban has even determined that transport by water is easier than transport by land by a factor of thirty. If one wanted to represent the economically relevant factors of the distribution of land and sea in their appropriate proportions, water routes would have to be reduced to one thirtieth of their length. Crete would then lie in close proximity to Italy, Greece, Turkey, Syria, Palestine, Egypt and Libya. Perhaps the explanation for the revolutionary changes on Crete is to be found in these countries.

One hundred years ago, when Arthur Evans began his excavations at Knossos, the parallels with developments in other countries around the Mediterranean were not apparent. For lack of knowledge, Evans was left with practically no choice but to regard the development of the Minoan civilisation as having occurred in isolation. The only country that had been thoroughly investigated archaeologically at that time was Egypt, and Evans linked the development of the Minoan civilisation with Egyptian chronology. Since then, however, our knowledge of prehistoric cultures in the eastern Mediterranean has expanded considerably. It is now appropriate to test the theories advanced by the pioneers in the light of modern knowledge. There are no longer any grounds for supporting the simple explanatory models that date from the early days of the study of Aegean prehistory.

Chapter 3

Climate:

History Cutting Capers?

Scholars are men who differ from ordinary mortals in that they take a delight in long-winded and complicated errors.

ANATOLE FRANCE

Did Climate Change Cause the Upheaval About 1200 BC?

In addition to tsunamis, ash-falls and earthquakes, drastic climate changes are also possible causes of far-reaching radical alterations in cultural history. In particular, archaeologists and scientists have tried to explain the end of the 'Heroic' Age, about 1200 BC, as the result of climate change and catastrophic drought. Such thoughts were expressed by W. Max Müller as early as the nineteenth century in his book *Asien und Europa* (*Asia and Europe*). He referred to an Egyptian temple inscription that stated that the Pharaoh Merenptah had to send grain to central Asia Minor because the harvest there had failed. This climate theory achieved considerable popularity at the end of the 1960s, approximately at the same time as Marinatos' catastrophe scenario. It was then that the archaeologist Rhys Carpenter from Bryn Mawr College in Pennsylvania published an influential booklet, in which he advanced the theory that Greece had experienced a drought that lasted for several hundred years, which removed the basis for agriculture and sustenance, and led to mass migrations:

> To my thinking, after puzzling for many years over this, the greatest still unsolved problem in Mediterranean history, there is only one solution that will meet all the varied aspects of the case, and that answer is – famine, a dropping of the food supply below the critical level for subsistence.

Carpenter asserts that there are no signs of external attacks on Mycenaean society. As a result, everything points to the Mycenaean population having left their original home on the Peloponnese of their own free will, virtually evacuating the region. He interpreted the undoubted signs of massive destruction that have been found in many settlements as looting of grain and food stores by the hungry population. As a result of this unrest (according to Carpenter) almost all the states in the eastern Mediterranean fell into a deep, cultural Dark Age, during which the knowledge of writing and of organised society were lost in many different places. According to Carpenter, the climate change in the eastern Mediterranean began about 1200 BC, and continued until 850 BC:

> And by famine I do not mean an occasional failure of several consecutive harvests, but such an enduring and disastrous destruction of annual yield as only a drastic climatic change could have occasioned.

Other researchers took up this theory of climatic change. In their view, the Mycenaean culture's way of life was based on an agriculture that was solely dependent on grain, itself extremely sensitive to poor harvests. As a result, major attacks or a series of crop failures would easily lead to unrest and raids on neighbouring states, and could have thus provoked an escalation of the situation.

During the last twenty years, this theory gained increasing significance among scientists in the USA and Great Britain as one of the most popular explanations of the cultural upheaval about 1200 BC. Many researchers developed the theory still further. They assumed that the effects of the catastrophic drought in Greece extended to Asia Minor, Syria and Palestine, and eventually also included Mesopotamia.

An example of the dramatic effects that even short-lived droughts may have is well shown by the Turkish province of Ankara in 1874. In that year, 81 per cent of the cattle, and 97 per cent of the sheep died. Through deaths and migration, the original population of this region was halved in less than a year. Ancient literature also contains innumerable accounts of droughts, crop failures and destructive storms that have occurred through-out recorded history and in all known regions of the world. Among them there are descriptions of droughts during the Dark Ages in early historical times – the period to which Carpenter refers. The Greek historian Herodotus mentions (1.94) a famine and epidemic on Crete at the end of the Trojan War that carried off men and cattle, until the land was so deserted that it was settled by new colonists. He also describes a terrible drought that affected Lydia in western Asia Minor during that period, and which lasted eighteen years and forced the inhabitants to separate and colonise new regions:

> In the days of Atys, the son of Manes, there was great scarcity through the whole land of Lydia. For some time the Lydians bore the affliction patiently, but finding that it did not pass away, they set to work to devise remedies for the evil ... In this way they passed eighteen years. Still the affliction continued and even became more grievous. So the king determined to divide the nation in half, and to make the two portions draw lots, the one to stay, the other to leave the land. He would continue to reign over those whose lot it should be to remain behind; the emigrants should have his son Tyrrhenus for their leader. The lot was cast, and they who had to emigrate went down to Smyrna, and built themselves ships, in which, after they had put on board all needful stores, they sailed away in search of new homes and better sustenance.

Even the small island of Thera, with which we are very familiar, was not exempt from this fate: 'Seven years passed ... and not a drop of rain fell in Thera: all the trees in the island, except one, were killed with the drought.' wrote Herodotus (4.151). The Bible tells how a drought forced Abraham to migrate to Egypt – when Palestine became fertile again, he returned. And on other occasions, Israel sent its children into Egypt to obtain grain.

In many cases, climate change is indicated by geographical names, which nowadays appear inappropriate. For example, in 865 AD, the Norwegian Floke Vilgerdson tried hard to establish a settlement on Iceland. Unfortunately, this attempt occurred during a cold epoch, and Vilgerdson had to abandon his plan during a particularly cold winter. He called the country the 'Land of Ice', in other words 'Iceland'. Some 120 years later, in a relatively warm epoch, Erik the Red discovered a new land west of Iceland, which, because of its flourishing vegetation, he called 'Greenland'. Climatic changes are therefore responsible for the names of Iceland and Greenland having precisely the opposite meanings from what they imply nowadays. During the favourable climatic conditions that prevailed in the 11th century AD, Norsemen succeeded in reaching North America by sea, by way of Greenland. Between 1200 and 1400 AD, however, there was a rapid deterioration in the climate, which was probably also the reason for the abandonment of the Norse settlements in Greenland. Because of the massive amounts of drift ice, the northern route to North America was no longer practical.

Discovery and Investigation of the 'Palace of Nestor'

When Rhys Carpenter described his theory of rapid climate change at the end of the Bronze Age, there were hardly any data from Greece relating to palaeoclimate, but this situation soon changed. At the beginning of the 1970s, new data were obtained that allowed the reconstruction of the climate of the region in the far southwestern tip of Greece. According to Homer, it was here that the palace of wise King Nestor – one of the leading Greek aristocrats at the Siege of Troy – was situated. In Homer's works he appears as a reputable, outstanding statesman of advanced age. His kingdom is shown to have been a powerful trading state from the fact that with ninety ships, his was the largest contingent in the Trojan War after that of Agamemnon, the leader. After Troy, Mycenae, Tiryns, Knossos and many other Bronze Age palaces had been discovered and excavated at the end of the 19th century, many archaeologists turned their sights on western Messenia, where the lost palace of Nestor must have lain, and where today various towns bear the name of the Bronze Age kingdom of Pylos. The Homer-inspired Heinrich Schliemann was the first to travel to the area to search for the remains of the palace, but he had to leave again without having achieved anything.

It was the American archaeologist Carl Blegen, who finally succeeded in tracking down the palace in 1939 – it lay farther to the north than had previously been thought. Because Blegen found Nestor's palace immediately before the outbreak of the Second World War, the start of the excavations was delayed until 1950. Mind you, on the very first day of their task, the excavators came across the palace archive with a total of more than 1200 preserved clay tablets, inscribed in the Mycenaean script. They were proof that a knowledge of writing existed on the Greek mainland in prehistoric times.

Shortly after publication of the inscribed tablets from Pylos, it proved possible to decipher the texts. The British architect Michael Ventris, an amateur cryptographer and a cipher expert during the Second World War, discovered that the so-called Linear-B script corresponded with an early form of Greek. It is true that the texts contain only details of taxes and other payments to the palace, but even such prosaic records often offer valuable insights into the organisation and economy of a kingdom. Study of the texts brought to light that the Palace of Nestor was the centre of a hierarchically and regionally organised system of various communities – in other words it was an early form of state. Within this state, about 50,000 people lived in two provinces, with approximately 200 settlements and small towns. When the Palace of Nestor went up in flames about 1200 BC, the state's structure and administrative organisation equally collapsed. This fire did, however, preserve the clay tablets with the Linear-B texts, which were obviously intended only for temporary use and which, without the fire, would long ago have disappeared. All the Linear-B texts consequently date from shortly before the catastrophe. The data about the economy that they contain confirm that, up to the very end, the palace had plentiful supplies of food at its disposal, and that, on average, the population had 128 per cent of the daily calorie requirements available. The theory advanced by Carpenter that the people of Mycenae were starving is thus shown to be completely untenable.

Pollen and the History of Climate

Whilst Carl Blegen excavated the Palace of Nestor in the 1960s, still using traditional methods, an interdisciplinary research team was already dedicated to the investigation of the overall environment in the palace's sphere of influence and its usage by the Bronze Age population. This University of Minnesota Messenia Expedition (UMME) represented a great step forward for Aegean prehistory through the multiplicity of methods that it employed. Geography, geology, metallurgy, pedology (the study of soils), agronomy, botany, chemistry, archaeology, historical sciences and linguistics – experts from all these fields pulled together to reconstruct the Bronze Age landscape.

Following the phase of increasing specialisation in the first half of the twentieth century, the rapid technological advances after the Second World War brought about a rapprochement between geology and archaeology. The field-oriented research disciplines for the study of the past came to be based on technology, and the number of scientists at excavations increased considerably. Robert John Braidwood, an American prehistorian who led an interdisciplinary project in northern Iraq, first proposed, in 1957, combining the mutual efforts of archaeologists and scientists in a new discipline. The term 'geoarchaeology', which eventually came to be applied to this field, first appeared in the 700-page investigation entitled *Environment and*

Archaeology – An Ecological Approach, by Karl Butzer, which was published in 1972.

The scientific research carried out for UMME provided new information about the effects of climatic change on early historical societies. Because plant communities are sensitive to variations in climate, the history of the vegetation reflects climatic change. Vegetation may therefore be enlisted as an indicator for the reconstruction of past climate. Details of the composition of former plant cover may be obtained for thousands of years in the past, because plants produce, year after year, vast amounts of pollen and spores, which are spread by the wind and insects. In this way, every individual plant community produces a specific mixture of pollen, which is almost as characteristic as a fingerprint.

As an organic material, pollen disintegrates in air; that is to say, it decomposes chemically or is eaten by microbes. As a rule, a pollen grain breaks up within a few weeks of it being released. There are, however, numerous geological environments in which this decomposition is prevented. Under favourable conditions in a desert, for example, there is no decay. This is why dinosaur eggs and recognisable embryos are found there. In ice, the low temperatures prevent molecules from moving. As we all know, food remains fresh in a freezer, and similarly, whole mammoths and humans (like 'Ötzi') may be preserved with their skin and hair. Finally, organic materials are also protected in the oxygen-free environment in bogs, which is why the so-called 'bog bodies' are sometimes found in them.

Bogs, lakes and marshes are also ideal storage sites for pollen. Under suitable conditions, it may be preserved there for thousands of years. Botanists take cores from the pollen-bearing layers with special coring tools, which preserve the fine structure of the sediments. The relative percentages of pollen in the individual layers of sediment reflect the changing composition of the plant community throughout the various individual periods in the past.

Basically, precise analysis of the vegetation history is desirable for all regional archaeological projects, but in the rain-poor Mediterranean region, suitable marshy areas are rare. One needs a certain amount of luck in finding a research area that contains lakes, lagoons, swamps or marshes that have remained damp over a long period of time.

The UMME botanists had just such a piece of luck, because at the northern end of the Gulf of Navarino lies a lake, several kilometres wide, known as the Osmanaga Lagoon. They were able to obtain cores from the sediments in this wetland area, from which pollen stretching back thousands of years could be recovered. The results of the pollen research produced a major surprise. What was established was that during the so-called 'dark ages' between 1100 and 700 BC – at a time when western Messenia was regarded as having been essentially uninhabited – there was the most intensive olive cultivation. Up to forty per cent of the pollen from that period came from olives. Left to natural devices, olives would never have reached such a high density. In one respect, then, the UMME results posed more questions than they answered.

The Pylos Regional Archaeology Project

Thirty years after UMME, Jack Davis, the successor to Carl Blegen at Cincinnati, devised a plan for investigating the surroundings of the Palace of Nestor once again, using the most recent archaeological and scientific field-research methods. The aim of this project was to compare the information obtained from the Linear-B tablets about the settlement structure in the Late Bronze Age kingdom of Pylos with the surface finds that are still encountered. This requires an area of approximately 250 square kilometres to be searched systematically. The method to be used – known as an 'archaeological survey' or, more colloquially, 'field walking' – was developed in the course of various investigations in Central America, and was first employed in Greece some twenty years ago. Jack Davis is one of the pioneers pressing this method into service.

The aim of such a survey is to record traces of former settlements, which may still be found at the surface, and then to reconstruct the history of the settlement from the sum total of the evidence available. In field walking, a group of five or six persons, spaced between ten and fifteen metres apart, sweeps fields and grassland, with their gaze kept firmly on the ground. Once they have covered a specific area, which often corresponds to an individual field, they meet to compare their observations and compile their notes. As they proceed, they collect all important artefacts and count all visible pot-shards. In their notes they record how many objects they have found in each survey area. Only the most important artefacts are taken back to excavation headquarters, where they are carefully dealt with and recorded.

Archaeological surface surveys have many advantages. One of these is the fact that *all* traces of former settlement are recorded, including farmyards, watchtowers, shepherds' huts, rubbish heaps, roads, and so on. In addition, a survey provides information on the overall period of settlement. The participants note down fifty-thousand-year-old stone tools, as well as defensive works from a recent war. Surveys thus indicate how the overall population in a specific area has evolved over the course of time. The organisation and implementation of such surveys are both cost-effective and flexible; in general, they can be completed within three years.

If the finds from a surface survey are compared with those from an excavation, the former are extremely unattractive. The spectacular objects that fascinate the general public are hardly ever found at the surface. Even the value of the data obtained by a survey is limited. If the search area is not well-defined geographically, for example by a range of mountains, there is always the possibility that an important inhabited site might lie immediately outside the chosen boundaries. And even within the area that is searched, a large part of the ground does not yield the desired information. Frequently, specific areas are not accessible, because they are excluded from the government permit. Others are impassable, because they are hopelessly overgrown, and yet others have been built over, eroded away, or covered with later sediments. Taking all these factors into account, it is obvious that only a restricted portion of the prehistoric surface will have remained undisturbed. For this reason, archaeologists must be cautious in drawing conclusions. Despite these objections, archaeology today cannot be imagined without surface surveys, and these form a completely natural element of regional archaeological fieldwork.

The project at Pylos that was envisaged by Jack Davis offered the possibility of investigating a landscape and its historical development under optimum archaeological and scientific conditions, using the very latest techniques. His request for me to act as leader for the scientific contributions was naturally bound up with questions regarding which methods would be of definite use and which experts should be invited to take part in the investigation. The UMME data had shown that the conditions for preservation in the Osmanaga Lagoon were suitable for pollen analyses. This established that we should invite a botanist, to determine the succession of vegetation over the past millennia as completely as possible.

Although the Osmanaga Lagoon was the best place in the whole of southern Greece for pollen research, this certainly does not solve all our problems. The careful examination of a pollen core requires a great deal of time – it corresponds to approximately as much effort as obtaining a doctorate. As a result, pollen experts – or palynologists, to give them their scientific name – are first, nearly non-existent; and second, have enough work to keep them occupied for years. If possible, however, the results of the analysis of the sequence of vegetation need to be available before evaluation of the archaeological finds takes place. How was I then to find an outstanding, yet affordable, pollen expert, but one who, above all, had some spare capacity? In discussing this with Jack Davis, I played what television commentators would probably call the 'Russian card'. The Soviet Union, which in 1991, when we were doing our planning, was still a single unit, had well qualified, highly motivated researchers in the traditional scientific disciplines, including palynology. I therefore suggested enlisting a Russian palynologist.

Jack Davis was amazed. The idea of collaborating with experts from Moscow for archaeological studies in Greece appeared quite extraordinary to him. Such a thing had never happened before in the field of Aegean prehistory. After all, the Cold War was still raging, and the last years of the Reagan era had been overshadowed by the planned introduction of the 'Star Wars' defence project. Naturally, Jack realised that I would hardly make such an unusual proposal if I did not already have a specific person in mind, ready and able to undertake the palynological work. He was right. Three years before, at a conference in Georgia, I had met the talented botanist Sergei Yazvenko. The circumstances under which we became acquainted were rather remarkable. Conference participants were expressly warned not to take any slides, being advised that there was no chance of any projection facilities. Naturally, I would not willingly have contravened the rules of the game, but my paper discussed the interpretation of satellite images in geoarchaeology, and I could not imagine how anyone could convey this topic with just words and gestures, so, without further ado, I stuck in a few transparencies. In Tiflis, in response to my request, a slide projector was indeed found, but an ancient model with such a weak lamp that it needed to be no more than two metres away from the screen. More problematic was the lack of power sockets, of which there was just one in the whole conference room. So the – absolutely faultless – simultaneous translation arrangements had to function without power during my talk, and the interpreter had to come up on to the stage, to translate each of my sentences into Russian. The projector was on the stage as well, and my future expert, Sergei, whom I did not know at that point, took on the role of projectionist. So my talk was a sort of audio-visual happening. On the last evening of the conference, I succeeded in escaping from the female KGB agent, who had been provided in the guise of an 'interpreter' from the Ministry of Geology, and spent the evening with three other foreign conference participants and some of our hosts and helpers. Sergei and I took the opportunity to begin to forge plans for collaborative projects.

The sponsors of the Pylos project still required a short written statement as to why this Russian–American combined operation made sense, but finally Jack succeeded in convincing them about the unusual composition of our team. Sergei was with us in Pylos by 1992, where he displayed his abilities to the full. We retrieved the first pollen cores, the results of which have already been published, and in the same year he obtained a grant from Canada, where he now lives and works.

Sergei brought a breath of fresh air to the methodology, testing new ways of solving certain notorious problems in palynology. One of these is the fact that certain types of pollen are overrepresented, whereas others hardly appear at all, even though the corresponding pollen-producing plants are present in large numbers. One may, for example, find practically no grape pollen right next to a vineyard. A pollen sample does not, therefore, enable one to draw conclusions about past vegetation without further work. If a sample contains equal quantities of pine and oak pollen, it does not by any means follow that pines and oaks amounted to equal fractions of the vegetation cover. To deal with this problem, Sergei searched for various plant communities that are part of the modern landscape, and marked out a total of 34 areas, each 25 metres square. Within each of these individual areas, he counted the occurrence of the larger types of plants, and estimated the smaller ones. Finally, he took a pollen sample from the modern surface, to determine ratios between the current plant population and the pollen count. In this way, he was able to determine that a pollen sample with forty per cent oak pollen corresponds to forty per cent oak trees, but that a pollen sample with forty per cent olive pollen represents twenty per cent olive trees. From these samples Sergei was able to develop mathematical equations, with which it is possible to calculate, approximately, the actual composition of past vegetation.

Our pollen cores from the Osmanaga Lagoon proved successful. Sergei gave the Pylos Project a continuous vegetation sequence for the past 7000 years. We found that the Messenia farmers were already practising extremely intensive agriculture in the third millennium BC. While the population density was low, they concentrated on the fertile ground in the valley meadows, which could be worked without a plough. When the population grew in the early Bronze Age, additional areas of land had to be created – deforestation began. Around 2000 BC, the pine forests were reduced to a fraction of their original size; between 1600 and 1400 BC – that is, in the first half of the Mycenaean epoch – they disappeared almost completely. The density of the deciduous oaks also decreased by half. Simultaneously, steppe and maquis types spread, until they covered about forty per cent of the overall surface. This sudden change in vegetation indicates massive overgrazing.

In the second half of the Mycenaean period – between 1400 and 1200 BC – the situation changed. The steppe vegetation, which had previously been widespread, retreated; in its place, useful plants, including olives, increased. In addition, many types of plants occurred for the first time, for example, barley, walnut trees and plane trees. At the same time, the soil became stabilised, and the erosion rates declined drastically. The countryside was obviously used systematically at this period, and was probably even stabilised with terracing.

After the collapse of the Mycenaean state about 1200 BC, the region appears to have been depopulated. During the centuries of this dark period, the plant cover shows less human influence than at any other time during the last four thousand years. It is only in the 8th century BC that the number of olives rises again – a sign of increasing agricultural development. Between 500 and 100 BC, olive production reached its peak, amounting to a quarter of the surface area.

The UMME botanist had, however, set the peak production of olives in the middle of the dark period – between 1100 and 700 BC. This was obviously the maximum that occurred five hundred years later in our cores. We had, however, corrected our radio-carbon dates for various distortions. If these corrections are applied to the UMME date, their olive maximum also falls in classical Hellenic times. So for thirty years a small error in the methodology had for thirty years caused Aegean prehistory to be haunted by an incorrect value – Messenia had never been used for intensive olive cultivation during the centuries of the dark age.

Climate or Humans?

The botanical investigations at Pylos have shown no hint of dramatic climatic change during the last five thousand years. All the far-reaching changes in the plant cover correspond in time with radical political and economic change. The inevitable conclusion is that it was human hands that determined the appearance of the west Messenian countryside. Carpenter's picture of a drought that persisted for centuries is disproved in every respect.

Even thirty years ago, Rhys Carpenter recognised the objections to his theory. For example, many of the towns that were destroyed contained stores of food that were left undisturbed by the attackers, and which instead were burned. Valuable objects and precious metals, on the other hand, had largely disappeared or been hidden. In addition, starving peasants would have had little chance against well-equipped and hardened palace troops. This is probably why there are no examples from historical times of widespread destruction by the hungry section of the population. Protests in times of hardship were, and still are normal, as occurred for example in ancient Rome, but not invasions or attacks. With regard to the end of the Aegean Bronze Age, it is, in any case, valid to differentiate between the economic and demographic collapse on the one hand and the complete disappearance of the Mycenaean culture on the other. In the Aegean region, the whole century between 1250 and 1150 BC was a time of great problems, and the individual destruction horizons at many sites merely emphasise this point.

Particularly dry years have repeatedly provoked waves of emigration. This happened for example, in Greece, in the 8th and 7th centuries BC. What tipped the balance then, however, was the population density, which caused the land to become exhausted. Any worsening of the weather increased pressure on the population. The descriptions of drought in the Bible may be interpreted in a similar way. Israel was not so densely settled as Greece in the 7th century BC, but lay on the margins of the desert. Any change in the weather in this marginal climate must have caused lasting effects on agricultural production.

Incidentally, the same applies to climatic change and droughts as to earthquakes. In the past four thousand years, thousands of catastrophic droughts, storms and floods have occurred – the German geographer Richard Hennig listed them as long ago as 1904 – but none of these events can be proved to have caused any radical cultural change. And even if such a cultural revolution were to have coincided with climatic change, the two processes were not necessarily causally linked.

To conclude this examination of various natural catastrophes, we may sum up by saying that the interaction between past cultures and their natural environment is not restricted to rare, catastrophic events. The extremely simplified explanatory models of the early generation of discoverers and patriarchal archaeologists, based on a single cause, no longer have any validity. The great pioneers' ideas arose at a time when knowledge of evolution was not common property, and classical antiquity was regarded as having arisen from nothing. Furthermore, the pioneers could base their theories only on the material that was then known – and this was extremely limited. They had no alternative but to search for simple explanations.

Nowadays, archaeology has far more data at its disposal, and there are also completely different techniques for searching for archaeological sites. In the second part of this book we will discuss past and present methods and, above all, the results of modern interdisciplinary archaeology. The discussion will bring to the fore, on the one hand, the interaction between people and the landscape and, on the other, the mutual stimuli that occur between different cultures.

Part Two

Archaeological Research
in the Twenty-first Century

Chapter 4

Techniques: Archaeology Past and Present

Just where it stops, science actually begins to become interesting.

JUSTUS VON LIEBIG

Nag Hammadi

My train journey south from Cairo has lasted fourteen hours before I finally reach my destination: Nag Hammadi. While the train slowly rolls to a stop, I check three or four times with Egyptian fellow passengers whether it really is Nag Hammadi, because there is no sign to confirm its identity. Finally, I open the carriage door. Outside, lies the green Nile valley, which for hours has hardly seemed to change, and which is a landscape that, despite a complete lack of rain, is blessed with an abundance of water. As far as the eye can see, sugar cane is growing. Here and there, mud-brick houses are visible, which any powerful storm would sweep away – except that here there are no storms.

There are only a few tourists on the train. A young Dutch girl, whose scanty travel clothes must appear blasphemous to any Allah-fearing Moslem, says, when I want to get off, 'My goodness, it's the end of the world.' Instinctively, I feel she's right. There is no station, just rusty rails, tumbledown mud huts, donkey carts and dust. I'm lucky and find an old car and driver that are free. 'Aluminium,' I say. He nods. 'Hotel Aluminium,' I repeat. He nods again. Together we load my rucksack into the boot, and set out.

In the 1960s, when there was close contact with the Soviet Union, this land of the Nile used Russian financial and technical aid to construct the Aswan Dam. Along with the dam's hydroelectric power station, Egypt also obtained a gigantic aluminium smelter. The raw material, bauxite, required to obtain the aluminium had, however, to be transported from the other side of the world – from Australia. A small archaeological research group, led by Kathryn Bard from Boston, is quartered in the guest hotel of this 'Aluminium City' in Nag Hammadi.

We cross the tracks, near an exhausted donkey that is struggling to pull a two-wheeled wooden cart over the rails. The load of sugar cane is about fifty times the size of the donkey, and, just now, heart failure seems closer than the other side of the tracks.

A few hundred metres farther on, a typical Peugeot taxi is blocking the right-hand lane. The French occupation of North Africa – and the Arab sense of the practical – mean that in this part of the world there is essentially only one make of car, which also means that obtaining spare parts ceases to be a problem. This particular representative of the Peugeot horde had been involved some time before in a head-on collision, and is standing – reduced to half its length but otherwise correctly positioned on the road – right in our way. It looks as though none of the passengers could have survived. We drove slowly past the wreck, as if nothing had happened.

After a while, we reach the guardpost at the entrance to the monstrous 'Aluminium City'. This unnatural industrial town and its guest-house are typical of the rapidly constructed, functional architecture of the 1960s. Although they were never properly finished, for years the buildings have been falling into decay. Despite this, the plant is the safest and most comfortable place in the whole of Upper Egypt, as a woman doctor at the Zurich Tropical Institute casually informed me when I had my hepatitis vaccination.

The archaeological team has already been hanging around for six weeks in this desert and industrial wasteland. They gratefully welcome the change that my visit brings. After talking far into the night, the next morning I get ready for work: searching for archaeological sites. For thousands of years, human settlement has taken place along the boundary between the green Nile valley and the sandy desert. This boundary is so sharply defined that one can, without exaggeration, stand with one leg in the valley and the other in the desert. Practically no archaeological remains are found on the cultivated strip. If there ever were any, they have been buried beneath the deposits of Nile silt.

In contrast, archaeological sites lie along the desert boundary like pearls on a string. We are searching this strip for a 6000-year-old settlement, hints of which are given by minor finds and cemeteries. Because of the intense utilisation of this border region between the desert and river, the prehistoric layers have, however, largely been destroyed. Those arch- aeological sites that have not been dug up and devastated in the course of thousands of years, have already been exposed in giant, hasty excavations by the Egyptologist Sir William Matthew Flinders Petrie. This English gentleman spent his honeymoon in the area, and excavated an Egyptian cemetery as he did so!

Abdel-Moneim Mahmoud, a young geologist from Cairo University, accompanies me on my first day in the field. We cross the Nile on a swing bridge, to inspect a gravel pit on the eastern side of the valley. Moneim knows the stratigraphy of this area from work for his doctorate, and gives me a short introduction to the regional geology.

As we are returning, I glance at the roughly drawn topographic map, lettered in Arabic. At one point, a low hill is shown in the middle of the Nile valley. Remains of early buildings might have been preserved there, and not been covered by the Nile sediments. Without telling Moneim my thoughts, I ask him to make a small detour. He happily translates my directions for the driver. We travel for several kilometres on a sand track across uneven fields. Away from the only tarmac road in the area, there are only sugar cane and irrigation canals. Only occasionally do we encounter a mud-brick house or a donkey cart. The countryside becomes more and more inhospitable and eerie. Moneim and the driver begin to wonder about my odd request. Finally we reach a tiny village and stop in the midst of the houses. If Nag Hammadi is not actually the end of the world, this is. Immediately our car is ringed by the inhabitants. Many of them carry rifles. In this part of Egypt, blood feuds still prevail.

Somebody knows the name of the spot that I am looking for. The sole tractor in the village just happens, as if by magic, to be crossing the square, and is stopped. A guide, Moneim and I have to climb up beside the driver. After about another kilometre, we reach the next village, which consists of just three dwellings. One of these is brightly painted with aeroplanes and other methods of transport, to indicate that its owner has made a pil- grimage to Mecca. At the entrance to the village stands an Egyptian with a Kalashnikov AK-47, with obvious signs of use. The driver briefly explains to him where we want to go. He nods. Moneim and I get down from the tractor, and follow the guide and the man with the automatic rifle. We cross a field of sugar cane, three metres high. The farmer is barefoot, and is wearing nothing except a short loincloth and his automatic. When a pair of loudly barking dogs follow us, he releases the safety catch and grins.

Suddenly, I see on the path what we are looking for: a potsherd – and another and another. So there was a settlement here after all. As we reach the small hill, we stop to look around, and discover the remains of a Roman fort. Marble columns, roads, defensive walls – most completely overgrown, but easily recognisable from their contours. The ground is covered with pieces of marble and pottery. Certainly no archaeologist has ever ended up in this area. Now even the inhabitants are surprised by the significance of the spot. The man with the gun is as happy as we are. The Metropolitan Museum ought to dig here, he says, hoping for work and wages.

When we return to 'Hotel Aluminium' and tell the rest of the team about the discovery, no one shares our enthusiasm. The find should have been three or four thousand years older.

Aegean Prehistory in Former Times

With experience, luck, and a few tricks, it is often possible to make significant finds in totally unknown areas. The pioneers of Aegean prehistory did undoubtedly have – at least to a certain extent – a nose for finds. Frequently, however, they did not need even that. In many cases travel guides already gave details about sites, well before they were discovered by science. In Roman times, scholars travelled through Greece searching for the ruins of ancient cities and temples. The notes that they made, and their subsequent writings, are still available today, at least in part. In the eighteenth and nineteenth centuries, philhellenes and military scouts followed the routes of their ancient predecessors. These early travellers also noted down their observations – and in many cases it was these notes that later led archaeologists to the various sites.

Nevertheless, the pioneers discovered innumerable sites that had not been mentioned by early travellers. The Palace of Nestor and many graves in the surrounding area are examples of this. How, then, were they able to locate these treasures? Frequently, they simply sought out the area's coffee-shops where the farmers met in the afternoon, and there obtained information about where pottery fragments were found in the fields. They probably also gave one or other of the locals a reward for leading them to the sites. As experienced archaeologists, they could generally decide immediately, on the basis of the surface finds, whether a site was worth excavating.

Most of the sites discovered in that way are now protected. Generally, an archaeological society has either rented or bought the land on which the site lies, and then put up a barbed-wire fence to mark the boundaries of the piece of land. These fences are naturally a blessing, but the blessing is mixed. They also imply that only the plot inside the fence is of value, and will be protected and investigated. As a result, for a long time archaeologists' attention was exclusively concentrated on the fenced-off areas. Over the course of the centuries, however, agricultural practices lead to erosion of the area outside the fence, causing archaeological remains in the surrounding area to be lost, and with them the chance for future generations to increase their knowledge of life in the past, which will possibly remain restricted to the closely confined central areas of known sites.

Even in the course of investigations within the fence, conventional archaeological methods inevitably encounter problems. Archaeology is perhaps the sole scientific discipline that exists by destroying its evidence. The context within which the artefacts occur eventually has to be destroyed during the excavation – even when important information is lost in doing so. To minimise this unavoidable damage, excavators have tried for a long time to record as many aspects of the associated area as possible in the finest detail. That, however, means that conventional excavations require a lot of effort, and expense. Whoever makes the grants, however, expects justification of the expense, and this is easiest to provide through spectacular finds. Archaeologists who carry out their excavations in the conventional way are therefore practically forced to choose sites at which spectacular finds may be expected. It is understandable that they should prefer palaces, temples and cemeteries.

Despite the technologies available today, the general public expects archaeologists to discover 'treasures'. Anthony Snodgrass, a professor at Cambridge, has likened their role to that of film stars, who would like to play *serious* roles, whereas their fans are only waiting for them to take their clothes off. As a result of this compulsion for sensation, after more than one hundred years of scientific archaeological excavations we know more about life in the former palaces than about the community as a whole.

To best clarify how the procedures originally employed in archaeology need to be expanded, let us imagine them applied to a later period. In the context of their own time, the archaeologists of the nineteenth century would have been largely restricted to the villas of industrial magnates, where they would have discovered splendid residences with spacious architecture, colourful paintings, and beautifully finished furniture and art objects. The commercial basis of the company, and the company as a whole would not, however, have been included. To obtain a more accurate picture of the function of the senior management of a company, a broader field of investigation and additional facets would need to be taken into account. In the nineteenth century that would have meant that one needed to know, at the very least, about the factories that were the source of a financier's riches. The machines in the factories would reflect the state of technology, and the raw materials employed and the finished end products would similarly express the needs and tastes of the time. Past town planning and the general level of culture would be revealed by the network of roads, and by the schools, churches, cemeteries and recreational areas.

In the past, however, archaeologists hardly showed any interest in the infrastructure of former societies. Their main attention was devoted to work with artefacts. During an excavation, thousands of pottery fragments need to be cleaned, labelled, classified, catalogued, drawn and photographed. This requires time – a lot of time. Archaeological excavations are thus generally among the most protracted of scientific research projects. The work at Olympia, for example, began almost 140 years ago, and is still going on. Because the appraisal of ceramics takes up such a lot of time, and is afforded such a high status, one is inclined to regard this task as being the principal part of scientific research. In fact, pottery should serve solely as the tool that gives us our first point of entry into the past. The actual scientific work must consist of the conclusions that may be drawn from the finds. Assessment of pottery alone can hardly provide the information that archaeologists want, because potsherds do not even reflect past societies, and certainly not the epochal events that determine the course of history. As one woman archaeologist has said 'Kings may come and go, but pots go on for ever.'

So, just as it would seem far-fetched to try to reconstruct and understand the last war in Bosnia using broken saucers, it is just as impossible to understand events that occurred some thousands of years ago, solely on the basis of pottery types.

Aspects of Modern Field Archaeology

Nowadays, the external conditions for field archaeology are, in many respects, less advantageous than they were formerly. In countries such as Albania, Algeria, Egypt, Libya or Syria archaeological fieldwork is possible, if at all, only with armed guards. Many university lecturers are unwilling to risk their students and themselves, and choose safer countries for their research. But even in many member states of the European Union experts encounter impediments, which hinder conventional excavations. Research on sites that have been known and preserved for a long time is only possible for selected groups. Working permits for excavations in Greece are divided between a dozen different nations, which all, from Denmark to Australia, have their own branches in Athens. The simplest and, in many cases, the only possible way of carrying out an excavation, consists of re-excavating a site that was archaeologically examined a long time ago by members of one's own country. So research work is restricted to those few sites where compatriots carried out excavations fifty or one hundred years ago. And because the choice of places does not depend exclusively on scientific arguments, archaeology runs the risk of reinforcing old prejudices, the sole aim of which was the recovery of artefacts rather than the answering of questions.

In addition, archaeologists nowadays do not always receive a friendly welcome from the rural population. Occasionally they are greeted by farmers with shotguns, who frequently even use them,. At the same time, many archaeological sites are plundered by robbers through illegal excavations, and innumerable others are destroyed by bulldozers. During the Pylos Project I was accompanying a survey team across an unprotected site, which was just about to be flattened by an earthmover. The village mayor arrived and screamed at us – not at the bulldozer driver – 'Clear off! This is an archaeological site. If you don't get away, I'll inform the Archaeological Service!' This threat was not necessary, however, because the woman who officially represented the Archaeological Service was among us on the spot.

Another Greek woman archaeologist has told me that she is often ready to give up her occupation, because so many sites are wilfully destroyed. Since the time of the great pioneers in Aegean prehistory, country folk have learned that archaeological remains beneath their fields are not a blessing, but rather a curse. The discovery of a site on a portion of land leads inevitably to a delay in building permission, increased costs, and even expropriation of the land. So the farmers try to ensure that there is nothing left on the land to discover. Whoever instigated this policy can have had little appreciation of the damage that it has caused.

Fieldwork in the Future

Because it is so difficult to obtain permission, as well as the necessary resources, for a conventional type of excavation, and also because of the limited information that may be gleaned from an excavation's finds, more and more archaeologists – particularly the younger ones – are turning to new techniques that allow larger areas to be searched for sites.

Surveys – field-walking, as I have described in connection with the Pylos Project – are being more and more frequently employed. In Greece alone, there are currently about two dozen such projects under way. Surveys have lower costs than excavations, and they generally require less time. As already noted, most such projects are concluded within three years. In addition, surveys not only provide information covering broad spans of time in the history of culture and over large areas, but also produce that information rather quickly.

Surveys and excavations may be combined effectively so that high-resolution detailed studies may be carried out simultaneously with regional investigations. Field archaeology first locates all the sites in a region by means of a survey, and subsequently investigates the most important places more thoroughly by excavation. This sort of multilayer approach with different methods of research covering areas of different sizes, may be extended, on the Russian-doll principle or like a collapsible telescope. The outermost area covered by a regional investigation is defined by the extent of the literature search carried out by members of the project. The chosen area needs to be as large as possible. For example, if the area being investigated is an island the literature search should include the neighbouring mainland.

Within this large area, covered by the literature search, a smaller area is chosen, generally amounting to a few hundred square kilometres. This needs to be an archaeologically interesting piece of country, defined by specific topographic boundaries. Within this area, the known archaeological sites are located, and then recorded and described in a uniform manner. The technical term for this technique is the 'extensive survey'. Apart from the known sites, spot checks are also made at specific locations that appear exceptionally well suited for settlement. In this way, a general, although imperfect, picture of settlement is obtained with the minimum amount of effort.

The 'intensive survey' – that is, the actual *surface survey* for archaeological sites – follows in a third, more closely defined region. The architectural remains and artefacts are located through systematic, fine-tooth-comb, field walking. Subsequently, the results of the intensive survey help to define the investigation's core areas, where excavations are finally carried out.

The Organisation and Requirements of Fieldwork

Archaeological fieldwork is nowadays accompanied by a whole host of natural scientists – in many cases their number exceeds that of the actual archaeologists. 'Science will generally become the key to new discoveries in archaeology', according to the archaeobiologist Hans-Peter Uerpmann from Munich. Geochemistry and biochemistry enable one to determine whether milk, olive oil or animal fats were once used in prehistoric cooking pots. The source of raw materials may be determined from trace-element concentrations. Fingerprints on clay containers permit ethnic groups to be identified, and even the genetic material of past individuals may be reconstructed from hairs and flakes of skin. This type of chemical and physical measurements from artefacts is known as 'archaeometry' – a field of research in which Germany is among the world leaders.

Scientific studies are no longer confined to individual finds, but deal with whole environments, which is why the term 'geoarchaeology' is used. In this discipline, however, Germany is at the bottom of the league. The gulf separating it from the level of knowledge in other countries is so wide that many German archaeologists have the impression that geoarchaeology does not exist. When I began to be interested in this field, some twenty years ago, I had to pursue my studies at a university in the USA. Unfortunately, the situation remains the same today. Because of the standards being set by international archaeological projects, however, we can expect that geoarchaeology will soon be actively pursued in Germany.

Over the years, certain ground rules have been established, which have proved to be of assistance in the preparation and logistics associated with geoarchaeological projects. I want to discuss these briefly here, because they contribute to ensuring that the involvement of scientists in regional archaeological projects is utilised as efficiently as possible.

To start with, any scientific investigation should pose a problem that is worthy of investigation. Although this sounds trivial, in very few scientific projects, publications and conferences is any emphasis laid on the real reason why they are actually taking place. It can be particularly helpful to set down the basic objectives or even publish them in the form of a project outline – preferably even before the project has begun. This document enables the aims, methods and scope of a project to be fixed in a concrete form. And this is precisely what is required when one considers the number of people directly or indirectly involved in all the various authorities, grant-giving bodies and research institutes.

The stated aims are of critical significance for the subsequent course of the project. They determine the choice of methods, the duration of work, the overall costs, and the type of specialists that will be consulted for the project. Later publications should refer to the original aims and describe how closely the project came to attaining them.

Naturally, most research projects produce unexpected results that exceed the original aims. This is precisely what makes science so fascinating. While concentrating on a specific task, one stumbles – more or less accidentally – across a surprising discovery, which may possibly be of greater significance than the goals originally envisaged. The word 'accidentally', however, does not properly convey the core of the matter. Such breakthroughs do not basically occur by accident but rather because the right people ask the right questions in the right place at the right time. Columbus was searching for a new ocean-trading route to India and found an unknown continent. Attempting to predict discoveries of this sort in advance would be preposterous, but that should not deter us from quietly striving for them.

The second step involves choosing the study area. Current practice nowadays in allocating an archaeological research permit means that the precise definition of the boundaries of the area to be investigated is essential. However, this generally means that the order of Points 1 and 2 is reversed. In most cases, it is obvious that there is a site for which a permit might be obtained, and it is only then that thought is given to questions that might be answered by investigations at that site. A truly scientific approach begins, however, by posing such questions. Will influential archaeologists in the future perhaps succeed in convincing those responsible for allocating permits of the importance of this principle?

It is self-evident that the study area must contain those elements that are central to answering the original questions. As a rule, this includes, among other things, fertile arable land, which would have attracted settlers at any period. Apart from this, the chosen region should be well-defined geographically. The size of the area to be covered is also of crucial significance. If it is too small – like most fenced-off archaeological sites – the outskirts and the hinterland are not included. If the study area is too large, the project will be unworkable. Experience shows that a square or rectangular study area with sides of between five and twenty-five kilometres in length provides good conditions.

Finally, it is necessary to assemble every conceivable piece of information about the study area involved. This includes any references and descriptions in ancient literature, the reports of early travellers who passed through the region in the eighteenth and nineteenth centuries and, naturally, all earlier archaeological, geological, geographical and botanical investigations. Details about the climate and hydrological data are also helpful, as are records of earthquakes and, frequently, information about current agricultural production as well. During this early phase of the investigation, this material serves as a fixed point of reference for the embryonic project.

Also, before the start of the actual field survey, a topographical map is drawn up, which will be used as the basis of subsequent work. Nowadays, this is prepared using software called Geographical Information Systems (GIS), which allows the study area to be represented as a three-dimensional image that may be viewed from various directions. Its true value, however, lies in the fact that it allows all landscape-related data, such as the results of the survey, to be stored digitally. Later, these data may be displayed and evaluated from different points of view. Finally, photographs giving a bird's-eye view, and satellite images, as well as existing topographical maps, all help to complete the desired model.

Before the individual field tasks are undertaken, the team leaders should have inspected the area. There are three main goals for this initial investigation. The first, naturally, is to establish whether the planned area is generally suitable for answering the basic questions being posed. Second, it is necessary to establish what methods may be used in the chosen area of country. Third, matters of logistics need to be settled. These include the choice of accommodation, the organisation of car hire, and the obtaining and furnishing of temporary offices as well as storerooms. Apart from this, this first survey of the area is a good opportunity to formulate working hypotheses, which are helpful in shaping the project's overall plan.

If the work of a geoarchaeologist is compared with that of a detective, the pilot season and the formulation of working hypotheses corresponds to the stage in which the first list of suspects is drawn up. Initially, the list may be very long, but it rapidly shrinks. An excavation team that invites scientific experts on to a project, naturally hopes to obtain expert advice about very concrete problems. The natural scientists, however, are, in most cases, reluctant to pronounce working hypotheses. Frequently, various possibilities are mutually exclusive. To an outsider it appears confusing when physical scientists contradict themselves, because the view that science is as clearly defined as the laws of mechanics is still widely held. It may be said, however, that at least as far as the earth sciences are concerned, they consist of a mixture of firm laws and free interpretation.

A comprehensive archaeological investigation frequently involves dozens of experts from various disciplines and countries. These experts require clear definitions of their tasks. Comprehensibility has to be one of the requirements for possible success. The aims, methods and provisional results should be known and available to each of the participants at all times.

The shape of the study area also needs to come in the category of 'comprehensibility'. If at all possible, it should be a rectangle, which is simple to subdivide and to depict on maps at various scales. Clarity is also essential in the hierarchy among those involved. This naturally does not mean that the traditional pyramidal hierarchy should be employed, with the 'excavation director' being solely responsible for all important scientific and technical issues – from the choice of participants to all consumables. Experience has frequently shown that a diversified system is the most efficient, with responsibility being assumed by many different people. The latter are responsible for individual aspects of the project. In the Pylos Project there were five co-directors; one each to deal with the prehistoric and historic periods, plus one each for the field-walking survey, the investigation of the artefacts, and the natural scientific contributions.

In contrast to other disciplines in the natural sciences, geoarchaeology does not have a standard repertoire of methods at its disposal. While most scientists have specialised to the extent of applying a specific method in many different places, a geoarchaeologist is concerned with one location, and has many different methods at his disposal – methods that have generally been established in other disciplines. Innumerable tools and procedures are available to investigate a tract of country, and because every area, taken on its own, is unique, every area requires a different combination of methods. In geoarchaeology, deciding which methods are best suited to a particular area is halfway to success.

The working hypotheses are an important aid in choosing the methods to be employed. For example, in a region where large areas are covered in recent meadow loam, cores are required to determine what lies under the alluvial layers. A landscape that is greatly eroded should, by contrast, be investigated by soil specialists. They are able to determine how much of the original surface has been lost.

It would naturally be ideal if all the methods that are significant in reconstructing a past landscape could actually be employed. Unfortunately, this is not always possible. Frequently, the scientists taking part in archaeological projects constitute – on cost or other grounds – only a more-or-less accidental selection, so that important aspects of the problem are not given any attention.

Techniques must not only be suitable with reference to the nature of the study area, but they must also be appropriate for the goals of the investigation. While one tries to avoid employing an insufficient number of different methods, one must also simultaneously take care not to become bogged down doing too many things at once – one is often walking a tightrope between the two. Many spectacular and currently fashionable techniques would possibly make no sensible contribution towards answering the basic questions being posed, so one can do without them. It would, for example, be senseless to employ ground-penetrating remote-sensing techniques to search for hidden architectural remains in an area subject to erosion. It would be equally foolish to search for small structures such as graves on low-resolution satellite images.

Only collaboration with highly qualified experts ensures that the standard of research corresponds to the current level of knowledge and technology. If an expert geophysicist using the most sensitive equipment is unable to detect any traces of structures below ground, then any further searching is superfluous. If someone using a simpler, or even the wrong, instrument came to the same result, then it would be uncertain whether there was really nothing there, or whether the inadequate equipment was not registering remnants of buildings that were actually present.

Nowadays, assembling the best experts generally means establishing a multinational team. For the scientific work at Pylos, for example, apart from the Russian botanist Sergei Yazvenko, a Bavarian hydrologist, an American soil expert, and a Greek physicist took part, and for the illustrations we engaged people from Canada, Great Britain and Switzerland.

In actually carrying out the project, in an ideal situation one begins with the techniques that enable one to sample the whole of the study area. This primarily involves remote-sensing methods, including the interpretation of satellite images and aerial photographs. Using these low-resolution methods, locations on the ground may be identified that appear to be worth investigating in greater detail. In contrast, high-resolution techniques, which include actual excavations, take place towards the end of the investigation. A basic principle, therefore, is to slowly increase the degree of resolution.

Archaeology Takes Off

What are the specific methods that scientists have at their disposal to scan for sites over the area of a regional archaeological project, which is, on average, some ten kilometres by ten kilometres in size? Because all airborne instruments are capable of scanning the whole study area on a broad scale, and thus of providing total coverage, a survey usually begins in space, using instruments on board the Space Shuttle or on satellites. Subsequently, investigations are undertaken from aircraft and helicopters.

First, an overall view of the most important topographical units of the area is required. Such detail is provided by the French SPOT satellite. The SPOT images have a resolution that corresponds to ten metres on the ground. Structures that are larger than this – including river beds, fields, villages, and made-up roads – therefore appear in the satellite images. These images may be read into the Geographical Information System, and be superimposed, like a tablecloth, on the three-dimensional model of the area that was obtained in the preparation phase.

Naturally, the search also applies to information that is less obvious. Data about properties of the surface, some of which may not be visible, are provided by the Landsat satellites. This includes infrared images. When the Chernobyl nuclear power station failed, the Landsat images immediately showed that abnormally hot cooling water was escaping from the plant.

The resolution of satellite images from Landsat-5 corresponds to thirty metres by thirty metres at the surface. On the ground, a square area of this size corresponds to a single pixel (picture element). Various data are recorded for each pixel, these corresponding to the amount of reflection at different wavelengths. Using computer programs, it is then possible to select specific features, such as fields of grain or olive groves, to separate them as different areas of the surface, and to evaluate statistically the amount of energy reflected. All pixels that have similar values are assigned the same colour. The most important features of the landscape, such as the distribution of fields, pasture, fruit trees, rocky outcrops and buildings, may be determined by this procedure, and subsequently printed out as a map. In most cases, such maps reveal information that is hardly visible (or even completely invisible) to the naked eye, such as the distribution of sediment in the sea or the course of coastal currents.

Both the SPOT and the Landsat satellites use passive detectors. They work with light that is reflected from the Earth's surface. At night, or when the sky is cloudy, they are therefore unable to obtain any images.

Additionally, none of their instruments are able to pierce vegetation or the ground surface. To overcome these restrictions, the European Space Agency developed a new type of satellite with an active radar transmitter: the so-called European Remote Sensing satellites (ERS-1 and ERS-2). On reaching the surface, the pulses transmitted by these satellites pass through any vegetation, and penetrate into the ground. There they are reflected and re-radiated, and eventually picked up by the satellite's detector. In dry areas, radar waves can 'look' several metres below the surface. In this way, for example, river beds dating from the last Ice Age are revealed beneath the sands of the Sahara.

A few months after its launch, ERS-1 helped to bring about a pioneering success for archaeological research. Radar images of the Arabian Desert revealed early caravan routes. This was possible because the ground along these tracks had been gradually consolidated underfoot, with the result that radar waves could not penetrate so deeply. Many such camel routes stretched like straight lines for hundreds of kilometres, and intersected at a point in the deserts of Oman. Archaeologists, who then examined this spot in more detail, discovered the lost city of Ubar – once the centre of trade in frankincense, the location of which had gradually fallen into oblivion over thousands of years.

To use radar equipment even more effectively, it may be mounted on an aircraft. From a height of three, rather than 785 kilometres, it naturally provides data with a much higher resolution. In addition, from this height, the radar waves can penetrate even farther into the ground. This makes dried-up river valleys and former roads more easily visible. A special aircraft belonging to the German Air and Space Technology Research Institute in Oberpfaffenhofen is able to scan an area ten kilometres square within a few hours.

Normal aerial photographs, which enable underground architectural remains to be detected from differences in vegetation growth, provide less useful data in areas around the Aegean than in northern and central Europe. In Greece and Turkey, the deposition rates are often so high that in a relatively short time foundations are buried too deeply for them to have any effect on plant growth.

More recently, additional methods have become available, which enable one to look deep below the surface – as far as 150 metres! At the Federal Institute for Geosciences and Natural Resources in Hannover, a scientific team is working with geophysical investigations from a helicopter. The helicopter trails a so-called 'Bird' beneath it. The equipment looks like a giant cigar and is fitted with various measuring instruments. Among these are magnetometers, which detect variations in the Earth's magnetic field.

The Earth's magnetic field does vary on a regional scale but, within an average-sized study area, the measurements generally remain relatively constant. Even there, however, there are still small fluctuations. They arise from changes in the composition of the bedrock and the soil. The soil consists of a mixture of very varied minerals, a small portion of which contain iron and thus possess magnetic properties. This natural magnetic background is disturbed by human settlement. If, for example, a particular area contains the foundations of a wall instead of weakly magnetic soil, this will create a negative deviation in the magnetic background, known as an anomaly. Many instruments that are employed for magnetometer measurements on the ground are so sensitive that they are able to measure deviations that are 1/50,000 of the Earth's magnetic field. Because the helicopter itself is made of metal and affects the measurements, the 'Bird' has to be flown at the end of a cable that is 45 metres long. The pilot flies the machine, at a speed of 140 kilometres an hour, so that the 'Bird' is just thirty metres above the ground. The whole study area is systematically scanned through a succession of parallel flight paths some one hundred metres apart. An area ten kilometres square requires measurement flights totalling a thousand kilometres, which corresponds to about a week of actual flying time.

Originally, the helicopter geophysical technique was developed to detect ore bodies in developing countries, or groundwater beneath deserts. It is now also used to locate industrial waste. Helicopter geophysics has not yet been used in archaeological research. The procedure would, however, be ideally suited for the detection of silted-up harbour basins, former canals, and settlements hidden behind sediments. Such structures would appear as magnetic anomalies on maps and profiles. Because the data obtained by the helicopter technique may be converted into three-dimensional images using computer processing, the subsurface may be viewed layer by layer.

Down to Earth

When the remote sensing has finished, and the archaeological team has begun the field-walking process, the scientists start their work on the ground. The data obtained by the remote sensing cover the whole of the study area simultaneously and provide valuable information to the researchers even before they have set foot on the area. Subsequent investigations on the ground are similarly directed towards covering the whole area as comprehensively as possible.

First, maps needed for the project are produced, showing the distribution of the different geological units. Normally, the geological maps prepared by the individual national geological services may be used as a basis for these, being adapted – if necessary – by appropriate observations in the field. The data from the remote sensing, the geological map, and the results of the area survey may be combined in the Geographical Information System. In many areas, a geomorphological map showing the distribution of the types of soils and landforms is also desirable.

All the methods employed so far have left the countryside unchanged – nothing has been destroyed and nothing taken out of its context. In the USA, this approach is known as 'Zero Impact', a concept that was first applied to mountain trips in the national parks, whereby after mountain-climbing and hiking the landscape is left exactly as it was originally. In future, zero-impact investigations will come to be increasingly employed in archaeology as well.

Nevertheless it is essential to put bores down into the surface as part of a geological programme. In principle, boreholes provide the same strati-graphical information as excavations, although they cover a much greater area and have a lower resolution. In our study model, cored stratigraphy would also be employed to check and calibrate the subsurface data obtained by the helicopter-based geophysics. The position of the boreholes is deter-mined, on the basis of theoretical considerations, to be as informative as possible. Instead of drilling the surface at random around a known archaeological site, it is advisable to lay out the boreholes in a straight line and at equal distances from one another.

When the remote-sensing data, the geological and geomorphological maps, the stratigraphical information from the boreholes, as well as the results of the field-walking survey and the pollen analyses are available, the project is already so well advanced that many of the original working hypotheses may be eliminated, and initial interpretations become possible. At the same time, it becomes evident that specific parts of the study area need to be the subject of additional, more detailed study. For example, archaeological sites generally occur on slight rises close to river meadows. The distribution of pottery in the vicinity of such settlements normally declines rapidly with the transition to the meadow sediments. This may mean that the lower part of the archaeological site is covered by later layers, beneath which additional artefacts and also the remains of walls may be hidden, so the original size of the settlement cannot be determined without further work. It can, however, also mean exactly the opposite; that is, that the settlement was first founded after the layers of soil had been deposited. The settlement layers, in this case, lie *above* the river deposits, and not beneath them. There are simple ways of finding out which of these two sequences of events is correct. All one has to do is drill some boreholes down into the meadow sediments and see whether settlement layers are to be found beneath the surface. This is an extremely reliable method of investigating the area round an archaeological site.

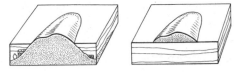

Do the sediments cover the settlement layers or the other way round?

At many archaeological sites, large numbers of pottery fragments are found on the surface, often with the remains of walls as well. Naturally this poses the question of whether other foundations are hidden below ground. To answer this, other geophysical methods are available. Many are similar to those used in the helicopter geophysical survey. However, ground-based measurements have a far higher resolution, which is why they are only able to cover a smaller area.

A magnetometer is usually so compact that it may be carried easily by a single person. The measurements are transferred to a computer and plotted on a map. The first magnetometer measurements generally reveal highly magnetic spots – with the false-colour palette generally employed nowadays, they appear as bright red points on a more-or-less evenly coloured blue background. These extreme deviations are nails, chains, tools, and other magnetic objects that have been lost in the fields. They must all be located, using a coordinate grid, and removed. As soon as the area has been cleaned, a further set of magnetometer readings is taken.

If any constructions produced by human hands do actually exist beneath the ground, magnetic mapping can produce amazing results. Under optimal conditions, it provides the layout of whole buildings or even of the entire settlement, even when the surface appears completely featureless. Effective computer programs enable one to determine the approximate size of the remains of buildings that are found, together with their depth.

Another extremely useful geophysical research technique is the measurement of soil resistance. In this method, four electrodes are screwed into the ground in a straight line at one-metre intervals. The resistance between alternate electrodes is measured, and they are then moved by one metre. After some thousands of measurements of this sort, a map is obtained of the electrical conductivity (or resistivity) of the soil. In a damp, saline area, such as a salt-water marsh, entire ancient settlements may be mapped using geoelectrical measurements.

When the geophysical measurements have been concluded, detailed information about the whole sub-surface area and the most important archaeological features is available. Inevitably, specific areas remain about which one would like to know more. These are the right spots, and this is the right moment, for excavations to begin.

The Limits of Technology

With so many marvellous technological methods available today, we must, nevertheless, still keep sight of all the dangers that accompany the use of these methods. Many of the new techniques, such as remote sensing or the Geographical Information System, have, when first applied to archaeology, been hailed as the ultimate tools for answering all sorts of yet unresolved questions – until it became obvious that these promising methods also have serious limitations.

Admiration for high-technology applications goes back, in part, to the pioneering discoveries that were falsely considered to have been brought about by these methods alone. For example, the discovery of the lost city of Ubar, already mentioned, was not solely the result of the interpretation of satellite radar images, because the site was by no means unknown. Young archaeologists working in Oman needed to obtain some practical experience with types of soil and pottery. This is why they decided to carry out test excavations for training purposes at a Roman site that had long been known. Among the Roman fragments, the archaeologists soon found other, much older, pottery. From this they concluded that an important city must have been there in pre-Roman times, and this was how the lost city of Ubar was discovered. The fact that their suspicions were subsequently confirmed by radar images did indeed help, but they emphasised the importance of the application of the latest radar technology because they wanted to get the international press on their side.

The successes ascribed solely to the use of the most up-to-date techniques are, therefore, not always what they seem. At the same time, there are also risks attached to the use of these techniques. Any researcher with sufficient means can buy an instrument to carry out chemical analyses, or acquire a

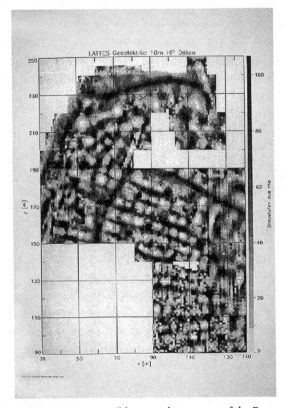

At Lattes (southern France) it was possible to produce a map of the Roman settlement from geoelectrical measurements

computer and a GIS program to produce three-dimensional models of the landscape. However, the use of such tools is questionable when the user does not have sufficient experience to interpret the results correctly. Outside the scientific field for example, it takes a long time to learn and practise driving a speedboat or a heavy lorry, because in inexperienced hands such machines can turn into deadly weapons. The law demands instruction, practical exercises, tests, official certificates and proof of competence from people who use the equipment that is potentially harmful, to reduce possible damage to a minimum. In science, it is quite different. In the best case, results that are produced by insufficiently trained users are simply useless. In the worst case, however, they may mislead whole generations.

Probably the best description of the dangers that lurk in the scientific method is to be found in Michael Crichton's best-seller *Jurassic Park*. Here are excerpts from a monologue by the mathematician Ian Malcolm – unfortunately, the words were omitted from the film.

You know what is wrong about scientific power? It is a form of inherited wealth, ... Most kinds of power require a substantial sacrifice by whoever wants the power, ... President of the company, Black belt in karate, Spiritual guru, Whatever it is you seek, you have to put in the time, the practice, the effort. You must give up a lot to get it. And once you have attained it, it is your power. It can't be given away: it resides with you. It is literally the result of your discipline.

Now what is interesting about this process is that, by the time someone has acquired the ability to kill with his bare hands, he has also matured to the point where he won't use it unwisely. So that kind of power has a built-in control. The discipline of getting the power changes you so that you won't abuse it.

But scientific power is like inherited wealth: attained without discipline. You read what others have done, and you take the next step. You can do it very young. You can make progress very fast. There is no discipline lasting many decades. There is no mastery: old scientists are ignored. There is no humility before nature.

Naturally, the highly developed technologies that are available to us today should, indeed must, be applied. They must, however, be carefully chosen and judiciously employed. No highly technical machine and no computer program is capable of providing satisfactory and reliable answers to complicated questions at the press of a button. Only the combination of several different methods – both traditional and modern ones – will help us to cast more light on the past. And even then, the real scientific work has to take place inside our heads. Despite all the highly developed technologies, success in science still largely depends on qualities that cannot be simply quantified: these include knowledge, experience, powers of deduction, talent and skill.

The use of various scientific technologies to answer archaeological questions changes our approach to the past as well as our understanding of it. The reduction of the hierarchical structure also affects methods of working. Where, once upon a time, great patriarchal figures were surrounded at excavations by hundreds of hard-working but submissive workers, nowadays highly qualified experts from all over the world undertake independent research. Their understanding of archaeology is less artefact- and more evolution-oriented. Instead of describing sculptures and pottery fragments, and viewing past cultures as isolated, more-or-less self-contained, static units, they regard civilisations as the results of multiple, mutually interdependent, development processes. In place of the dramatic scenarios of natural catastrophes proposed by the pioneers, it is now a question of the long-term complex interrelationship between human beings and the environment. The fascinating insights that these new approaches afford are the subject of the next chapter.

Anyone who is able to grasp five thousand years of human history to any extent, won't be surprised by anything.

ROMAN HERZOG (1993)

Vanished Landmarks

In 480 BC, the Persian army under the leadership of Xerxes marched through Greece. The High King wanted to avoid the mountainous interior and to maintain contact between the foot-soldiers and his warships. He therefore commanded the army of more than one-hundred thousand soldiers to march south from Macedonia along the coast to Attica. Approximately 150 kilometres north of Athens, near Thermopylae, his troops reached a narrow pass between the steep cliffs and the sea. If one believes the Greek historian Herodotus, the width at this point was just wide enough for a single cart to pass. Directly behind the pass, the Greek king Leonidas had posted approximately one thousand elite soldiers. Despite their overwhelmingly hopeless inferiority, they succeeded in halting the advance of the Persian army for two days; long enough for Greek ships to engage the Persian warships under favourable circumstances.

Anyone who sees the 'Pass' of Thermopylae today can hardly recognise the ancient countryside. A five-kilometre-wide coastal plain stretches out below the steep cliffs. In the modern landscape, Leonidas and his soldiers would probably have been able to delay the advance of the Persian troops by little more than a moment.

Slow processes such as erosion, deposition, tectonic displacements and changes in sea level cause lasting effects on the landscape. Even though such processes are hardly perceptible, their effects over a long period of time may be far greater than those caused by natural catastrophes. Above all, the alterations in the landscape caused by human activity have, over the millennia, had serious consequences for the overall composition of the countryside. For this reason, we need not be surprised that many former natural features, such as the Pass of Thermopylae, are hardly recognisable.

In trying to reconstruct past events, archaeological and historical experts repeatedly encounter information that no longer agrees with the present-day landscape. There are innumerable examples: Bronze Age sites in the barren mountains of northern Greece, where today only steppe-type vege-tation and maquis grow, contain bones of wild boar and deer – animals that must have lived in dense woodland. Otter bones show that there must once have been rich, freshwater streams where there are now merely dry river beds. Lakes and swamps that were described by travellers in Roman times have long since disappeared. A town like Pella, the capital of Greek Macedonia, had a busy seaport – today it lies thirty kilometres from the coast, deep in the interior. Impressive remains dating from Roman times of settlements, agricultural terraces and aqueducts are found in Libya, Tunisia and Algeria, indicating a once fertile countryside. Nowadays, unproductive, desolate wastelands prevail.

The Exhaustion of Natural Resources

Our awareness of the fragility of the natural environment seems to have first arisen in the last few decades. After the bitter years of food shortages and ruined cities at the end of the Second World War, the industrial recovery in the 1950s and 1960s brought about an economic miracle in the whole of Western Europe, as well as the so-called 'consumer age', and the 'throw-away society'. Events such as the dropping of the first atomic bomb in 1945, the launch of Sputnik in 1957, and the Moon landing in 1969, merely served to strengthen belief in people's unrestricted power over nature. This spirit of *Homo faber* was expressed on both a large and small scale. Governments undertook giant, highly technical projects, dammed rivers to create gigantic lakes, fitted ships with nuclear propulsion, hacked satellite towns out of the countryside, robbed streams of their meanders and flood-plains, and forced them into concrete culverts. The population disposed of their rubbish along the sides of country roads and many unthinkingly changed their sump oil in the middle of the woods.

A change of direction occurred in 1972, when the Club of Rome, with its study, *Limits to Growth*, first pointed out that such irresponsible over-exploitation of nature and its resources must have lasting consequences for the future. This appeal introduced a new era of ecological awareness. Suddenly, it was realised that nature is a fragile web: a dynamic balance that has evolved over a long period of time, and more gradually it came to be understood that human intervention in this balance threatens to destroy the very foundations of life for future generations.

Since then, everyone, including those in industry, commerce and politics, has become convinced of the necessity for ecological awareness in modern society. Many parliaments include parties that have adopted respect for nature as part of their policy, and no business can allow itself to appear negligent towards the environment. Environmental protection has become a trademark.

This socio-political development in recent decades might give the impression that environmental awareness is a recent achievement. People have, however, always had a conscious relationship with their natural environment, because their existence, like that of all other living things, is dependent on an intact biosphere. Although, thanks to our technical means, it is now possible to settle every region of the globe, the availability of clean air, water, food supplies, shelter and fuel are, as before, of more fundamental significance. Before industrialisation, the availability of these primary resources determined whether a particular area was generally habitable or not, the most important prerequisite for the siting of permanent settlements being the availability of water. As a rule, fertile soil constituted another requirement for successful settlements, because those who tilled the fields did not, preferably, want to travel long distances. Other natural resources, such as wood, grain, fruit, nuts, game and seafood, were also desirable.

Until the beginning of trade in mass-produced goods, not only the fate of individuals and small groups but also the political and economic success of whole states largely depended on the available natural resources. Above all, non-essential resources such as ores, precious metals and a favourable geographical and political situation determined whether a state did, or did not, thrive. It was only with industrialisation that other factors, such as expertise, a willingness to innovate, capacity for work, and financial strength, could assume a higher value than sources of raw materials.

In many respects, therefore, human beings are no different from other living things. Like other organisms, we search for a habitat that comes closest to our requirements. The form and characteristics of the landscape determine where we settle down. We enjoy a beautiful view, which, in an emergency, provides us with a strategic vantage point; we seek out a sunny spot and also the vicinity of springs, rivers and lush vegetation.

To appreciate how closely we humans are linked to our natural environment, we only have to imagine taking a trip in the Rocky Mountains. When the sun sets, we start to look out for a suitable spot to pitch the tent. There needs to be a tree in the vicinity, so that we can hang our food out of the reach of bears. In addition, the tent needs to be on slightly higher ground, in case it starts to rain in the night. Is there a stream nearby? All the better, because then we will have a source of drinking water, and can wash in the morning. There also needs to be a site for the camp fire, protected from the wind. If so many aspects of the environment need to be taken into account for a stop of just a few hours, how much more planning does the choice of a permanent settlement require?

People have always recognised the advantages offered by a specific location. They chose sites that most closely satisfied their requirements. It is not for nothing that estate agents state that the three most important factors in the choice of a property are: Location! Location! Location! Patterns of settlement therefore correspond not to chance but reflect a complex system of requirements. Archaeologists who attempt to reconstruct the pattern of past settlement want to understand how this system works.

While people were exhausting nature's bounty, they were simultaneously altering their environment. To a continually greater degree, they imposed their ideas on the landscape. Many natural resources, including fertile soil and groundwater, are not renewable or require very long periods of time to regenerate. Other resources, such as wood, require careful planning and investment for their long-term maintenance. Without far-sighted measures, the quality and quantity of natural resources continuously decrease. This creates an imbalance between civilisation and the ecosystem. Just as the land is subjected to exploitation by people, and correspondingly changes, people also have to adapt to the changes in the land that they themselves have partially brought about. Settlements are abandoned, because their original advantages have been lost, and in their place new settlements are founded at sites that offer greater advantages under the changed circumstances.

A good example of the interrelationship between land and settlement is shown by coastlines. Thousands of years ago, Mediterranean woods were already giving way in the face of agricultural demands. New arable and pasture land was required; wood was used as a fuel or building material. Deforestation led inevitably to soil erosion; the eroded loose material was mainly deposited at the mouths of rivers, causing them to silt up. When it was founded about 1000 BC, the Italian port of Pisa lay directly on the coast. By the classical Greek period, the latter had already shifted by 3.7 kilometres; now it has become 12 kilometres. Ravenna, a port and naval harbour at the time of Augustus, now lies eight kilometres from the sea. Adria, the 6th-century BC Greek port, is now 24 kilometres from the sea, and the important coastal town of Spina is now 25 kilometres inland. Cleopatra's fleet was still able to enter the harbour of Tarsus in southern Asia Minor, but today the town is 20 kilometres from the sea. When it was founded in the sixth century BC, Arles must have lain on the open sea – now this historical town is fifty kilometres inland.

Challenges for Geoarchaeology

To reconstruct how the landscape has evolved; what natural changes it has undergone; how people first used, then exploited, and finally overexploited it; how different cultures have tried to repair the errors they have made in its management – all these are the tasks of geoarchaeology. The point of departure is always the current landscape, because, like a constantly changing provisional result, it has been created by past processes.

The current landscape still contains, in part, many indications of its past state. Work in a new area, therefore, initially throws up a whole series of questions. What does it mean if the current plant cover consists solely of low, heath-like shrubs – the 'maquis', so widespread in Mediterranean countries? Does it imply that there were never any woods in the region, or that they have been cut down? How should we interpret the fact that there is no land suitable for farming in an area? Was there none in prehistoric times, or has it all been lost through erosion since then? What can we conclude from the fact that, in a particular area, there are no rivers that flow all the year round? Does it mean that there was no surface water in earlier times, or that the sources have dried up?

Geoarchaeology's favourite area has, from the very beginning, been Greece. Thanks to active tectonics and a complicated coastline, Greece possesses an extraordinarily diverse landscape. In prehistoric times, this region was the point of contact with the dynamic, advanced cultures of Asia Minor, and thus experienced political and technical changes more quickly and more strongly than Central Europe. In addition, it has been extremely thoroughly researched. Numerous projects in the fields of geography, geology, archaeology and ethnology have provided a mass of detailed information about the mutual relationships between people and the land.

Because we, just like any other organism, are subject to an untold number of external factors, investigation of the historical interaction between humans and the environment is extraordinarily complicated. To be able to get some sort of general grasp of it, the environment must be divided into individual aspects. Among others, these include: the climate, the geological composition of the landscape, its ore deposits, the topographical relief, the geomorphology, the soils, the water reserves, the shape of the coastline, the fauna and the flora. Examination of these different components is first carried out individually. Only towards the end can the results of the individual investigations be combined to give a comprehensive picture of past dynamic processes.

In small archaeological field-projects, frequently just a single person represents the scientific side. They therefore need to be able to grasp the individual aspects of the landscape, all on their own. Because the various components depend on one another, it is advisable to begin an investigation with the geology of the bedrock, because this is the single individual aspect of the landscape that does not undergo any changes – or at least no changes that are obvious to us human beings. At the same time, the distribution of the rocks determines many other aspects of the landscape, including the relief. As a rule, hard rock types produce ridges, whereas more easily eroded material generally gives rise to topographic hollows. Tectonic faults in the bedrock may also determine the shape of the landscape, and this has further effects on human exploitation of the countryside. Steep slopes are generally used neither for settlement nor for agriculture, although there are exceptions to this rule. The population frequently retreats from fertile coastal plains that are exposed to piracy or attack, or that are liable to enemy invasion, into areas that cannot be cultivated or are mountainous. Other aspects of land-use and topography are also interrelated. Olive trees, for example, will not flourish above a certain altitude.

The distribution of the various geological units also largely determines the quality of the soil. Again, these are of the greatest significance for the landscape, because they form the basis of all life on dry land. For non-geologists it is often hard to understand what the term 'soil' generally embraces – it does *not*, in fact, as is often assumed, refer to any deposited material. Instead, soil formation describes the complex processes that operate, over the course of time, on the ground surface. These include weathering. Through the changes in temperature and humidity that occur between night and day, and between summer and winter, the surface alters

Phira, the principal settlement on Thera, lies on the edge of the cliffs

Excavated Minoan houses in Akrotiri. This is 'Triangle Square', with the Western House on the left-hand side

Minoan houses in Akrotiri

Excavated and partially reconstructed portions of the palace at Knossos

This 600-tonne coral block was thrown on to dry land by the tsunamis caused by Krakatau

The tilted foundation stone at Amnios

An area near the railway station at Merak, a village on Sumatra, after its destruction by tsunamis

In Niru Chani, even walls that are just the width of a hand have remained standing

The Minoan settlement at Gournia

The excavations at Mochlos lie on an island

The Minoan palace of Kato Zakros lies in extremely dry eastern Crete

The Mycenaean township of Tiryns should have suffered from major earthquakes

The archaeological site of Monastiriki (centre) in the Amari Valley

North of Monastiriki stretches fertile meadowland, which is, however, more or less impossible to farm

A Linear-B tablet

The excavated foundations of the throne-room of the Palace of Nestor

A SPOT satellite image of the Trojan Plain

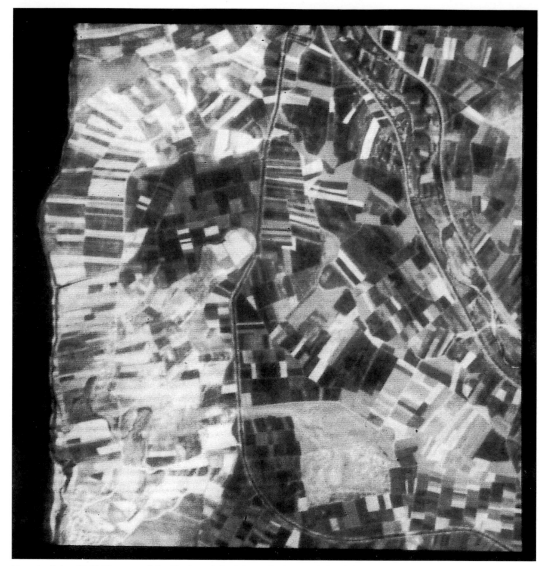

Detail of the SPOT image of the Trojan Plain. Towards the top left of the image centre, a reclaimed marsh appears as a dark patch

The results of the magnetometer survey of the Palace of Nestor

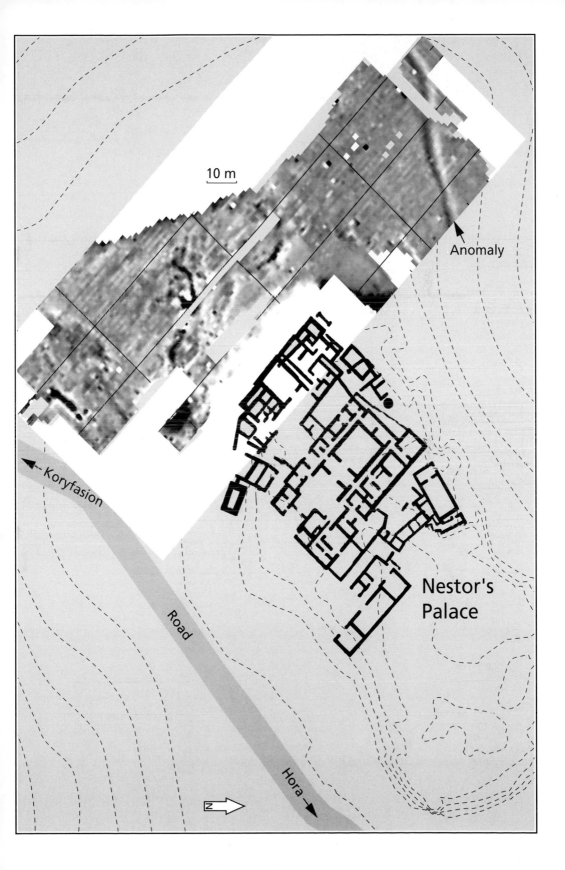

10 m

Anomaly

← Koryfasion

Road

Hora →

N →

Nestor's
Palace

A radar satellite image (from ERS-1) of the Dardanelles with the island of Imros on the left-hand side of the image

A Landsat image of the eastern half of the Peloponnese. The complicated coastline helps to make Greece an ideal region for geoarchaeological research

The term 'soil' is applied to the thin layer above the bedrock. This is not a sedimentary deposit, but material produced by weathering

The large stones are the remnants of ancient agricultural terraces

The Skourta Plain is on the northern side of Parnassus is extremely sparsely settled

Athens, south of Parnassus, is a concrete jungle

The whole of Thera's caldera may be seen from Oia at the northern end of the group of islands

The tilted stone on the right-hand side of the foundations of this building in Amnisos is supposed to have been moved by a tsunami

The walls of the sixth city of Troy – here seen on the eastern side – show no sign of damage from earth tremors

The Lion Gate at Mycenae has stood, undamaged, for thousands of years

with time. In dry regions, water-soluble materials migrate toward the surface, where they are precipitated as the water evaporates. In areas with heavy precipitation, the situation is reversed, because the rain washes particles out of the uppermost layer, which then become concentrated somewhat lower down in the soil. Clay particles migrate within the soil in this way too. Over the course of time, horizons thus arise, which may indeed outwardly bear some similarity to layers of sediment, but which arose differently, namely through modifying processes that took place *after* the rocks were deposited. Although soils may require very long periods of time for their formation, they are also fragile and may erode very quickly. Their maturity is thus a sign of their age. Because in the Mediterranean region it takes thousands of years for readily visible soil horizons to become established, intact soils indicate stable landscapes. However, the state of the soil does not just reflect the past, but in many respects also determines the future of the countryside. Indeed, if the soils are once eroded away, then a dense plant cover can hardly ever be re-established.

The predominant limestone mountains in the Mediterranean region normally develop into a clay-rich, dark red soil, known as *terra rosa*. If these soils are irrigated they are very fertile but, on the other hand, without artificial irrigation only olives and almonds are able to flourish. In addition to this, they are generally stony and thus difficult to work. More easily tilled soils occur in hilly areas and valleys. The minerals and nutrients that these soils may perhaps lack can be provided nowadays by artificial fertilisers. Best of all for agriculture are the valley soils. In general, there is also adequate water, so that real vegetable plots may be established.

When all relevant aspects of the environment have been individually investigated; when the botanists, palynologists and palaeo-ecologists have determined the vegetation's history; when the geoarchaeologists, geologists and soil specialists know the stability and instability of the soils; when the hydrologists and hydraulic engineers have determined the water balance; when the archaeozoologists have reconstructed the evolution of the fauna; and when the archaeologists have assembled all available information about the history of settlement; then the time has arrived to combine the data gathered into a single, panoramic view of landscape and culture.

Existence in the Garden of Eden

Living things are able to thrive only under specific climatic and geographical conditions. If the environment remains unchanged, then they can exist practically unchanged for millions of years. If, however, the environment changes, then they must adapt to survive. In this way, the speed of environmental change determines the rate of biological evolution. Slow changes favour adaptation, whereas rapid ones may cause some forms to be driven out or even lead to their extinction. Periods in which the Earth underwent dramatic changes in its land-masses or climate were therefore frequently times of mass extinctions of both plant and animal life forms. At the same time, however, many new types first appeared during such epochs.

The evolutionary spurts in the predecessors of modern humans also occurred at times when the Earth was undergoing substantial changes. When, about four million years ago, the central African forests shrank in size, the primates living there had to adapt to life in the savanna, which probably proved the spur to the evolution of upright gait. The next major step for hominids – the use of stone tools – ensued with the beginning of a new geological era, namely the Ice Age, about two-and-a-half million years ago. The duration of the Ice Age, known to geologists as the Pleistocene, matches the duration of the Early Stone Age, or Palaeolithic. Throughout the whole of the Pleistocene – in other words, for more than two million years – the cultural level of the ancestors of modern humans remained essentially unchanged. But then, in the last 150,000 years, climatic change at European latitudes became so drastic that these areas were abandoned by hominids. At subtropical latitudes in Africa, the climatic variations were not so strongly expressed, so hominids there were able to adapt to the new environment.

South of the Sahara, the first, anatomically modern humans (*Homo sapiens sapiens*) evolved about 100,000 years ago. They proved to be the most adaptable form to appear in the whole of Earth's history – the only form that succeeded in settling in every environment, from sandy deserts to icy wastes. During later warmings, the cold regions became temperate and the temperate ones tropical. The vegetation belts shifted accordingly, and humans adapted to this natural evolution. Their competitive advantage was so great that nowadays their biomass is more than that of any other life form. If all the individual members of a species were piled up in a heap, none of the piles would be as large as that of *Homo sapiens*.

The first humans enjoyed an environment that comes close to being described as Paradise. Streams provided large amounts of pure water, plant cover was dense and corresponded to the natural vegetation community, while the fauna provided plentiful food. Humans took advantage of this supply and, in doing so, intervened in the complicated balance that had been built up by nature in the course of evolution. Through their intervention, the simple Palaeolithic cultures probably did more damage to the environment than modern industrial society. At any rate, worldwide examples show that the extinction of large mammalian fauna followed the spread of Palaeolithic settlement.

During the last major phase of the Ice Age, 18,000 years ago, humans probably had similar abilities and skills at their disposal to those we have today. This means that they displayed the same biological characteristics, possessed the power of speech, and had a knowledge of music, painting, mythology, and medicine. They still, however, gained their food through hunting and gathering, and thus had to live in small groups. The low population density tended to minimise social contact, meaning that there was practically no exchange of information, and specialisation was virtually impossible. All of their time and energy needed to be employed in surviving.

At that time, sea level was about 120 metres lower than at present. The continental shelves were dry and formed wide plains, which prevented easy access to the water. Such a low sea level forced people to become oriented towards inland areas – anyone who has ever tried to go for a swim at low tide in the North Sea knows the problems.

The Ice Age and Palaeolithic ended about 11000 BC, when the most rapid and far-reaching environmental changes in all of Earth's history occurred, which finally led to the rapid rise of civilisation during the subsequent, warm interglacial period. The temperature and sea level rose rapidly, and the vegetation belts shifted. The rising sea level flooded the coastal plains (water flooding into the mouths of rivers and their valleys) and thus led to the creation of innumerable natural harbours. A high sea level invited people to climb aboard boats and cross the sea, thus accelerating the exchange of information between different peoples. Knowledge about new discoveries and achievements spread more rapidly and the advance of culture received a major boost. In the Australo-Pacific region, in northern Europe, and in the Aegean, seafarers replaced the inland-oriented cave dwellers.

Soon after, the first settled cultures arose. It is probable that the Mesolithic seafaring cultures, which had themselves arisen in response to a stimulus from the environment, acted as a catalyst to the rise of civilisation. Civilisation arose primarily in those areas of the world that were, to some extent, linked to one another. Isolated peoples in South America, Africa and Australia remained without any developed technology until recent times. The Mediterranean lands, in contrast, took on a leading role in cultural history because they possessed a favourable climate and lay in a particularly advantageous geographical location, forming a link between three continents: Europe, Asia and Africa. The far-reaching exchange of goods and ideas that went with this location, favoured the cultures in Mesopotamia, Syria, Palestine, Egypt, Asia Minor and Greece for thousands of years.

About 11,000 years ago, the interior of Greece was covered in thick evergreen woodland. Bears, foxes and hyenas inhabited this undisturbed forest. Humans lived on the coast, only venturing farther inland when hunting antelopes and deer near wild-animal tracks and rich stretches of water. Many types of animal, including wild ass and ibex, vanished from Greece at about this time. Archaeologists today, during the course of their field surveys, still stumble across temporary campsites where the hunters prepared their stone tools for cutting up their kill. For example, during a project on the Peloponnese near Mycenae, we discovered a Mesolithic archaeological site on the slopes of a steep gorge that led into a fertile valley surrounded by mountains. It was obvious that people had not entered the valley itself. They had simply used the narrow entrance to hunt herds of animals that were passing in and out. Although the site had obviously been occupied only seasonally, we found many thousands of stone tools that had served to divide up the kill.

In a cave on the southern coast of Cyprus, the effects of Mesolithic hunters on the mammal population are even more clearly shown. There, archaeologists discovered stone tools, together with innumerable bones of the pygmy hippopotamus. Obviously, on this section of the coast, the animals were not only hunted but slaughtered on the spot, and in vast numbers. Since then, these animals have become extinct. In Africa as well, a mass-extinction occurred between 15,000 and 10,000 BC – in the last phase of the Acheulean culture. Climatic change does not provide a plausible explanation for such radical alterations, because the animals would simply have followed the shifting climate zones. In addition, the couple of dozen reversals between glacial and interglacial periods in the previous two million years had not led to any comparable reduction in diversity.

The Move to Settlement

After the hunter-gatherer societies of the Palaolithic and the short interlude of seagoing peoples during the Mesolithic, a completely new type of culture arose in the Neolithic, when one person had the idea not to kill the goat he was hunting but to capture and keep it. The impetus for this most successful idea of all time may have been the fact that large mammals had become so rare because of overhunting that there was hardly anything left to hunt.

Keeping stock requires settlement, and this straightaway makes it impossible to feed a large population by gathering fruits and seeds as well, because the area surrounding a settlement would soon be exhausted. The domestication of animals therefore also demanded the cultivation of plants for food. Fruits and seeds were no longer just collected, they were also planted.

Because the wild forms of the animals and plants that were first domesticated occur as natural (or 'wild') communities in the area known as the 'Fertile Crescent' – the region from Palestine to Syria, and then across southern Asia Minor to Iraq and Iran – the origins of animal husbandry and agriculture could only have occurred in that region. There is much to indicate that the first domestication took place in southeastern Turkey – not in Mesopotamia and certainly not in Egypt. Initially, the settlers just kept only goats, but soon there were sheep as well. As early as the 8th millennium BC, we find both species together. Cattle and pigs followed in the 7th millennium BC. At the same time, many farming settlements appeared around the western and central Mediterranean. The material remains of these settlements resembled the first farming villages in the Fertile Crescent. Whereas the seagoing people in the Mesolithic had essentially spread along the coast, from the start these early farming communities sought out fertile plains in the interior. In Greece, the new settlers chose the wide plains of Thessaly, where there was plenty of water and where the soil was light and could be worked without a plough.

The nomads of earlier millennia lived in small groups and could acquire only portable objects. The interval between births must also have been correspondingly large, because a family could carry one child at the most. Settlement meant that these restrictions were no longer valid. In addition, the space required per capita decreased by a factor of 500. From then on, it sufficed for just a few of the community to be engaged in agriculture to feed the whole group. The others could devote themselves to different tasks. So areas of activity such as crafts, art, trade, politics and religion came to occupy an increasingly important role. The continuous supply of food also led to a population increase. Soon after the introduction of settlements, the first towns appeared in the Near East.

Agriculture and animal husbandry introduced a completely different use of the environment. In an undisturbed natural environment, hundreds of plants occur in close proximity. Agriculture, however, seeks to reduce this multiplicity, because it aims to give useful plants the optimum conditions for growth and, on the other hand, to restrict as much as possible the success of all other plants so as to produce the maximum amount of food from a given space. The inevitable result is the destruction of the natural plant community.

Initially, the farming communities used only the best soils, namely the fertile loams in the flood-plains of perennial streams. There, they practised the simplest form of agriculture. They tilled each field only for as long as adequate yields could be obtained; then they shifted cultivation to another area. This migratory agriculture required the farmers to have a certain degree of mobility and also demanded a relatively large area in proportion to the population. So the system worked only as long as there were few people living in a particular region, who did not, therefore, require a great deal of food. Only with the introduction of letting land lie fallow were farming groups able to settle in a fixed location. In this system, different portions of arable land were left uncultivated every year, so that they might regenerate.

Because for thousands of years agriculture in the Neolithic was restricted to the few fertile valley lands, the rest of the vegetation remained in its original state. For example, in the Argolis – the region that later became the centre of the Mycenaean culture – about eighty per cent of the land continued to be covered in evergreen oaks. In remote areas, far from towns and villages, it is still possible, even today, to find remnants of the plant communities that flourished in the Neolithic. In these areas, the rich terra-rosa soils may also be preserved, forming the basis for a dense plant cover.

In the late Neolithic, a flourishing agricultural society had developed in Greece. The farming families lived in simple houses made from sun-dried clay bricks, which had only a restricted lifetime. Because the houses had to be repeatedly rebuilt, over the course of time high settlement mounds arose, which still overlook many fertile plains in countries around the Aegean.

The introduction of agriculture gave many incentives for technical and economic innovations. Although the wild ancestors of the cow provided just a couple of decilitres of milk a day, dairy farming was nonetheless established. The result: today a cow produces as much as 15,000 litres of milk over the course of her lifetime. Sheep were kept not just for the production of meat, but also used as sources of fertiliser and wool. Then, a sheep gave about a kilogramme of wool – now, it gives as much as twenty kilogrammes. Spinning and weaving developed into important craft activities in the Early Bronze Age. The cultivation of grapes and olives also began, and oxen were used as draught animals.

The plough was first employed in Greece about 3000 BC. Suddenly, far greater areas than before could be cultivated. With the improved food supply that this facilitated, the population once again increased. To be able to feed this increased population in the long term, new fields and pasture had to be laid out. People began to clear the oak woods on the hills.

Even today, not all scientists believe that this deforestation actually took place, and certainly not that this caused major environmental damage. These researchers maintain that forest fires can cause similar devastation, and that nature recovers from it. But deforestation caused by human hands has completely different effects from those created by natural forest fires. The latter cause the seeds of many plants to germinate, and stimulate the regeneration of many different plants and herbs. In addition, insects, parasites and fungi are reduced. If forest fires are completely absent, the result is that the vegetation becomes too dense, the amount of combustible material rises, plants grow up that are unable to withstand fire, the vegetation's diversity declines and old trees predominate. This causes the range of different plant growth to be restricted. Forest fires are thus a natural and necessary factor in maintaining the ecological balance. Even the deforestation produced by human hands, however, would probably not have caused lasting damage to the environment if pastoral agriculture on the cleared areas had not, in the long term, prevented the vegetation from recovering. Pines, heather and hornbeam began to grow on the cleared land instead of oaks.

The progressive deforestation had immense effects on many other factors in the environment, including, among others, the climate and the water retention of the soil. Even if precipitation in prehistoric times was no greater than today, the forests would have produced a great deal of evaporation and thus raised the humidity of the air. In addition, the dense plant cover protected the soil from erosion by rainfall. The clay-rich soils retained the precipitation and only released the water very slowly. As a result, rivers flowed throughout the year. Without a dense cover of vegetation, rain falls directly on to the soil and damages it. In heavy downpours, it is practically impossible for the subsoil to absorb the water because its pores are full of air, which cannot escape fast enough. So the water runs across the surface. Rivulets flow in to small hollows and change into streams, which cut deep into the soil. Without the grip of roots, sloping soils slide, layer by layer, into the valleys. Fertile soils, which have been formed over thousands of years, are thus washed away. This sort of erosion, known as 'soil erosion', is basically caused by human activity. Without human intervention, it does not occur naturally.

Anyone who believes that in prehistoric times humans lived in harmony with nature has not the faintest idea of what really happened. Whichever region one examines, the first phase of human-induced environmental instability was the most destructive, because it was at the very beginning that the most soil was lost. Once the balance is destroyed, the interval between individual phases of soil erosion becomes shorter. Despite this, less and less material is set in motion, because most of the fragile soil has already been lost. The massive extension of agriculture caused millions of tonnes of previously fertile earth to be washed down into the valleys, where it was laid down by the rivers as loams. The Stone Age and Early Bronze Age settlements in the valleys vanished under metre-thick layers of mud.

Our geoarchaeological research in Greece has shown that the episodes of extensive soil erosion occurred in different regions at different times. In the centres of Neolithic agriculture, the ecological balance had been lost by the 4th millennium BC. Less densely settled areas first suffered damage from the expansion of agriculture in the 3rd millennium BC, and even more distant regions were not affected until thousands of years later.

The change from natural forested areas to agricultural land had probably progressed substantially by the Early Bronze Age. By the Late Bronze Age, the Greek vegetation already had a similar composition to the one found today. Dense woods may still have been present in the interior. Wild boar, deer, and possibly even a few lions lived there, the presence of all these animals being confirmed from bones found in excavations.

Between 1200 and 800 BC, the population density in many areas of Greece declined drastically. Subsequently it increased again, reaching a maximum in classical antiquity. Even the most remote fields had to be worked to feed the population. By this time, however, people had already developed technical methods of stabilising the soil. They restricted the flow of streams through small check-dams; they protected the soil on slopes by terracing. Using such simple methods they were able to reduce soil erosion substantially. Extremely solidly constructed terraces, with blocks of stone that are too heavy to be moved by a single person, are found in many areas of Greece. These terraces were probably constructed in classical times.

There are, however, stretches of land around the Mediterranean that have escaped the exploitation of nature and also soil erosion. One such intact landscape is that of the Skourta Plain in the Parnassus range of

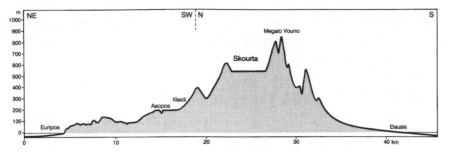

The Skourta Plain on the northern side of Parnassus is extremely sparsely settled

mountains, halfway between Athens and Thebes. For long periods of Greek history it was a frontier region between the opposing kingdoms of Boeotia and Attica, belonging to Attica but more easily accessible from Boeotia. Because Boeotia did not need to use the area and hardly anyone from Athens managed to get there, the land was spared misuse. The Greek historian Thucydides tells of an oath taken by the Athenians and Boeotians that none of the two peoples would live in the area. Even today there are hardly any villages there.

At an altitude of more than 500 metres above sea level, in the middle of the mountains, there lies an extensive plain with extraordinarily fertile and well-preserved soil. Olives no longer flourish at this height, so the soil is used for the cultivation of cereals and vines. On the mountains around the valley the soils are also well preserved. Dense mixed woods cover the slopes. Satellite images show that the distribution of woods corresponds approximately to the boundary between Attica and Boeotia in classical times. When the traveller George Wheler arrived in the area in the seventeenth century, he encountered wild duck, wolves, bears and wild boar. Even today, the area is notable for having (for Greece) an extremely rich variety of animal life – while busy Athens, with its five million inhabitants, lies just a few kilometres farther south.

The Untouched World of Albania

At the end of our investigations in Pylos, Jack Davis was looking for another project. Because Albania had been freed from Communist dictatorship and had been opened up to the outside world, it seemed the obvious time to reveal the country's archaeological treasures to a greater public. Unexpectedly, Jack invited me to take part in a week-long pilot project in Albania.

A few weeks later, I met him and his team at Gate 56 at Zürich-Kloten

Airport, and we flew together to Tirana. After two tiring days going around offices, we were driven over deeply rutted roads for four hours – which here corresponds to one hundred kilometres – to the ruined city of Apollonia in the south. Greeks from Corfu and Corinth founded a colony here in 588 BC, which later developed into an important trading and university city, lasting for nearly one thousand years. Hardly had we entered Apollonia, than a tangible sense of relief spreaded through the team. A fantastic excavation house, erected with funds from France, awaited us. The rooms opened inwards on to an atrium, but on the outside they were surrounded by high walls of natural stone. The small garden outside the house was protected by a wrought-iron fence, and was illuminated at night. Guards with machine-pistols stood inside the fence, day and night.

On the very first evening, I looked out from the veranda, fascinated by the coastal landscape. I scanned it with binoculars, and discovered that there were people in practically every field. They were sitting, gossiping, in small groups beneath trees or on large worked stones from the ancient ruins; taking individual cows to pasture, herding sheep, gathering hay, cutting grass with scythes, or weeding vegetable plots. Hundreds of people were still in the fields as darkness began to fall. The landscape was alive. It looked like a painting by Pieter Brueghel. This is what life in the country must have been like before our time.

It was only a few days later, during a long exploratory trek around the immediate neighbourhood of Apollonia, that I realised what drew me – and possibly the Albanian inhabitants as well – back repeatedly to the countryside. It was the background 'noise', that fascinated me so much. You do not hear a single machine: no cars, no tractors. All fieldwork is carried out by hand. Instead of the normal busy roar of a city, you can still hear frogs croaking, cowbells ringing, birds singing, cicadas chirping, asses braying, sheep baaing and horses neighing – dozens of different sounds filling the air, mostly drifting across from a distance. From time to time there comes the sound of children's voices from the nearest village, where the women – as in Homer's time – still do their washing in the village well. A couple of days living in the countryside in Albania would, it seems to me, be a cure for the ubiquitous 'achievements' of civilisation. Most of the inhabitants that I speak to, however, appear to be happy to do without the romantic side to their countryside. They want to get away as quickly as possible.

Just as the background noise and work on the land in Albania recalls life in earlier centuries, the soil, the flora and the fauna are, in comparison with the rest of Europe, relicts preserving former diversity. In the Albanian mountains there are still brown bears, wolves, lynx and jackals.

Until recently, access to the former acropolis at Apollonia was forbidden even to Albanian archaeologists. This, the highest point of the town, was declared a military security zone. Now, it appears that the whole of the acropolis is riddled with underground bunkers. It was from here that the Albanian general staff would have overlooked the coast if, as the dictator Enver Hodja feared in the 1970s, western troops had threatened to invade Albania. Hodja had thousands upon thousands of these bunkers built along the coast: they ruin an otherwise intact landscape.

In the area that we examined around Apollonia, the authorities have placed broad areas of land under conservation orders. To prevent undiscovered archaeological sites from being damaged, ploughing will never be allowed in these areas. The soils have therefore been preserved intact. Even the fragile, humus-rich uppermost layer is still present. Anyone who ever doubts that human activity is the main cause of soil erosion should take a trip to Albania. Wherever the fields have been tilled by hand, using the simple techniques that have endured since the Late Stone Age, the countryside has remained intact.

Chapter 6

Engineering Knowledge:
The Control of Water and Town Planning

Contrary to well-meaning advice, I avoided restricting myself to a statistical enu-meration of what was capable of being proved at the time. Such a position is as irrefutable as it is unproductive and unscientific: it does not accord with the fact that science, as a continuing process, has to rely on new initiatives and impulses. Anyone who is facing new ground, must also step on it.

HERMANN KERN (*Labyrinthe* (*Labyrinths*), 1982)

Technical Reconstruction

When people no longer simply exploited natural resources, but instead began to exhaust nature's stored potential as much as possible, they had invented technology. The development of the latter is closely linked to that of contemporary society, culture, politics and agriculture. Throughout the history of civilisation, technology has taken various forms, and adopted various paths to a solution, but it has always adhered to the principle of rationality in attempting to achieve its aims. Rational solutions may be reconstructed by adopting the perspective of past engineers, and taking account of their tools and potential. Because the forces and laws of nature have since been established, it is possible, from the remains of former installations, to measure the extent to which the natural laws were under-stood in earlier times. This method has been called by the Essen architect Horst Leiermann, 'technical reconstruction'.

In technical reconstruction, all the information that is available is taken into account simultaneously – documents, objects, even mythological trad-itions – irrespective of their different interpretations. In this, the engineers' and scientists' approach to research differs from that encountered in con-ventional archaeology. The latter is rigidly divided according to the nature of the material. Architectural monuments, texts, artefacts and sculptures are, at any one time, investigated by specialists in different disciplines. In addition, the remains recovered are also differentiated according to their

125

country of origin and handled in individual subdisciplines (Egyptology, Ancient Oriental Studies, Assyrian Studies, and so on). With technical reconstruction, this division is not needed. The single distinguishing criterion here is how a culture, irrespective of its origin or language, could cope with the laws of nature.

To find plausible solutions for past technical problems, modern-day engineers, technologists and architects start by using their experience to reconstruct former technical installations. In many cases, this method requires consideration of a variety of working hypotheses and approaches towards an explanation, until, eventually, one interpretation crystallises into being the most plausible solution. Lacking proof that a particular installation was actually used in the way it appears to have been employed, technical reconstructions can only remain in the realm of theory. Whenever new information comes to light, they must be reconsidered. In favourable cases, however, they help to bring further components of the prehistoric and historic technological constructions to light. If such components are then found where they were predicted to lie, the assumption that the technical reconstructions are correct is reinforced.

Hydraulic Engineering in Mycenaean Times

Water management is an almost ideal subject for technical reconstruction. Because water, alongside air, is the most important natural resource for human beings, water management and hydraulic engineering played a prominent role in nearly every region of the globe and at almost every period in the history of human culture. Remains of water-engineering projects dating back to prehistoric and early historical times have survived in many different places in the countries around the Mediterranean. Artificial irrigation of fields had been common practice since the 4th millennium BC (at the latest), and by the 2nd millennium BC complicated drainage systems were employed in Egypt and Greece. About the same time, many cities in Mesopotamia, Egypt, Asia Minor and Crete also already had ingenious water-supply and waste-management systems.

Jost Knauss, Professor of Hydraulic Engineering at Munich Technical University, has studied the hydraulic installations in Mycenaean Greece, and has written five books and over thirty other publications on the subject. His research has shown that many, if not most, important Mycenaean settlements benefited from artificial water-management systems. It turns out that the Mycenaean engineers' knowledge must have reached a high level, because their technical solutions corresponded precisely with the hydraulic requirements. Jost Knauss has concluded that they even surpassed the state of knowledge in classical antiquity, a thousand years later.

In the 1930s, archaeologists discovered an artificial dam several kilometres east of Tiryns, the Late Bronze Age city on the Argive Plain that was the heartland of the Mycenaean culture. The dam was as high as a three-storey house, and many times as long. It stretches right across a river bed and thus blocks the natural watercourse, so it was intended to divert the river. An artificial canal, 1.5 kilometres long, leads from the dam to the next natural watercourse, and at the base of the dam, massive walls partly survive that were meant to protect the lower portion, at least on the side in contact with the water. The style of these walls is characteristic of the Mycenaean period. It was therefore clear that this construction was built at about the same time as the cities of Mycenae and Tiryns in the Late Bronze Age.

Seventeen years ago, on behalf of the German Archaeological Institute, I began research on the history of the landscape in the Argolid. Naturally I was particularly interested in why the river had been diverted. The obvious assumption was that this was unavoidable to protect the lower part of Tiryns from flooding, because the original river bed ran directly towards the city. Because practically no sediment could have been deposited around the Late Bronze Age city since the time of the diversion, I began by finding out the structure of the subsoil in the vicinity of Tiryns from both hand and machine cores. The results of the stratigraphical investigation were amazing. It turned out that large parts of the lower portion of the city had been buried by mud-flows in about 1200 BC, and were now hidden as much as five metres below the surface.

Although the flood disaster took place about 1200 BC – that is, at about the time that palace society began to collapse – afterwards there was obviously still enough expertise and political leadership on hand to plan the dam and canal, and carry out the construction. The aim of the installation was clearly to protect the lower part of the city of Tiryns permanently against future floods, a task that it fulfilled in every respect. The dam even far outlasted the settlement at Tiryns. When the last inhabitants left, seven hundred years after the dam had been built, the diversion was still doing its job. Today, 3200 years after its construction, it is the oldest still-functioning piece of hydraulic engineering in Europe.

The hydraulic engineer Jost Knauss also examined the river diversion at Tiryns. In particular, he pointed out the excellent choice of location. Obviously the Mycenaean engineers thoroughly understood the hydro-

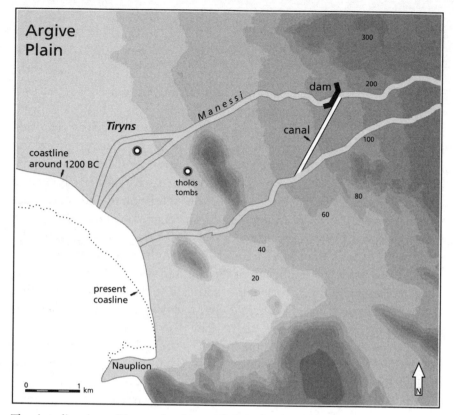

The river diversion at Tiryns – the oldest, still-functioning piece of hydraulic engineering in Europe

logical properties of the catchment area. Over eighty per cent of the total flow was diverted.

Other centres of the Mycenaean culture also possessed hydraulic systems. Directly downstream of Mycenae, Jost Knauss investigated the remains of a massive wall that stretches across the bed of the Chavos. It had been thought that this wall was the remaining portion of a prehistoric bridge. Jost Knauss recognised, however, that it was the remains of an artificial storage dam. Remnants of waterproof clay still remain in the cracks between the stone blocks. Just below the stone wall there are circular depressions in the bedrock, and it is conceivable that these were introduced as basins for washing laundry. Probably jets of water were allowed to escape from the reservoir at specific points, to fill the basins and agitate the water within them. Such natural 'washing machines' are still sometimes used in Greece to clean flokati rugs.

There are passages in ancient Greek literature that suggest that in Homer's time – or shortly before then – washing was carried out in such hollows. Jost Knauss quoted the following passages in his reconstruction of the installation. In the *Odyssey*, Nausicaa, the beautiful princess, goes outside the city to wash expensive clothes:

> They reached the lovely river with its never-failing pools, in which there was enough clear water always bubbling up and swirling by to clean the dirtiest clothes.

And in the *Iliad*, Hector flees from the wounded Achilles past the springs of Troy, of which it says:

> Close beside [the springs], wide and beautiful, stand the troughs of stone where the wives and lovely daughters of the Trojans used to wash their glossy clothes in the peaceful days before the Achaeans came.

At various places the Mycenaean engineers also constructed systems that enabled them to divert excess water from the winter and spring rainfall, or else to store some of it to irrigate the fields during the dry summer months. There are many dry valleys in the Greek countryside that rapidly turn into lakes after heavy downpours in winter. The water generally finds natural outlets through fissures in the limestone. If these fissures are blocked, however, the lake persists in the valley, possibly even throughout the summer.

The Mycenaean engineers had many reasons for interfering with these natural reservoirs. Among others, the valley floors contain fertile soil, and in a country dominated by barren limestone mountains these are valuable agricultural areas. But most of the fertile soil could not be worked, because for most of the year it lay beneath standing water. Even if it dried out at the end of the summer, this was too late for sowing. People therefore shied away from siting their farms and settlements in these valleys, because of the threat of flooding on the one hand, and because the damp areas provide the ideal breeding grounds for mosquitoes – and thus malaria – on the other.

The hydraulic-engineering solution to this problem was as simple as it was effective. Part of the excess winter and spring rainfall was retained in reservoirs, so that the water was available for irrigating the fields in the dry summer months. The rest was led away through artificial watercourses as quickly as possible. To this end, only a small portion of the valley needed to be partitioned off with a long, narrow dyke from the rest of the area. The water was retained behind the dyke, and the remainder of the valley dried out.

A particularly striking example of a water-supply and drainage system is that found in the Kopais in central Greece. This riverless basin in Boeotia once consisted of marshland and lakes, which covered 150 square kilometres, roughly the size of San Francisco Bay. To reclaim the fertile agricultural land, and reduce the danger of malaria, the Mycenaeans first constructed a simple system, similar to that found in many other valley basins in Arcadia at that time. In the 14th and 13th centuries BC, the Mycenaean engineers then improved upon this system. On the northern margin of the plain, a large canal was constructed, 25 kilometres long, 40 metres wide, and 2–3 metres deep. This carried the combined waters of two rivers and several streams to a natural outlet on the opposite side of the valley. Massive dykes, thirty metres wide and two metres high, separated the canal from the rest of the plain. In case of extreme floods, there were spillways and relief reservoirs. The whole system dealt with 700 million cubic metres of water every year. The canal was so efficiently designed that the existing polder system, which had dykes just one metre high, could be retained. During the rainy season, water was directed towards the basins, which filled to become reservoirs. The excess water flowed away through the canal. In this way, the farms and towns, as well as the agricultural land, had a constant supply of water throughout the year. In addition, the canal could be used as a waterway to transport goods from the interior to the coast.

After the collapse of the Mycenaean state, the drainage of the Kopais also fell into disrepair, and marshland returned. In Roman times and, eventually, in the nineteenth century, the Mycenaean attempts at drainage were repeated. Today, the Kopais is a dry plain, skirted by a motorway.

A Granary Becomes a Desert

The consequences that follow from a breakdown in the system of land management may be seen in the wadi landscape of central Tunisia. In Roman times, North Africa was known as the 'Granary of Rome'. Today the region is a wasteland, inhabited by a few nomads only.

Some time ago, at the invitation of a Danish archaeological and historical team, directed by Søren Dietz, I visited the Zaghouan valley, an area in northeastern Tunisia. Because two geographers were already part of the project, I seemed to be regarded as a sort of guest. In any case, I had been given so little information that I did not even know where the research area lay. I was told that was not necessary, because I would be met at the airport.

When I arrived five hours late, at about one in the morning, in Tunis, I could count the people who were still in the airport on the fingers of one hand. It was obvious that there was no Danish archaeologist among them. But the information desk was still manned. 'No, we have no message for you' they told me.

What should I do? I needed to find a hotel for the night – but the next day was the last day of Ramadan. All public institutions, offices, archaeological institutes and excavations were closed. So the next day I wandered around Tunis, took a taxi to the ruins of Carthage, and then visited the airport again to ask, in vain, about any messages.

Finally, I remembered a casual remark of Søren Dietz's: 'This time all of the team will be accommodated on the coast.' The previous year there had been two sets of accommodation, one on the sea and the other in the mountains. I needed to go where the mountains are close to the sea. So I took a taxi to Hammamet, the largest tourist centre on the coast, to look for a hotel there, hire a car and then search for the archaeological team. I tried to find out from the driver how many hotels there were in Hammamet. 'More than a hundred,' came the answer – so it was likely to be a long search.

The driver set me down at the crossroads where there were no less than four hotels. An extremely smart hotel was prepared to let me stay one or two nights. Exhausted, I signed in the guest-book. As I did so, I thought to myself, 'Why not start my search right here?' So I said to the porter, 'No doubt you know this area really well.' 'Yes, naturally,' he said. 'Then you have probably heard of the Danish archaeologists.' 'Of course,' said the cheerful man behind the counter, 'they are living here!' 'Indeed!' I thought, and then asked 'So then you know Søren Dietz?' 'He's living here as well!' At that very instant, my eyes fell on my own name farther up the page in the guest-book. I had just managed to hire the very room that had already been reserved for me! Søren Dietz and his team greeted me like a long-lost son.

The fieldwork in the interior also hides a series of similar surprises. The survey team had discovered well over one hundred Roman villas and farmsteads, many of which had lavish bathhouses. In Roman times, water from springs in the Zaghouan Mountains had been carried to Carthage through aqueducts fifty kilometres long. Smaller streams were restrained with weirs, and fertile ground was terraced. The inhabitants captured some of the rainfall in cisterns, to store it for dry periods. These methods enabled the relatively low rainfall to be used in the most efficient way, and the soil to be preserved for agriculture over a long period of time. We discovered no signs of soil erosion between the end of the last Ice Age and the end of the Roman period.

Today, the landscape looks very different. Metre-thick layers of alluvium have accumulated in the wadis – sediment derived from once fertile soil that has been washed away. During the rainy seasons, the rivers flood about a quarter of the countryside. During the dry seasons, these extensive areas of land lie fallow beneath dense growths of thistles. Nearly everywhere these recent sediments show no signs of layering, so they must have been laid down in a very short period of time. Later we found a late Roman mausoleum, which was probably built in the 5th century, directly on soil that was at least 10,000 years old but which today is buried under sediments five metres thick. A wadi has cut into the recent deposits and revealed the mausoleum. The latest pottery in the sediments above the mausoleum dates from the 7th century.

The mausoleum was built at the end of the Roman period, when the landscape was still intact, thanks to the numerous stabilisation measures that had been undertaken. Subsequently, Roman domination of Tunisia was lost, and during the next two centuries the works controlling the landscape also collapsed. The result was massive soil erosion, causing the land to become almost completely barren.

Of Ports and Men

At all periods, people have used their technical knowledge to gain economic advantages. With their drainage measures, the Mycenaean hydraulic engineers increased the extent of the ground that could be used for agriculture and provided a supply of water during the dry summer months. Because the wealth of the Late Bronze Age kingdoms – not just in Greece and Crete, but also in Asia Minor, Syria, Palestine and Egypt – rested on foreign trade in luxury goods, it would have been sensible for the Mycenaean engineers to have employed their expertise in facilitating this foreign trade – in other words, building protected harbours for the trading ships.

Previously it was believed that this had not happened and that the first artificial harbour installations were constructed several centuries later. They would have been unnecessary in Mycenaean times – according to the assumptions made by most experts in Aegean prehistory – because the rowers would have been able to pull their ships ashore very easily on to the sandy beaches. After all, just such a procedure is described by Homer in the *Iliad*. Nevertheless, it should be noted that in the Bronze Age there were different types of vessels. Small fishing boats and boats that were used for local trade, together with the fast, slender warships that were used to attack enemy lands, could certainly simply be hauled up on to the beach. But this was not possible with the large trading ships. Many Late Bronze Age ships, such as the trading vessel from the 13th century BC that was discovered wrecked off Ulu Burun on the southern coast of Turkey, could not have been just pulled ashore. This ship had been laden, in metal alone, with over six tonnes of freight. The fact that the other cargo (including Canaanite amphorae, African ebony, stone anchors, elephant tusks and ostrich eggshells) originated from various countries in the eastern Mediterranean, suggests that a series of coastal cities possessed installations suitable for large ships, and the corresponding facilities for handling freight.

There are enough indications of such installations. There was a massive mole and sea wall as early as the 3rd millennium BC in the Early Bronze Age harbour at Limantepe in western Turkey. Pharaoh Amenhotep had a rectangular, artificial harbour of unbelievable size – one kilometre wide by one-and-a-half kilometres long – built on the west bank of the Nile at Thebes in the 14th century BC. Frescos at El Amarna, the Egyptian capital in the 14th century BC, show Syrian ships lying next to one another alongside a quay.

Early ports along the coast of Palestine have been investigated thoroughly. The Israeli archaeologist Avner Raban has been studying them for several decades. In his opinion, the question of whether a harbour was built or not, did not depend in any way on the available knowledge – that was obtainable anyway – but on whether there was a commercial need. If a city needed a protected harbour to carry out trade all year round, then such a harbour was built. But if the population needed moorings only during the warm summer months, there would have been no sense in building an expensive harbour. Where there were artificial harbours, there were various standard solutions, depending on whether the harbour's main function was related to passengers, ore, grain, or large objects.

During the Pylos Project, we eventually succeeded in discovering by far

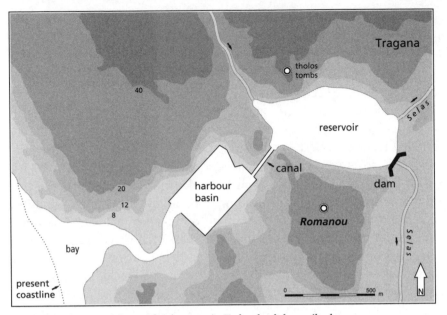

Nestor's harbour and the artificial reservoir. Today, both have silted up

the oldest artificial harbour in Europe. The harbour basin was about five kilometres southwest of the Palace of Nestor and about ten times the size of a football field. The discovery of this installation indicates that the Mycenaean engineers definitely used their knowledge for maritime construction, and also that they possessed outstanding expertise in this respect.

About five hundred metres inland of the shoreline, the Mycenaean engineers dug a rectangular basin, which was joined to the sea by a canal that followed an ancient river bed. To prevent the basin from silting up, it needed to be scoured by a constant flow of clean water. To achieve this, the builders artificially dammed a nearby river to make a reservoir. In it, the river water came to a standstill, and any sediment that it carried consequently sank. Clean water from the top of the reservoir was then carried off through an artificial channel to flush the harbour basin. This sort of 'clean water flush' was widely used in the Middle Ages. No one had suspected that such a useful mechanism had been recognised and employed two thousand years earlier, but had subsequently been forgotten.

In the *Odyssey*, Homer describes in detail how, ten years after the end of the Trojan War, Odysseus' son Telemachus makes his way to the court of the wise King Nestor at Pylos, but he does not say a single word about his ship having to enter a large artificial harbour. Why not? In Homer's day – four hundred years after the Heroic Age in the Late Bronze Age – the

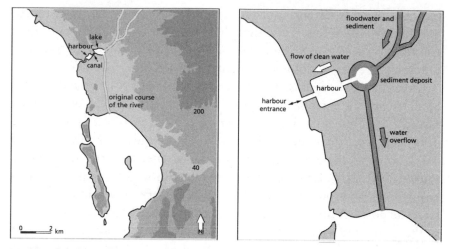

Working drawings of Nestor's harbour

Mycenaean hydraulic installations had long since fallen into disrepair. At best, silted-up basins or functionless dams might still have been recognisable. The Greek population of the 8th century BC no longer possessed any knowledge of hydraulics, which, had they done so, would have given them a true idea of the Mycenaean engineers' achievements. Even the erection of the fortifications at Mycenae appear in tales as the work of giants; that is, of the Cyclopes. The construction of hydraulic works was also ascribed to demigods. So, some of the labours of Hercules may actually refer to hydraulic works. His successful fight against the Lernaean Hydra could, for example, be an account of the drainage of the Lernaean Lake in the Argolid. The heads of the monster would then be the streams that fed the lake. Every time one of these streams was cut off from the body (the lake) a new one arose.

Urban Development

The construction of Late Bronze Age harbours was not the only field that required forward planning and technical engineering skills. Laying out cities must also have been a science in its own right. To continue to function for hundreds of years, cities must be provided with a complicated infrastructure. A city is like a living organism, with various essential organs. Among the most important components are the administration and organisation of water supply and drainage; the production and distribution of food and other essentials; communal institutions, including administrative centres and religious areas such as temples and cemeteries; and, finally, the industrial quarters. Even though many cities appear chaotic, their construction needed to follow a plan. Without a functioning sewage system, for example, every cloudburst would have turned into a disaster.

If a city had to be reconstructed after destruction by a fire or at the hands of an enemy, the most obvious thing was to ensure that the population's essential requirements, at least, were met as far as possible. Even in those days, there were undoubtedly definite, basic rules governing the layout of cities. Some of these are actually mentioned later by Aristotle (*Politics*, 1326a–1327b, 1330a). He states that a city must, above all, be difficult for an enemy to occupy, but must simultaneously be easy for the inhabitants to leave. Its position must be such that it is easy to reach from any direction, so that grain and wood may be transported easily to it, and news carried easily to any particular destination. Naturally, a city also needed to have a functioning water supply. Aristotle wrote all this in relation to the cities of his time – that is, of the 4th century BC. But what, in concrete terms, did Late Bronze Age cities one thousand years earlier actually look like?

Mysterious Labyrinths

In the winter of 1877, a 6th-century-BC wine jar was found near Rome, with a remarkable inscribed design. It included seven riders, seven infantrymen, and a labyrinth. In the outer ring of the labyrinth was the word 'TRUIA', meaning 'Troy'. As a result, the archaeologist who first published details of this jar interpreted it as an outline plan of the city of Troy, the dominant Late Bronze Age trading centre in northwest Turkey.

Nowadays, we think of a labyrinth as being like a garden maze – a complicated, confusing network of passages and cul-de-sacs that make it difficult, or even impossible, to find the right path to one's actual goal. Originally, however, the term 'labyrinth' had a completely different meaning; intersections and cul-de-sacs were only added a few hundred years ago. In antiquity, and throughout the Middle Ages, labyrinths depicted just a single path, and there was therefore no chance of getting lost. It follows that the depiction of the labyrinth must originally have had a completely different meaning and function than it has nowadays.

The geometrical form of the labyrinth therefore only actually makes sense if it is interpreted as an architectural plan. It thus symbolically represents a model of a city. The lines in the labyrinth correspond to boundaries, which generally consisted of walls or hedges; the space between

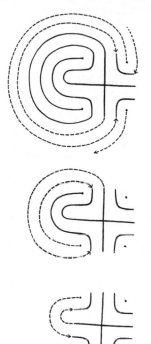

How to draw a labyrinth

them is the pathway. Overall, the labyrinth represents an inner space separated from the outside world, from which entrance is gained only through a small gateway. Finally, the path from the entrance to the centre follows the longest possible route, which means that travelling along this path to the centre requires the maximum time and effort. There are neither intersections nor possibilities for any alternative route.

The basic design of the labyrinth consists of a cross. In each of the four sectors there is a right-angled corner, and within that again, a point. The cross is first joined to the end of one of the corners. Subsequently, taking the next two elements of the basic design at any one time, they are linked together in pairs. The complexity of the labyrinth increases according to how many right-angle corners are placed within the arms of the cross.

Most labyrinths are found around the Mediterranean, and it is probable that the design originated in this region. The word 'labyrinthos' may be traced back to the 3rd millennium BC; its roots lie in western Asia Minor. The *-nthos* ending is characteristic of the Luwian language. The Luwians and Proto-Luwians were a people in western Asia Minor, who, in the Early

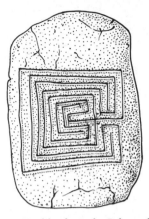

Labyrinth on the back of a Linear-B tablet from the Palace of Nestor

Bronze Age, exerted a great influence on the islands of the Aegean, and over the region of modern-day Greece.

One of the oldest, firmly dated examples of the labyrinth comes from the Palace of Nestor in Pylos. It was scratched on the back of a clay tablet – possibly to pass the time whilst writing. Another labyrinth appears on the fragment of a clay tablet that was found at Tell Rifa'at in Syria. Both labyrinths come from a period about 1200 BC. At that time, both cities, Pylos and Tell Rifa'at – like Troy – suffered destruction, which also marked the end of the Bronze Age and the beginning of the Iron Age. These two examples show that at the end of the Bronze Age the labyrinth was a recognised pattern around the eastern Mediterranean.

But what does the labyrinth have to do with Troy? The period of the Luwian culture in western Asia Minor, the 2nd and 3rd millennia BC, was also the period when Troy was in its prime. At about 3000 BC, the Trojan sphere of cultural influence took shape as the first of the Bronze Age cultures in the Aegean. Because of its geographical location, Bronze Age Troy must also have been Luwian – and, in fact, the sole preclassical inscription found so far at Troy is in the Luwian script and language. Troy collapsed as a trading centre at the same time as Pylos and Tell Rifa'at about 1200 BC, and was subsequently sparsely populated. Later, the place became a sort of shrine to the 'Golden Age', until it was finally completely abandoned in the fifth century AD, upon the collapse of the western Roman Empire.

A Magical Dance

A couple of hundred years after the collapse of Troy, the labyrinth reappeared in the form of specific areas set aside for dances and rituals. The drawings on the Italian wine jar from Tragliatella, mentioned earlier, illustrate this ritual, which was known in antiquity as the 'Trojan Dance'. It was mainly performed in early Italy, primarily when cities were founded, and then typically before any walls were erected. The chosen dancers were often the adolescent sons of aristocratic families. The armed riders and foot-soldiers in the drawing on the wine jar have just left the labyrinth, and have thus completed a complicated, choreographed set of movements. The various figures of their dance symbolise magic protective walls, which will complete the physical protection of the city. The labyrinth should exhaust and confuse both physical attackers and harmful spirits, and make it impossible for them to penetrate into the interior.

Because the labyrinth in its classical form was associated throughout the whole of antiquity with the name of the city of Troy, experts anticipated, as many as fifty years ago, that a labyrinthine arrangement would be rediscovered in the layout of the city of Troy. Unfortunately, the most important central portion of Troy was lost when the area was levelled in Roman times. Despite this, it is obvious that the buildings of this, the sixth city of Troy, were actually arranged on ring-like terraces. In principle, therefore, the city might well have been laid out in the form of a labyrinth. Possible boundaries may have been walls, ditches, canals, natural cliffs, terraces and wooden palisades.

In recent years, geophysical investigations in the lower part of the city clearly revealed two massive anomalies. Subsequent follow-up investigations showed that these abnormalities were caused by artificial ditches hewn out of the bedrock. These ditches are similarly circular in shape, and arranged around the central temple and palace area. So Troy was actually laid out in a circular fashion. It is, however, hardly conceivable that the whole layout of Troy strictly followed the plan of a labyrinth. Daily routine movements would have been far too time-consuming, especially for the aristocracy, whose mansions were in the centre. The walls and other boundaries must have been broken by gates and bridges to facilitate everyday traffic. Such shortcuts would not have lessened the symbolic protection in the least. Sensibly planned and constructed, they could even have increased the confusion of strangers.

The ring-like layout of the city of Troy also reflects the military organisation. In the Hittite kingdom, the neighbouring state in central Asia Minor in the 2nd millennium BC, the armies similarly assembled in concentric rings, where the arrangement corresponded to the status of the individual soldiers. The inner ring, around the king, consisted of elite soldiers and bodyguards armed with spears. The next ring was formed by the hand-picked 'Golden Spear' guards. Simple soldiers with bronze spears and other heavy weapons formed the outer ring.

The equivalent to the ritual of the Trojan Dance is found elsewhere in western Asia Minor in the Bronze Age and early Iron Age. Herodotus describes how the people of Sardis, in western Asia Minor, had carried a lion around the city, to protect it against evil spirits. The Roman philosopher Seneca also confirms that similar rituals were performed at Troy, in particular as expiation for the city, and to bless it.

This might clarify a key scene in Homer's description of the Trojan War. The *Iliad* reaches its climax in the fight between the Greek hero Achilles and Hector, the chief warrior of the Trojan army. Achilles slays Hector, ties the corpse to his chariot, and drags it three times around the walls of the city. He probably did this not because he wanted to desecrate the corpse, but to break the Trojan city's magical protection. He must, therefore, have gone round anticlockwise – widdershins, the direction of death. Here, Homer is conveying a deeply symbolic act. The walls of Troy have lost their supernatural protection and will soon be destroyed.

A thousand years after the Trojan War, during the Hellenic period, the original sense of the labyrinth had long been forgotten. The design remained, however, as well as the dance movements. Both were regarded as being irritating and confusing. Neither the dancers, nor the general public, understood the meaning of the movements that were carried out.

After the true meaning of the labyrinth had been forgotten, people began to conceive of it as a single, imposing construction, with complicated paths and passageways. The ruins of the Minoan palace at Knossos were included, even though nothing found there could be correlated with the original form of the labyrinth.

In Roman times, the labyrinth was still closely connected with the Bronze Age city of Troy. It served as an example of a fortified town, together with protective walls, towers and main gate. In later centuries, too, the name of 'Troy' remained inseparable from the concept of a labyrinth. In Sweden, there are hundreds of labyrinths, or 'Troiburgen' as they are known. In general, they are marked out with stones on the ground, or cut into the turf. In England, the same sorts of design are known by the names of 'Troy Towns' or 'Walls of Troy'.

Future Prospects

After this long circuitous route, starting with old-style excavations, and proceeding through modern surveys, the methods of geoarchaeology, remote sensing, the historical relationship between culture and landscape, and the technical reconstruction of past water engineering and town planning, we find ourselves back in the labyrinth! What an appropriate metaphor. Despite all our efforts at synthesis, we are faced with innumerable individual observations and phenomena, which seems to be an unavoidable situation in archaeology, because this is the only way in which prehistoric cultures are handed down to us. There are no comprehensive descriptions of events. Or are there?

Ever since the great discoverers brought the discipline of Aegean prehistory into being one hundred years ago, so much new knowledge has been gained that a critical reassessment of the schools of thought that arose then appears overdue. We should critically examine not only our supposed 'knowledge', but also our 'ignorance' – everything we do not know. Mediterranean archaeology is full of unsolved problems, some of which may be mentioned here. The rise of the Minoan and Mycenaean cultures is one of them, but so is their collapse. There are questions about the origin of Early Iron Age peoples such as the Philistines, the Phoenicians and the Etruscans, as well as themes such as Atlantis, the Phaistos Disc, the origin of the 'Sea People', the historical basis of the Trojan War, and many, many, more.

In recent decades, there have been no noticeable advances to report in clearing up these problems. This was not so much because the available information was insufficient to tackle the questions, but rather because they did not form the main focus of archaeological interest, and were even, in many cases, regarded as taboo as far as serious science was concerned. This attitude also stems from the discipline's early days, and has, in my opinion, now been overtaken. If Aegean prehistorians had concentrated on the major problems of Mediterranean archaeology, these would probably have been solved long ago.

In the following chapters, I attempt an approach to formulating answers to some of these questions. My main concerns in doing so are not to present 'solutions' but rather to provide a stimulus to new ways of finding solutions. Detailed treatment of the major, still open, questions, may possibly also help us to assemble the individual pieces of information gained so far into a harmonic whole. We begin with by far the greatest and most notorious problem in archaeology: the foundering of Atlantis.

Chapter 7

Atlantis: The End of a Legend

If the circumstances for a scientific discovery or a technological advance are right, then it will be made, and whether it is by Tom, Dick, or Harry is quite irrelevant.
JULIUS BELOCH (*Griechische Geschichte* (*Greek History*), Strasbourg, 1912)

A Gruesome Find

How, using just simple means, can one create the greatest possible excitement? The best method is perhaps to take an unusual object, remove it from its original context, and put it into a completely new, unexpected location. After a while it must be discovered by some unsuspecting person who cannot possibly identify it correctly. The general public will be informed and, not long afterward, wild speculations will spring to life: the thing is of extraterrestrial origin; it is unequivocal evidence of a CIA or Mafia conspiracy, an impending environmental catastrophe, the Last Judgement, or something even worse.

An innocuous Coca-Cola bottle, left in some inappropriate place, is sufficient to unleash such a chain reaction, and cause endless nights of discussion, as in the film, *The Gods must be Crazy.* A Coke bottle falls from a plane on to the African savanna. Bushmen pick it up, and eventually resolve to return the precious object to where it must inevitably belong – to the Gods.

Not that long ago, something similar happened in the United States. In St Louis County in the State of Mississippi, the police found a twenty-litre glass flask containing a gelatinous organic substance, consisting of two parts. One was about seven pounds in weight, resembled muscle tissue, and was dark like liver. The other was elongated, like a tongue or a tentacle, and had regular grooves. The police gave their mysterious find to the local health authorities. These first checked whether it consisted of human tissue – it did not – and then had it examined by marine biologists, who could not identify it either. If the media had found out about this rather gruesome find, there is not the slightest doubt that there would have been headlines such as 'Life from Mars Already Found on Earth?' or 'Are Scientists Hushing Up a Horror Experiment?'

Those in charge acted responsibly, however. They appealed directly to the general public and thus met the media on their own ground. The mystery was soon solved, because a female employee at a French restaurant recognised the strange lump of material. Eight years before, she had been experimenting with vinegar, and she had left the flask in a dark corner of a cellar where she had forgotten about it. When she found it again, the vinegar bacteria had produced large amounts of cellulose. She wanted to get rid of the horrible mess – and so, through a chain of coincidences, it wound up in a ditch, where the police found it.

What does this story have to do with archaeology? Well, two important lessons may be learned from it. First, even the most bizarre events may have remarkably simple explanations. Second, the circle of obvious experts does not always include the people best able to solve a problem.

Lost in Space and Time

Later generations are often helpless and (of necessity) sceptical when faced with objects and stories from earlier times because, throughout the history of culture, knowledge has not only been gained but has also been repeatedly lost. Every advance first makes proven procedures outdated, then gradually causes them to become superfluous, and then finally results in their falling into complete oblivion. Simple mechanisms follow on from more expensive, manual methods of production, and are replaced by machinery. Film-setting replaces lead typesetting, databases replace card files. The list could be continued almost indefinitely. Retrograde steps, or more frequently, cultural upheavals, do, however, cause an even more dramatic loss of knowledge. In times of crisis, the level that has been reached is not replaced by a higher one but by a lower stage. The fall from the 'Golden' Age of the Late Bronze Age into the 'Dark' Age of the Early Iron Age is a good example of this. The people who lived in Greece during the 'Dark' centuries were not competent to deal with the water-management systems left from the Bronze Age.

Because archaeologists' work involves every era in the history of culture, as well as every region of the Earth, they encounter large numbers of baffling objects and inexplicable phenomena as part of their daily routine. It may seem easiest to ascribe many of these phenomena to extraterrestrials – which was what Erich von Däniken proposed. If the solution to a problem is not immediately obvious, amateurs eagerly consider colliding planets, sunken continents, cosmic catastrophes, epidemics, 'earthquake storms', or invasions by mysterious hordes. Even the catastrophe theories that the pioneers of this discipline developed to account for the collapse of the Aegean Bronze Age, adhered to this pattern. Luckily, archaeologists seldom turn to such simplistic explanations nowadays, no matter how spectacular they might be. Normally, they consult other experts before they make sensational announcements to the general public. And, in the main, these experts are natural scientists. Because of their different training and experience, their alternative points of view, or even their different research methods (which had not previously been considered), they may possibly be able to get closer to solving the problem. In general, the greater the effort put into such investigations, the less spectacular the results. Just as in mathematics, where a complicated equation may be made more manageable, and often even soluble, by removing terms from within the brackets and cancelling others out, so some of the unknown terms in archaeology's hierarchy of theories may frequently be cancelled out by means of scientific investigations.

When analysing my work in the Argolid in April 1990, I had an idea that I thought might conceivably contribute to the solution of what is probably the most-discussed problem in archaeology. I had already investigated the river diversion at Tiryns, and established that parts of the lower city had been buried by a mudflow about 1200 BC. According to the excavator, Klaus Kilian, a major earthquake occurred at Tiryns practically simultaneously. Similarly, the collapse of the Mycenaean culture started about this time. Floods, earthquakes, and the collapse of a heroic age – all these events reminded me of the end of legendary Atlantis. I began to investigate further.

When I published the results of my thoughts on the matter two years later, a female Swiss television reporter asked a series of people on the street what 'Atlantis' meant to them, and obtained a wide range of answers: a myth, a utopia, a hit from the Sixties, the search for a long-lost knowledge, the description of the end of the world, dreams of the next world, a legendary city that disappeared in Greek antiquity ... The story had long become divorced from its origins and had become self-perpetuating.

To most people, Atlantis is a fabled, drowned land that long ago sank

147

below the waves in an immense natural disaster, and which, today, evokes a longing for a perfect, former world. Hordes of scientists and amateur researchers have swarmed everywhere to track down the place where this Paradise may have lain, and have returned full of 'discoveries'. According to them, Atlantis lay on Heligoland; at Uppsala; on Spitzbergen; on the Canary Islands; in Mongolia; on the Bahamas; in Bolivia; in Australia; or beneath the ice of Antarctica. But the lost Paradise must have existed; of that all the 'Atlantologists' are convinced – after all, the story came down from no less a person than the Greek philosopher, Plato.

Plato's Most Ambitious Project

Like the forgotten jar of vinegar, the story of Atlantis obviously lay so long in a dark place – in Egypt – that its expiry date had long since passed. After many hundreds of years, a highly respectable person – the Greek, Solon – stumbled across it in this odd place. By then it seemed utterly mysterious, and thus all the more spectacular. The discoverer carried it across the sea to Greece, and there tried hard to fathom its true meaning. In doing so, he altered some of the original concepts. More generations passed before the tale again came to the attention of a credulous person; this time, the philosopher, Plato. Without being able to determine its true meaning himself, he used the details to support his own political ideas. This chain of remarkable circumstances gave rise to one of the greatest mysteries in history – one that has eluded any plausible solution for 2500 years.

Everything that we know about Atlantis comes from Plato's text. About 350 BC, the philosopher began to draft what was intended to be a three-volume work on the natural sciences and history, which was intended to be recited by three (largely historical) figures during a festival in Athens. The three books thus came to be known by their principal speakers (*Timaeus, Critias, Hermocrates*). The presenter and fourth speaker was Socrates. The discourse did not, however, actually take place; Plato merely put words into their mouths. Such fictitious discussions by people who actually existed were part of the currently accepted literary forms. Unfortunately, Plato did not complete the trilogy; it breaks off in the second volume, shortly before the end of the Atlantis story. It is his sole unfinished work, and to this day we do not know why he failed to complete it. Illness or death did not stop him, because he subsequently wrote the *Laws*, yet another comprehensive book.

In the prologue to the work, Plato has Critias recount the tale of Atlantis (*Timaeus*, 22B–25D). In it, he declares that this early high culture came closest to his conception of the 'ideal state'. The actual description of the city does not, however, agree thematically with the first volume of the trilogy. So the speaker, Critias, has to refrain from giving his discourse until it is his turn. With the exception of this prologue, the whole of the first volume is delivered by Timaeus. He deals with astronomy, physics, biology and anatomy – rather unusual themes for Plato. Plato's concern in this book is to summarise current knowledge of the natural sciences as accurately as possible. He was himself a friend of many contemporary natural philosophers and had personally visited their schools in Sicily, southern Italy and western Asia Minor. The book gave him the opportunity to acknowledge the achievements of these friends, to bring to light important historical information and, at the same time, to interpret these from the perspective of his own particular philosophy. The *Timaeus* was thus a collection of traditional and contemporary concepts in natural philosophy and, as such, provides an important description of knowledge in the 4th century BC.

The other two volumes of the trilogy, *Critias* and *Hermocrates*, were intended to recount the history of humanity and the development of culture. Because Plato finished only part of the *Critias*, the content of the remaining portion of the work is largely speculative; we can, however, assume that he intended to write two all-embracing discussions on the same principles found in the *Timaeus*. The contents of the *Critias* and *Hermocrates* would therefore have consisted of a mixture of verbally transmitted tales and various writers' accounts of history. Although some of these contributions were probably already known, the trilogy as a whole formed Plato's most ambitious work, because, with it, he was trying to produce a comprehensive, scientific picture of the past.

Plato chose a chronological approach for the structure of the *Critias*, the second volume in the trilogy. He begins with the description of the geography of his home of Attica in the dim and distant past, obviously as he had heard it through oral tradition. As with our current reconstructions of past landscapes, the consequences of deforestation and soil erosion occupy a prominent part of Plato's discussion. He compares the eroded lands, as they appeared even in his day, to the bones of a wasted body, attacked by disease: 'all the richer and softer parts of the soil having fallen away, and the mere skeleton of the land being left'. After another elaborate transitional passage, Plato finally turns to the detailed description of Atlantis (*Critias*, 113C–120D). The connection in which this description of an earlier high culture occurs is completely plausible, coming just at the right place in the chronologically arranged *Critias*, because the principal theme of the second volume of the planned trilogy is the history of Greece and neighbouring countries. With this account of Atlantis, Plato had incorporated a comprehensive description of past high cultures. The other material envisaged for this book, including the traditions regarding prehistoric Attica, may have been interesting but were by no means so detailed or spectacular as the story of Atlantis. Moreover, it would hardly have sufficed to fill a whole volume. Plato therefore had to rely on the Atlantis tale, and so turned it into the central element in the trilogy. Because Atlantis was said to lie in the Atlantic (and thus in the west), on top of everything the story fitted harmoniously with Plato's chosen, westward-looking theme for the trilogy. Two of the three speakers came from Sicily and southern Italy. It was there, and in western Asia Minor, that most of the schools of natural philosophy were to be found in the 4th century BC, and there that the knowledge discussed in the Timaeus originated. It was to the west, where a sense of change and a spirit of discovery reigned, that Plato repeatedly found himself attracted.

Plato's Role as a Disseminator of Ideas

Plato recounts how he obtained the story of Atlantis from his ancestor Solon. Solon was a renowned Greek statesman and general, who lived six generations before Plato. Because of his achievements as the highest official in Athens, he was considered to be the 'wisest of the Seven Wise Men'. By peaceful measures, Solon had brought a new order to the endangered Athenian city-state; he reformed the constitution, the legal code, and the system of weights and measures. After his political activities, Solon devoted his time to travels, one of which took him to Egypt, and it was there that he first heard the tale of Atlantis. The country of the Nile was then enjoying a period of independence and stability. Its government was concerned, however, about the increasing strength of Babylonia, which had extended as far as Palestine and thus reached Egypt's borders. As a counterbalance, Egypt built strong ties with Greece, and encouraged Greek soldiers to found colonies in the Nile Delta. Greek traders naturally followed the armed forces. In the western Nile Delta they founded the trading city of Naukratis, which at the time of Solon's visit in the 6th century BC had already grown into the most important trading city in Egypt.

Just sixteen kilometres away from Naukratis lay the then Egyptian capital of Saïs, where the official priesthood was located. Solon's position as a respected politician from Egypt's closest ally meant that a visit was inevitable. According to Plato, the priests received their guest with great reverence. Extensive talks took place in a relaxed atmosphere, the theme of which must primarily have been about economic and military questions. Eventually, however, they must have got round to the latest ideas in natural philosophy and their different perceptions of history. The Egyptian priests reminded Solon that there was no continuous historical record in Greece that could be compared with the Egyptian one. On the contrary, they intimated, the Greek people had only recently emerged from the Dark Ages. As a result, they did not yet realise that there had been a high culture on their own territory. The achievements and heroic deeds of the former Greek states were still regarded with great admiration in Egypt. Behind all this, however, there loomed a momentous event: how the Greek states had once combined and entered a war, which, after long hard battles, they had finally won, and in which their opponent had been the fabled 'Atlantis'. This defeat of 'Atlantis' by Greece had, however, finally averted an ominous danger for all the Mediterranean peoples.

The story, which Solon eventually heard in all its details, made such an impression on him that he wrote it all down in his travel diary, so that he could later turn it into an epic poem. After his return, he did actually begin this work. In accordance with the spirit of the time he 'greekified' proper names. In other words, he substituted a Greek equivalent – or what he took to be one – for foreign names. Probably Solon, or Plato, introduced the name 'Atlantis', which is, in fact, a Greek word. The historical writer Hellinikos of Lesbos, who lived at about the same time as Plato, even published a complete work entitled *Atlantis*. Unfortunately, it has not survived. Similarly nearly all of Solon's writings have been lost. He was, in any case, unable to finish work on the Atlantis text. Plato held the view that had he done so it would have made him as famous as Homer.

After Solon's death, his writings presumably were preserved by his family and handed down from generation to generation. Obviously they eventually came to Plato, the distinguished director of the Academy. At least this is how Plato describes it, and he was fully convinced that he had obtained an authentic historical account.

Fiction or Fact?

Plato's text describes Atlantis as an island in the Atlantic Ocean, a few hundred kilometres in diameter, on which, some 11,000 years ago, there was a thriving, fabulous city, but which fell to Greek forces and eventually,

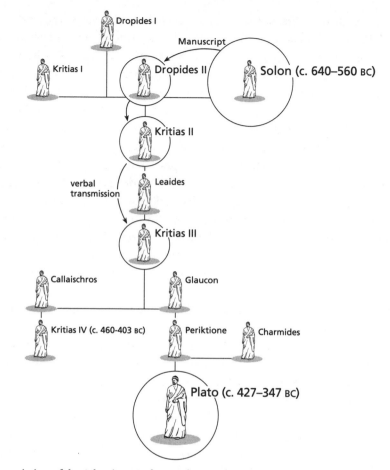

Transmission of the Atlantis story from Solon to Plato

in a natural catastrophe, sank into the sea in just a single day. Even these few details suffice to establish that the story told by Plato cannot have any factual basis. On geological grounds alone it is impossible for a whole continent to disappear overnight. Even plate-tectonic movements take place so slowly that, over a period of ten thousand years, they hardly amount to more than a hundred metres. And 11,000 years ago, when Atlantis is supposed to have flourished, there was no culture anywhere in the world that was as advanced as that described by Plato. It could conceivably have been involved in a war against Greece, because at that time the Greek population consisted of a few fur-clad cave-dwellers, whose technological knowledge was hardly advanced beyond that of producing stone tools. The story of Atlantis, as told by Plato, simply cannot be incorporated into any plausible historical framework. It simply does not add up, as we now know without a shadow of a doubt – despite all the attempts of 'Atlantologists' to teach us otherwise.

There are two possible explanations for the story: first, Plato may have made it up; and second, it may contain a core of historical events overlaid by later distortions. Both views may be supported by very sound arguments. Plato could, quite simply, have devised the story himself, because he was a great inventor of similes and allegories. Whenever it seemed appropriate, he experimented with different ideas and made up suitable legends. These differ, however, in all respects from the Atlantis tale. To make these differences more apparent, the Austrian language researcher Wilhelm Brandenstein cites two examples of similes that Plato devised. On one occasion, he claimed that crickets were once people who became so captivated by the singing of the Muses that they forgot to eat and drink, and died. The Muses then changed them into crickets, who neither eat nor drink, but just sing as long as they live. On another occasion, Plato gave a poetic account of how sexual attraction arose in people. According to this, every individual was originally round, with four arms, four legs, and a head with two faces. Because of this, people were so strong that they did not know what to do with their strength. When they eventually attacked Heaven, Zeus decided to weaken them, and so he took a knife and cut them in half down the middle – just as one cuts fruit in half. On the cut side, the skin was pulled together and sewn up at the navel. Since then, each half has been filled with longing for its other half, so that the two might be joined into a whole and thus overcome their deficiency.

As far as Atlantis is concerned, Plato had plenty of grounds for making up suitable tales for his own ends. After all, he puts it forward as a satisfying illustration of his 'Ideal State'. So it is not surprising that in various elements of the introduction, and also at the end of the Atlantis account, Plato's philosophy is expressed unambiguously – so unambiguously, indeed, that it gives the impression that the long-winded description in between is no more than a political-philosophical myth. Anyone who does not believe in the historical authenticity of Atlantis, can pick a sentence from the introduction or from the end of the twenty-page text and try, on that basis, to ascribe the whole tale to some genre of literature.

Such attempts, however, have all failed. Individual excerpts may well fit into a literary genre, but the tale as a whole is too inconsistent for that. Let us take, for example, the most widespread interpretation of the Atlantis story, namely that it is a morality tale. According to this, prehistoric Greece should be regarded as a model state, which punished Atlantis for the latter's increasing decadence. This interpretation ignores the fact that, in the first place, the story does not deal with Greece but with Atlantis. It is, therefore, not a depiction of the 'ideal state' but of its adversary. In addition, it is first and foremost Greece that suffers from natural catastrophes – and it is quite incomprehensible why, in a morality tale, the 'good' side, of all people, should primarily be the one punished.

Other interpretations also remain unsatisfactory, because they either do not take account of Plato's actual words, or even turn them on their heads. According to the French ancient historian Pierre Vidal-Naquet, Plato put forward the tale of Atlantis 'as a fable, a myth'. But Plato specifically states the opposite, namely that the story is true 'in every respect'. He does not once employ the word *mythos*. Instead, he uses a concept that he exclusively reserves to indicate a structure that may be rationally understood. He says, in fact, that the story is a *logos* (*Timaeus*, 20d, 21a, 21c, 21d, 26e, 27b; *Critias*, 108c) and thus a true event.

People have also frequently attempted to class Atlantis as a 'Utopia', just as Burchard Brentjes has done recently in *Atlantis – Geschichte einer Utopie* (*Atlantis – The Story of a Utopia*). The concept 'utopian' is applied to a form of society that does not experience injustice, oppression, or a despotic ruler. But the city described by Plato does not accord with this in any respect. Atlantis is subject to a totalitarian monarchic regime. Kings can execute anyone they like – only when they have one of their own rank in mind do they have to seek approval from the council of elders. In addition, Atlantis has certain oriental characteristics, which Plato regards as out-landish, such as when he talks about the apparently 'barbaric' decorations of the temples or the primitive rituals of sacrificing bulls. Admittedly, Plato acknowledges respect for the technical achievements of the population of Atlantis, but the structure of their society is, to his mind – as an enlightened Athenian democrat – dreadfully old-fashioned. Certainly, Atlantis is not a place where Plato would have liked to live, and it definitely was not a utopian state. On the contrary, the type of society described by Plato could virtually be portrayed as an 'anti-Utopia'.

In an invented story, the course of events should, at the very least, be consistent, so that it appears largely believable. But in the Atlantis story the suggested historical background is utterly absurd, even though the description of the city seems to be consistent and completely plausible. In descriptions pages long, Plato devotes himself, above all, to the architectural details of the palace and temple buildings, to the structure of the military apparatus, and to the hydraulic engineering works. In the field of water management, alone, Atlantis surpasses the state of knowledge in Greece in Plato's time. But how could a philosopher, with no training or experience in city planning, engineering methods, business, or knowledge of materials, have *imagined* such a complex, exotic city? To combine the vast number of individual elements about Atlantis into a harmonious whole in this fashion, Plato would have needed to be a city planner or engineer.

Many other arguments suggest that Plato had based his account on an already existing description of a historical city. What is decisive is that he could not have improved the credibility of his model of an 'ideal state' with a *fictional* story. It is as if a head of state were to try to encourage the population to behave as an 'ideal society', and then give as an example the tiny village (which we all know) in which Astérix and Obélix lived. His appeal would be the greatest embarrassment of all time. If, however, his appeal referred to a *historical* state, for example to ancient Athens, it would be quite appropriate and not at all out of place. It was only by using a real example that Plato could enhance the weight of his arguments, yet everything suggests that he found himself unable to set the content of the story in the correct historical context. Perhaps this was because he had battened upon the first ever canard in the history of the world?

Apart from the points mentioned, there are numerous further indications that the story was not freely invented but represents a distorted reflection of a historical event. For example, Plato repeatedly stresses that the story, despite its strangeness, 'is by no means a fabricated tale, but is a true story in every respect'. He gives added weight to his statement, by referring to numerous different authorities, including Solon, the 'wisest of the Seven Wise Men'; the goddesses Athene and Neith; the brother state of Egypt; the revered king Amasis; and the latter's respected priests. Moreover, Plato's story contains solid scientific observations – for example concerning the consequences of soil erosion on hydrology and agriculture – which would be quite inappropriate for a fictional account. Yet again, the Atlantis story occurs in a textbook about astronomy, physiology and early history – if it were a purely fictitious parable it could hardly have been given in a less appropriate place. It is also far too long to be of use as an example, and it is peppered with far too many trivial details, which only divert attention from Plato's alleged topic. The genuine similes that Plato invented are always short and concise, wonderfully relevant and, above all, readily recognisable as similes.

We now come to the contradictions. Atlantis was destroyed by Greek forces and, in addition, was then saddled with a natural catastrophe! Although Atlantis lay in the Atlantic Ocean, the same catastrophic event affected Greece – at the other end of the world! Atlantis is said to have lain in the Straits of Gibraltar, but there is absolutely nothing to show that the distribution of land and sea was significantly different in prehistoric times! When Atlantis sank it was supposed to have produced quantities of mud, which rendered the strait impassable. But the Straits of Gibraltar are almost three hundred metres deep and have been passable for millions of years! Further, one of the priests at Saïs claims that Egypt has the oldest culture, only to confess shortly afterwards that the Greek culture is a thousand years older! If Plato had really wanted to find some simile, he would undoubtedly have found a better one. Finally, the story breaks off in the middle of a sentence, Plato eventually giving up work on the trilogy. Had it revolved around an invented simile, however, it certainly would have fitted with Plato's conception, and there would have been no cause for coming to a full stop. So there are many grounds for suggesting that Plato did not invent Atlantis, and equally there is only one basis for believing that he thought up the whole story by himself: the lack of a reasonable explanation of where and what Atlantis might have been.

In all this, the fact should not be overlooked that the school of thought that Plato invented Atlantis arose about the middle of the nineteenth century. At a period, then, when nowhere in the world had there been a single scientific excavation of any sort. Pompeii and Olympia, Thera, Troy, Mycenae, Tiryns, Knossos – all these discoveries lay in the distant future. The existence of prehistoric cultures (as described in the Atlantis story) was absolutely unthinkable to the historians of the time. As a result, it was quite impossible for them to place Homer's 'Golden Age' within any actual historical framework. It is hardly surprising that they relegated Troy to the status of a myth. According to the then current view, Homer's books were recounting a solar myth, in which the Greeks represented the Sun and the Trojans the dark clouds. These concepts are so deeply rooted that, even today, many experts are not prepared to accept that the archaeological site at Troy is identical with the city proclaimed by Homer. Burchard Brentjes, for example, writes 'To this very day it has not been proved that "Troy" ever existed.'

So where does that leave the growth in our knowledge over the past 150 years? We now know that as much as a thousand years before the classical Greek period there were highly developed, literate cultures in Mesopotamia and Egypt, on Crete, on the Greek mainland, and in Asia Minor. We need to judge the interpretation of Plato's Atlantis against the *current* state of our knowledge, and not try to fit it to the nineteenth-century conception of the world.

Past and Present Explanations

Previous attempts to find a historical and geographical framework for the Atlantis legend have almost all come to grief on the most striking event in the story: the description of the natural catastrophe that destroyed Atlantis. According to the interpreters of the Atlantis legend, if there really had been a natural event of this magnitude in the past few thousand years, further evidence or recollections of it must have been preserved. They overlook, however, the fact that our current understanding of the destruction of Atlantis has little in common with Plato's – so little that many 'Atlantologists' carefully avoid citing the corresponding passage in the text. It runs as follows:

> But afterwards there occurred violent earthquakes and floods; and in a single day and night of misfortune all your warlike men in a body sank into the earth, and the island of Atlantis in like manner disappeared in the depths of the sea.
>
> (*Timaeus*)

Plato is here repeating the words of an Egyptian priest. Addressing his Greek listener, the priest says that the whole Greek army sank into the earth together, after the Greeks had returned from their attack on Atlantis. So the natural catastrophes therefore occurred in Greece. So, if we want to locate Atlantis on the basis of natural catastrophes, we need to search for traces of 'violent earthquakes and floods' in *Greece*! Atlantis is only mentioned in passing, and the claim that the island 'in like manner disappeared' is not very convincing – it had already been sacked by the Greek army. We thus attach a far greater significance to the natural catastrophe than Plato. He devoted just a couple of words to the allegedly world-shaking event. Given that the whole Atlantis text occupies some twenty printed pages, more than 99 per cent of the information that he includes is unused if one tries to locate Atlantis by relying solely on the catastrophe scenario. By contrast, an interpretation of the story from an archaeological point of view must aim to track down as many points of agreement as possible between the overall content of the story and the current state of *archaeological* knowledge.

Many scholars of the humanities, who have interpreted Plato's text as a corrupted description of a historical event, have followed this path. There is, however, no unanimity regarding which event or which place is concealed behind the Atlantis story. One scholar (G.R. Morrow) recognises that Plato never distorted facts in the interests of his construct of ideas. An Egyptologist (J.G. Griffiths) finds indications that the story actually originated in Egypt. Another researcher (F. Gidon) notes that Plato's Atlantis fits perfectly into the Bronze Age. Several experts (A.E. Taylor, P. Frutiger, H. Herter and A. Giovanni) also think that Atlantis may have been identical with Helike, a city that disappeared in an earthquake in 373 BC. Others (J.B. Skemp, W. Welliver) view the conflict between Greece and Atlantis as the Persian War. Some (O. Rudberg, U. Wilamowitz-Moellendorff and C. Corbato) see parallels with the Sicilian city of Syracuse, which Plato once visited. One scholar (O. Kern) takes the tale to be an echo of the Eleusinian War; another (E.D. Philips) finds indications of Carthage; and several (K.T. Frost, J.V. Luce, S. Marinatos, W. Brandenstein and M. Pallotino) think that Atlantis may be rediscovered in Minoan Crete.

Despite the plethora of suggestions, none of these proposals has had a lasting effect on archaeology. Even the most popular historical explanation – that the eruption of Thera could have left its mark in the story of Atlantis – did not provide prehistory with any useful stimulus. The towns on Thera were victims of a volcanic eruption – but Atlantis suffered earthquakes and floods, none of which occurred in the eruption of Thera. Thera had at its disposal neither extensive, fertile, agricultural land, nor the major reserves of wood and metal that were such a feature of Atlantis. We do not know of any fortifications, defensive walls, or watch-towers at Akrotiri, and certainly no ship canals. Thera's population showed no inclination towards the display of arms and warrior-like behaviour like that found in Atlantis. It was not a 'barbaric' land, nor an enemy of Greece, and certainly was not destroyed by a war. The idea of equating Thera with Atlantis appears at least as far-fetched as making the eruption of Thera responsible for the collapse of the Minoan culture.

Prehistoric Greece in Plato's Text

Because the details of date and place in Plato's text are not credible, in theory Atlantis could have existed anywhere in the world and at any period.

This gives the 'Atlantologists' free rein to search for the drowned culture as far afield as India or beneath the ice in Antarctica. The key to locating Atlantis does not lie in the description of the sunken city, so much as in the depiction of the *Greek* culture that opposed Atlantis in the war – even though the latter is not the main theme of Plato's description. With respect to the Greek forces opposing Atlantis, we know where they were to be found; only the date at which they were active needs to be determined. If the culture described by Plato more or less accords with our archaeological knowledge of prehistoric Greece, all that remains to be done is to identify a specific adversary, and we shall then have taken a major step to placing the vanished island kingdom.

In the prelude to the *Timaeus*, Plato provides numerous details of the Greek constitution at the time of the great war. The Egyptian priest at Saïs describes a heroic age, when the Athenian state 'was first in war and in every way the best governed of all cities, is said to have performed the noblest deeds, and to have had the fairest constitution of any of which tradition tells, under the face of heaven'. The priest compares the constitution of prehistoric Greece with that of Egypt. Priests, artisans, shepherds, hunters and husbandmen all represented their own castes, and the artisans were subdivided into groups according to their crafts. Even the warriors formed their own group 'and are commanded by the law to devote themselves solely to military pursuits' said the priest. The equipment of the soldiers is particularly helpful in dating the Greek culture. Bronze weapons are mentioned in the text, together with horse-drawn chariots, as well as archers kitted out with shields, men with sling-shots and spear throwers. A particularly notable sign of the early Greek culture was nevertheless a knowledge of writing.

Thanks to these indications, it is not difficult to find a corresponding image in ancient Greece. The description agrees perfectly with what we now know about the Mycenaean culture. In Mycenaean times there were well-organised states in Greece with a hierarchical society. The weapons were made of bronze; spears, shields and chariots were part of the normal equipment. In the 14th and 13th centuries BC, when the regal houses of Mycenae, Tiryns, Pylos, Argos, Thebes and Athens were at the peak of their power, the culture prevailing in Greece corresponded in all respects with that described by Plato. The Mycenaeans even possessed a knowledge of writing, which Plato could not have known about. What has remained the *outstanding* event of Mycenaean times, even for us today, was the Trojan War. What is more, the Egyptian priest in Plato's account describes this event early on, so we immediately link it with the Mycenaean culture:

> Many great and wonderful deeds are recorded of your state in our histories. But one of them exceeds all the rest in greatness and valour. For these histories tell of a mighty power which unprovoked made an expedition against the whole of Europe and Asia, and to which your city put an end.

The combined Greek forces conducted a war outside Greece, which finally went in their favour – and the details of this event agree with what we know about the Trojan War. According to Homer, it was the Greeks who sent 1186 ships into battle – in Plato, it was the enemy who had a fleet of 1200 ships. In Plato's story, the enemy of the Greeks is called 'Atlantis' – today we call it 'Troy'. So is Atlantis then Troy? Were the Egyptian priests simply recounting a slightly different version – namely *their* version – of the story of the Trojan War?

The radical changes about the time of the Trojan War had considerable effects on the culture and the economy in Egypt, so much so that it is perfectly feasible that recollections of these crucial events would have been preserved. Naturally, we should not expect the Egyptian version to agree in all its details with the account handed down in Greece. These differences alone could have led to the true basis of the story becoming obscured.

The Egyptian priest emphasises the fact that at the end of the war between Greece and Atlantis a cultural collapse took place, in which the impressive knowledge of the Greeks was once again lost. 'There have been, and will be again, many destructions of mankind arising out of many causes; the greatest have been brought about by the agencies of fire and water, and other lesser ones by innumerable other causes', he said. So the 'Golden Age' was followed by a 'Dark Age'. Only the illiterate and uneducated, the 'herdsmen and shepherds who dwell on the mountains', survived; the towns, in contrast, fell into decay. The Egyptian priest summarised the consequences of the cultural collapse in the following words:

> You do not know that there formerly dwelt in your land the fairest and noblest race of men which ever lived, and that you and your whole city are descended from a small seed or remnant of them which survived. And this was unknown to you, because, for many generations, the survivors of that destruction died, leaving no written word.

His description of the cultural collapse in the 12th century BC and the subsequent 'Dark Age', could hardly be bettered. When the Mycenaean culture collapsed, the whole culture gradually decayed. Only the peasants survived – at a lower cultural level. Much of the acquired knowledge was lost, and had to be rediscovered at a later date. We can hardly imagine a more striking description of the history of Greece from an Egyptian priest of the 6th century BC.

But why were the parallels between Atlantis and Troy not recognised much earlier, if everything is so simple? There are various reasons for this. In the process of translating place-names and units of measurement from ancient Egyptian into ancient Greek, errors crept into the text. Basically, only four words were completely incorrectly translated or interpreted, but this sufficed to obscure the historical foundation of the story. In addition, Atlantis could be equated with Troy only after the Late Bronze Age culture of the Aegean had become known – in other words, from about 1905 onwards. Subsequently, many people realized that the key to the Atlantis legend lay in the Bronze Age Aegean. In doing so, however, they tried to discern traces of the Minoan high culture on Crete, and not the Mycenaean culture on the mainland.

Not least, the interpretation of Plato's tale was rendered more difficult because the text cannot easily be assigned to any of the usual modern-day disciplines. Plato wrote it down in the 4th century BC, and documents of this date normally fall within the scope of historical linguistics, ancient history or philosophy. The Atlantis story, however, describes events that occurred a thousand years before, so the credibility of its contents needs to be assessed by *prehistorians*. The latter, though, are not normally concerned with classical texts. Careful examination of the Atlantis tale therefore requires a collaborative effort by an interdisciplinary team. Unfortunately, it has never been accorded such attention, so its investigation still has to be undertaken by individuals.

Critical Translation Errors

Although the Greek state described in the Atlantis story may be correlated with Mycenaean Greece without any problems, the identification of Atlantis with Troy is not immediately obvious from the dialogue in the *Timaeus*. According to this, the war between Greece and Atlantis would have taken place 8000 years before the discussion between Solon and the priests at Saïs, but the Trojan War must have been about 1200 BC, and thus only about 640 years before Solon's visit to Egypt took place. Atlantis apparently lay on an island in the Atlantic Ocean and was larger than Asia and Libya combined. Troy, on the other hand, is not an island, lies to the east of Greece, and definitely was not larger than Asia and Libya combined. The details of places and dates in the *Timaeus* do not, therefore, on the whole, agree with what we know about the Trojan War.

In fact, all the translation errors that have caused the text to be misinterpreted for so long have crept into this one section. For this reason, any previous approach to picking out the key details and determining from them the actual location has been doomed to failure. It is precisely these key details that have been distorted during transmission, yet these very distortions actually emphasise the authenticity of the story.

Let us consider the dating. Atlantis apparently existed 8000 years before Solon's visit to Egypt, and therefore some 11,000 years before the present day. The opponents of a historical Atlantis suggest that Plato had set his metaphorical tale in dim and distant prehistory, to emphasise that this was not a truly historical account but a myth. Franz Susemihl, for example, wrote in the year 1855:

> At the same time, however, setting the myth in that extremely far-off time, no historical recollection of which remained, even among the Egyptians, avoids any misunderstanding that a real historical fact was the basis . . .

Five generations later (and after 150 years of research), historical linguistics continues to rely on arguments from the century before last. The Tübingen scholar Alexander Slezák, for example, recently wrote:

> It does take some literary ignorance to overlook the fact that these statements [about dates] . . . are there to simply exclude the questions that may arise concerning any possible historical content of the story.

If, however, we examine the statements of *historians* from Plato's own time, it is obvious that they employed the same time reckoning. The suggestion that they intended to 'simply exclude' the 'questions that may arise concerning any possible historical content' from their statements, is hardly likely to convince anyone. Herodotus, the 'father of historical writing', maintains that the pharaohs had reigned for 11,340 years. This statement rests, like those of Solon, on discussions with Egyptian temple priests, who claimed that their written records covered this whole period of time.

A completely similar timescale is present in another work of Plato's, namely in the *Laws*, which was written later. There, the philosopher states that the Egyptian culture is 10,000 years old – and at this point we may absolutely exclude any suggestion that the information is given in a mythological context. One person, who would, after all, be in a position to know best, because he was himself an Egyptian temple priest, was the historical writer Manetho. He also reckoned the age of the Egyptian civilisation as either 11,000 or 11,985 years – in other words, his figures are nearly identical to those given by Plato and Herodotus. Manetho, however, states extremely clearly – and not once, but three times – how these apparently incomprehensible numbers arise:

> We may assume that in statements about dates we are dealing with lunar years, which consist of thirty days: What we now describe as a 'month', was previously known to the Egyptians as a 'year'.
> Overall it was 11,000 years, but this means lunar years, and thus months.
> So it thus came about that the times of the Gods who reigned amongst you over six generations in six dynasties, were reckoned in years, each of which was a lunar year, consisting of thirty days. The overall duration in lunar years amounted to 11,985 or 969 solar years.

So the incomprehensibly large figures given by Manetho, Herodotus and Plato are lunar years – that is, months. In Egypt, various calendars were in fact in use simultaneously, and the temple priests were generally in the habit of using the original lunar calendar. To convert the high figures into the chronology normally used nowadays, they should be divided by 12.37.

If, however, we divide the value of 8000 years given by Plato by 12.37, then the cultures described in the Atlantis story occurred at a time 647 years before Solon's visit to Saïs, and therefore about 1200 BC. This date agrees perfectly with the state of cultural development described by Plato. It was *only* at this period that a culture flourished in Greece that simultaneously possessed bronze weapons, chariots, fortifications, and a knowledge of writing; which excelled in handcrafts, art and warfare; and about which heroic epics circulated hundreds of years later. The war between this prehistoric Greek culture and Atlantis falls squarely in the time of the Trojan War. The Greeks' enemy could, therefore, basically have only been Troy, because the Greek forces could hardly have fought in two places at once, and have caused one victory to be celebrated in Greece and another in Egypt.

The second error – that Atlantis was an island – is also characteristic of translations from Egyptian hieroglyphic texts. The hieroglyph for 'island' basically means 'foreign land'. In Egypt during the New Kingdom, the whole of the Aegean, including the surrounding mainland coasts was described as 'the islands'. Even the island-free coast of North Africa was known as the 'Islands of the West'. Atlantis, therefore, was not necessarily an island in the modern sense, but was more likely simply a foreign land on some distant coast.

The third translation error involves a local name, which is mentioned in the description of the location of Atlantis. The Egyptian priest describes the surroundings of Atlantis precisely enough:

> in those days the sea was still navigable; and there was an island situated in front of the straits which are by you called the Pillars of Heracles; the island was larger than Libya and Asia put together, and was the way to other islands, and from these you might pass to the whole of the opposite continent which surrounded the true ocean; for this sea which is within the Straits of Heracles is only a bay, having a narrow entrance, but that other is a real sea, and the surrounding land may be most truly called a boundless continent.

Atlantis, therefore, should have lain in front of straits that 'are by you [that is, in Greece] called the Pillars of Heracles' – a term that, in classical antiquity, was applied to the Straits of Gibraltar. From this it was concluded that Atlantis lay in the Atlantic Ocean. However, the text states, that Atlantis in fact lay in front of the straits and not beyond them. The legendary state must, therefore, have lain among the countries around the Mediterranean – the Greeks' influence did not actually extend any farther even in Solon's time. A state outside the Mediterranean could not have been a threat to Greece, because it would have been unknown to the Greeks.

In addition, the whole description of the location of Atlantis does not seem to be at all applicable to the Straits of Gibraltar. The latter is not in any sense an 'entrance' and was never impassable. The area of the Straits does not appear like a 'bay' and similarly does not have a 'narrow entrance'. There is no 'island' near the Straits of Gibraltar, and certainly not one that is 'larger than Libya and Asia put together'. To which other 'islands' could they have sailed from Gibraltar – and why? How could they have arrived at the idea that the Atlantic Ocean was 'surrounded' by a continent? And where in Spain would a natural catastrophe have occurred so that a whole subcontinent disappeared into the sea? There are two possible explanations

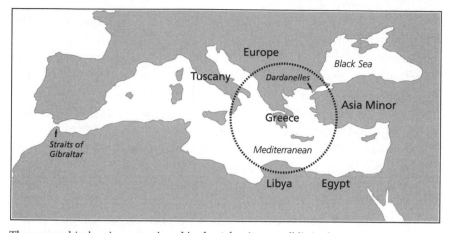

The geographical regions mentioned in the Atlantis story all lie in the eastern
Mediterranean – only the Straits of Gibraltar lie outside this area

for these discrepancies. Either the description is false, or the name 'Pillars
of Heracles' has been wrongly attributed.

This example also shows how the details given in a text over three
thousand years old cannot be transposed willy-nilly to our own time.
Atlantis existed in an era that was long before Solon's visit to Saïs. As a
result, the world-view described in the story must also be appropriate to
the date at which the text originated – which means that it must be *reduced
in size*. About 1200 BC, the sphere of influence of Greek ships stretched, at
most, over the central and eastern Mediterranean, but not, as yet, as far as
the Straits of Gibraltar. For this reason, many archaeologists were ready to
accept Thera as a possible candidate for Atlantis. The suggestion that the
realm of that former enemy lay around the coast of the Aegean is far more
plausible than any other explanation.

If we leave the mention of the 'Pillars of Heracles' aside for the moment,
the location of Atlantis agrees perfectly with the position of Troy, and the
geographical configuration of the Hellespont, the entrance to the Dardanelles, and the Black Sea. The Black Sea is a proper 'ocean' that is
enclosed by a 'continent', and its entrance lay within the range of activity
of Mycenaean ships. In the Late Bronze Age, 'the sea was still navigable';
subsequently, the knowledge of how the strong currents in the Dardanelles
could be countered was lost for centuries. Troy lay, like Atlantis, 'in front
of the straits'. From the narrow entrance in the Dardanelles, which is like a
bay, one could travel to the foreign lands around the Sea of Marmara, and
from thence to the mainland coasts that surrounded the whole of the inner

sea. In Plato's original text, the agreement between the description of the location of Atlantis and the entrance to the Black Sea is all the more striking, because for the 'ocean' Plato uses the term *Pontos*; the same term that the Greeks applied to the Black Sea. To the Greeks, this sea was of far greater significance than the Atlantic. In the Late Bronze Age, important goods arrived in the Aegean from the Black Sea – apparently horses and metals above all – and in classical times many Greek colonies stretched along the Black Sea coasts. So it is not surprising that Herodotus (4.85) says that 'There is not in the world any other sea so wonderful.'

So we are left with the question of why the term 'Pillars of Heracles' occurs in Plato's text when what apparently was meant was the entrance to the Black Sea? The Greek geographer Strabo suggested that Homer transposed many place names from the Black Sea to the Mediterranean because, between the 12th century BC – that is, at the time described in his epic – and his own time (the 8th century BC), the Greek world had expanded. The Russian geographer Abraham Sergeievitch von Noroff described this as early as 1854 as follows:

> Strabo says, when speaking of the geographical knowledge of the Homeric period, that people had then generally regarded the Pontine Sea as another ocean, and viewed voyages on it as reaching distances that were as great as those beyond the 'Pillars of Hercules'. Because the Greeks considered the *Pontus* as the greatest of the seas that were accessible to them, so they tended to call it 'the sea', just as Homer was called 'the poet'. To comply with the general consensus, Homer transferred pontine localities to the Ocean.

In the same year, these words were summarised by a German scholar in the statement that 'the words "Pillars of Hercules" in the story recounted in Plato's *Timaeus* should not be interpreted as the present-day Straits of Gibraltar, but as the Thracian Bosphorus'. A similar conclusion has also been handed down from Roman times, the grammarian Servius having remarked that 'We travel through the "Pillars of Heracles" into both the Black Sea and into Spain.'

So the 'Pillars of Heracles' in the Atlantis tale could perfectly well have been the entrance to the Black Sea – the region in which Troy lies and which precisely corresponds with the description in the Atlantis text. This concept was probably only later extended to the Straits of Gibraltar with the expansion of the Greeks' world-view.

There remains only the question of how the concept of the 'Pillars of Heracles' generally came about. There are no topographical features either at the Hellespont or at the Straits of Gibraltar that resemble pillars. So where does this idea of pillars come from? Well, even in the very early days of sea travel, moorings and harbours were marked by pillars. One of the non-Homeric descriptions of the Trojan War, the *Lesser Iliad*, mentions such pillars as a special feature of the harbour of Troy. On a relief from the Roman period, which shows the Greek fleet at the siege of Troy, one of these pillars is clearly recognisable. So this may explain the 'Pillars', but why 'Heracles'? Many prehistoric water-engineering works were ascribed to the magical powers of this demigod, but nowhere was Heracles so active as at Troy. There, according to the epic, he had redirected entire rivers. The pillars that marked the entrance to the harbour of Bronze Age Troy could therefore have been the origin of the 'Pillars of Heracles'.

The fourth and last translation error concerns the extent of Atlantis. In the *Timaeus*, it is said that the state is larger than Asia and Libya combined. In the *Critias*, it is then claimed that the plain below the capital city is 3000 by 2000 stadia, which corresponds to about 540 by 360 kilometres, roughly the size of Ireland. These enormous dimensions have obviously arisen during the conversion of units. Such misunderstandings frequently occurred, because there were no unified systems of measurements in antiquity. Plato himself interrupts the tale at one point to note that the length of the water-engineering works does not agree with the size of Atlantis; despite this he continues his task, and describes the facts as they were transmitted to him.

And what about the natural catastrophe? If we consider the Atlantis text as a whole, the natural catastrophe is completely subordinate in significance. It is mentioned only once in passing, obviously only to bring the story of the former cultures to a plausible conclusion. For Atlantis, the catastrophe would, anyway, have had no serious consequences, because the city already lay in ruins, after the Greek forces had destroyed it. Some form of sudden or enduring change in the landscape must have occurred, however; otherwise the priests would hardly have resorted to such an explanation.

Probably these changes in the landscape were not natural catastrophes in the true sense. The highly developed hydraulic-engineering works near the most important Late Bronze Age palaces caused the kingdoms to be sources of wonder. Such engineering works offered attackers a means of causing great destruction for the minimum effort. When, about 1200 BC,

Mycenae, Tiryns, Pylos, Gla, Troy and many other cities were burnt to the ground, portions of the lower city of Tiryns disappeared under layers of mud, several metres thick. Elsewhere the hydraulic works suddenly broke down. The harbour at Pylos filled with river gravel, for example. Who can discount the fact that these technological installations may also have fallen victim to enemy action? Major landslides and floods would have been the result.

To sum up, it should be said that equating Atlantis with Troy does not produce one hundred per cent agreement between the text and our archaeological knowledge. Despite this, it differs favourably from the solutions proposed previously, in which an attribution was made solely on the basis of selected individual features. With these earlier methods only a vanishingly small portion of the complex text could be interpreted. Assessing the content on an *archaeological* basis, we can, on the other hand, fit more than 99 per cent of the story into a plausible picture. The remainder is restricted to a few words which are typical of translation errors between ancient Egyptian and ancient Greek. Plato's story of Atlantis is no different in this respect than either his other works or other ancient historical descriptions. Hardly any ancient text is likely to be completely free from translation errors, and even the content of a modern-day news report never attains more than 99 per cent accuracy.

Features of Atlantis

The passages from Plato's Atlantis account mentioned previously, into which translation errors have crept, all come from the short, general introductory speech at the beginning of the *Timaeus*. When Solon impatiently asked the Egyptian priests for more details of the Greeks' glorious past, one of his hosts said: 'The exact particulars of the whole we will hereafter go through at our leisure in the sacred registers themselves.'

The actual description of Atlantis then follows in the *Critias*, the second volume of Plato's incomplete trilogy. The account given there is so full of detail that it is quite possibly a translated excerpt from the Egyptian original text. Computer analysis has actually shown that the style of the *Critias* differs greatly from that of Plato's other works, as if the volume had not been penned by him.

How does the precise information in the *Critias* stand with respect to the theory that Atlantis may be Troy? Previous attempts to locate Atlantis have been restricted to stressing general similarities between Plato's text and some specific place on the globe. Equating Troy with Atlantis, however, adds a new perspective to the matter: every individual detail in Plato's *Critias* fits with Troy – 'archaeology's fateful mound' as some journalists have called it. Even Troy's individual characteristics, of which there are quite a few, are mentioned in the Atlantis story, giving a corresponding emphasis to their significance.

Let us begin our comparison with the very name of the city: 'Atlantis'. This word is of Greek origin, and so would not have come from the original Egyptian text. It is possible that Plato even introduced the word, because a work with that title (in the Hellenike anthology) was being talked about just at that time. 'Atlantis' derives from the name of the Titan Atlas, and means roughly 'Daughter of Atlas'. This suggests that Atlas and his daughter founded the legendary city of 'Atlantis'.

But Atlas and his daughter were supposed to have built Troy. The complete line of descent for Troy up to the time of the Trojan war was: Atlas, Electra, Dardanus, Erichthonius, Tros, Ilos, Laomedon, and Priam. According to Homer, Priam led the Greeks' opponents during the war, and his father, Laomedon, ordered the fortified walls to be built. Homer states that Erichthonius was the richest man in the world; and the people of Troy, Ilius and Dardania were the Greeks' adversaries in the battle for Troy. So Homer incorporated the names of six out of the total of eight legendary founders. It is not surprising that there are still older traditions that hark back to the original founder of the city and his daughter 'Atlantis'. Because of them, English historians, including Jacob Bryant and William Gell, used the term *Atlanteans* for the Trojans as late as the nineteenth century.

Gell refers to Herodotus, when he says that the *Atlanteans* in western Asia Minor were extremely skilful in the sciences. It was Herodotus, too, who stated that the Egyptians had always considered that they were the most ancient people in the world, until an investigation by the priests of Saïs – a few years before Solon's visit – had found that the peoples of western Asia Minor were even older. This recognition is mentioned in the Atlantis story, when, on the one hand, the priests look back with pride on their long tradition, and on the other, admit that there are still more ancient peoples.

According to Wilhelm Brandenstein, the root of the word 'Atlas' probably lies in *antlos*, a term that is much older than the name of the Titan. *Antlos* denotes a particularly strong current. In the whole of the Mediterranean region, the strongest current is found in the Hellespont, where the excess water from the Black Sea floods into the Aegean – exactly in the region where Troy lies. If we remember that most of the other states had contact with Troy by sea, it is understandable why the presence of an extremely strong current might have been significant when the place was given a name. The name of the Titan, 'Atlas', seems therefore to have arisen from the original place name, and not the other way round.

In ancient Greece, landscape and place names were generally derived from mythological founder figures. For example, the Greeks called the Peloponnese after Pelops, a grandson of Zeus and forefather of the Pelopids. However, if a name for a region or a city had already become established, they had no inhibitions about finding some founding figure. This is how they derived the name 'Kreta' (Crete) from a fictional Kres, the son of a nymph from Mount Ida and Zeus. For Atlantis the sequence appears to have been: 1. Antlos; 2. Atlas; 3. Atlantis.

One specific feature of Atlantis was the presence of two springs, one hot, the other cold. Poseidon, the guardian god of Atlantis, had specifically arranged this:

> He himself, being a god, found no difficulty in making special arrangements for the centre island, bringing up two springs of water from beneath the earth, one of warm water and the other of cold . . .

Poseidon was also the protector of Troy. As god of the sea and horses – both emblems of Troy – he jealously observed his city's fate. When it finally collapsed, he punished Odysseus for his trickery with the Trojan Horse. Not only that, Troy was the sole city in antiquity to possess a hot spring and a cold spring – just like Atlantis. Homer describes this pair of springs in the *Iliad* as follows:

> One of these two springs is warm, and steam rises from it as smoke from a burning fire, but the other even in summer is as cold as hail or snow, or the ice that forms on water.

Another particularly characteristic feature of Troy is the occurrence of strong north winds that, even today, plague excavators and visitors. Troy is the sole place in the Bronze Age that was recorded as being 'windy'. Homer uses this adjective more frequently than any other to describe the capital. And, of course, the north winds are also mentioned in the Atlantis story. The fertile plain below the city stretched, as at Troy, towards the south, and was thus 'sheltered from the north [winds]'.

The royal succession in Atlantis is another striking characteristic, because it was extremely complicated. It was not the eldest son of the ruling king but the oldest member of the whole royal house who had the rights to the throne. On the death of a ruler, a brother or a cousin of the former king might succeed him. In addition, a council of elders ruled alongside the king. There was just such a senate in Troy. In Atlantis the council of elders had ten members, the same as in Troy. The Austrian archaeologist Siegrid Deger-Jalkotzy has written:

> The institution of this council of elders alongside the king is a further characteristic of the Trojan social structure. Together with the king, the elders determined the city's public affairs, as well as its political and military actions. It is true that they did not take part in the war, but they had overall command of the troops, together with Priam.

Plato describes Atlantis as an extraordinarily prosperous city, with beautiful houses, parks, sports stadia and busy markets, where traders came from all over the world. The king and the senate lived in the central temple and palace quarter of the city. Comparing the description of Atlantis with the view of Troy that has been handed down to us reveals how the two cities resemble one another. The palace area of Atlantis was laid out as follows:

> In the centre was a holy temple dedicated to Cleito and Poseidon, which remained inaccessible, and was surrounded by an enclosure of gold; this was the spot where the family of the ten princes first saw the light ... Here was Poseidon's own temple which was a stadium in length, and half a stadium in width, and of a proportionate height, having a strange barbaric appearance. All the outside of the temple, with the exception of the pinnacles, they covered with silver, and the pinnacles with gold. In the interior of the temple the roof was of ivory, curiously wrought everywhere with gold and silver and orichalcum; and all the other parts, the walls and pillars and floor, they coated with orichalcum.

And this was how Troy appeared, according to Raoul Lefèvre in *Sammlungen Trojanischer Geschichten* (*Collections of Trojan Histories*) from 1464:

> There was then no city in the whole world that was so large and in such beautiful surroundings ... It had rich palaces without number, the fairest that there had ever been, and the finest houses, prosperous and in splendid settings. In many parts of the city there were parks and sports arenas

for competitions and games. The city was frequented by tradesmen and craftsmen of all sorts who came from or travelled to all parts of the world. Through the centre of the city flowed a wide river, on which ships could pass and which was of great convenience to the citizens ... There were also many games and much conversation, for example board games, games of dice, and many others. On the most impressive position, on the edge of a cliff, King Priam built his opulent palace. It was called Ilion and was one of the most immense and luxuriant palaces that the world has ever seen. Its height amounted to five hundred steps, that is without the towers, of which there were many and which reached so high that from a distance it appeared as if they stretched up to heaven. And in this luxurious palace, King Priam had built the most sumptuous chambers anywhere in the world at that time. There his magnificent throne was to be found, together with the table from which he dined and held court with his princes and noblemen. And everything was of gold and silver, of precious stones and ivory.

The two passages are like descriptions of one and the same city from two different points of view. The towers, the palaces, and the sports arenas – all these features are present in the one and in the other. Unfortunately, the appearance of the central palace quarter of the sixth city on the site (Troy VI) may no longer be confirmed by excavation, because this area was flattened in Roman times.

In those sections where the incredible wealth of Atlantis is mentioned, Plato's account seems almost fabulous: Atlantis was a land where excess reigned. In the 5000 years of the history of culture, however, there have repeatedly been cities that succeeded in amassing unimaginable riches. Generally their leaders were able to exploit valuable deposits or use the favourable geographical location of their realm to control international trade. Examples of people with such inconceivable fortunes include numerous Egyptian pharaohs, the Queen of Sheba, and King Solomon. Why should the description of stinking-rich Atlantis not conceal a historical state, the rulers of which had been able to use the international economic situation to their advantage for some time? Indeed, the Atlantis story emphasises that many objects arrived in the city from distant lands – without, however, specifying whether this meant goods, taxes, donations, gifts, bribes or sacrificial offerings, or whether they were simply accepted, acquired or exacted by the kings of Atlantis. The fact that many of the goods came from afar, must, on its own, have made them unusually valuable.

Apart from imports, the immediate surroundings of Atlantis provided all the necessities of life that the population required. Even this statement in Plato's tale reflects a situation that was typical of the flourishing societies of the Late Bronze Age. The population could feed itself from the fertile countryside without problems. However, legendary riches – as we know from Egyptian Thebes, Troy and Knossos – presupposed additional, active foreign trading. Here the goods traded were generally characteristic of their country of origin: Egypt provided gold; Mycenae produced fine ceramic wares and valuable oils; Crete exported precious stone jars; and the Lebanon traded useful cedar wood.

By far the most important trade goods, however, were metals. If there was one factor that bound all the countries in the eastern Mediterranean together in the period between 3000 and 1200 BC, it was their lively interest in raw metals. It is not for nothing that this period was later named the Bronze Age. The first known tin-bronzes in the world appeared towards the end of the 4th millennium BC – and that was at Troy, the history of which as an influential trading port precisely corresponds with the duration of the Bronze Age. Initially, various cities in the north-eastern Aegean, including Poliochni on Lemnos and Thermi on Lesbos, competed for control of the trade in metal. The first urban settlements also occurred in this region. Eventually, Troy succeeded in gaining a monopoly, and became the only one of these cities to flourish during the entire Bronze Age, thus amassing even greater wealth.

The supplies of tin, crucial to the preparation of bronze, were obviously mainly obtainable via the Black Sea. By controlling the entrance to the Black Sea, Troy also controlled the trade in metals and other goods between Central Europe, the Baltic, Siberia and Central Asia on one hand, and the Cyclades, the Greek mainland, Crete, Egypt, Libya and the central Mediterranean on the other. The city developed into a world trading metropolis, where raw materials and finished goods were traded. In times of political tension, this control of foreign trade assumed a high strategic value. No Bronze Age state could become rich without being involved in the trade in metal: access to ore deposits; experience in mining and processing; trading and finishing – these were the principal economic factors in the Late Bronze Age. Troy would therefore have been able to impose trade embargoes on its enemies. Probably this is why, over its two-thousand-year history, the city was destroyed many times.

Of Atlantis we are told that it possessed not only imported ores, but also its own deposits in abundance – and this again agrees precisely with the

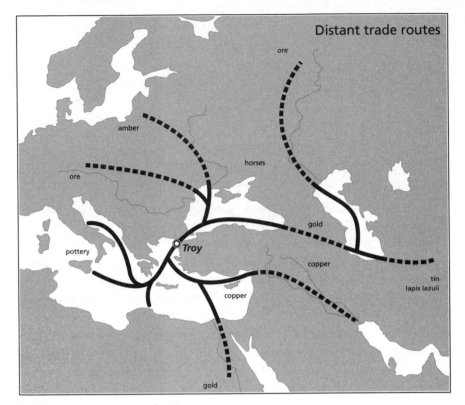

Distant trade routes

ore

amber

ore

horses

gold

pottery

Troy

copper

copper

tin
lapis lazuli

gold

Many trade routes converged at Troy

region around Troy. Far more mineral resources occur in the Trojan hinterland than in any other region of the eastern Mediterranean. There are sources of lead, copper, zinc, arsenic, mercury, antimony, gold and iron.

Alongside the normal metals, the Atlantis story mentions another, mysterious material, which evidently was found only in Atlantis. Plato remarks that by his time all that was remembered was its name: orichalcum. Earlier, when Atlantis flourished, it really did exist, and at several places in Atlantis it was even dug directly out of the ground. So orichalcum was not some artificial alloy but was valued more highly than any material other than gold. Here is yet another statement that sounds like a fantasy or fairytale, and, unsurprisingly, the mention of this mysterious metal has stimulated the imagination of many 'Atlantologists'. To them, 'orichalcum' stands for the supernatural force that was lost when the city was engulfed. The Russian occultist Dimitrii Mereschkovskii considered 'orichalcum' to be the magical formula that is the origin of all things. A similar, far-fetched interpretation arose during the Third Reich, when confessed Nazi ideologists and scientists were taken with the idea of shifting Atlantis on to German soil. Because there are not very many sources of ore along the coasts of the North Sea and the Baltic, without further ado they equated the metal, orichalcum, with amber!

Mind you, mysterious metals like orichalcum are not a rarity in ancient texts. The Egyptian term (*asem*) for electrum, an alloy of gold and silver, developed into *asimos*, which later became *asima*. The last is tantamount to meaning 'the unknown'. Another metal shrouded in mystery and with a similar name (*asium*) originated in the region of western Asia Minor, known itself as Asia, and was covered by an export ban. One trader landed in prison because his caravan was smuggling asium. Was asium perhaps another name for the mysterious orichalcum?

The way and manner in which orichalcum was used makes this raw material seem even more improbable. The ornaments inside the palace consisted of orichalcum, intermingled with gold, silver and ivory. In addition, certain outer and inner walls, columns and plinths were supposed to have been covered in orichalcum. It is said that, in the sunshine, they shone like fire. Walls with a coating of metal? Again that sounds like a fairytale. In reality, however, it involves a favoured technique in the Bronze Age. Egyptian goldsmiths covered not only valuable wooden objects with bronze, but they also clad the tops of obelisks with gold or electrum, so that they glittered like flames in the first rays of the morning sun. Even today, the two largest obelisks in the world, at the temple of Karnak, retain such a coating of electrum.

Metal coatings for walls were also not unusual. Hesiod speaks of 'houses of bronze', 'bronze doors' and a 'wall of bronze', and Homer also mentions that 'walls on either side were of bronze from end to end'. Herodotus described the west-Iranian city of Ecbatana as being surrounded by ring-like walls, where each wall had a different colour and the two innermost were clad with silver and gold. So in this respect, yet again, Plato's depiction of Atlantis fits with the picture that other authors give of a metropolis in ancient times.

The same may also be said for another way in which orichalcum was used in Atlantis. The stelae on which the text of the city's laws were inscribed, were also supposed to have been made from the mysterious metal. In fact, texts of particular importance in the Late Bronze Age were often recorded on sheets of metal. For example, a peace agreement between the High King of the Hittites and Pharaoh Rameses II – probably one of the most important treaties of the period – was inscribed on sheets of silver. Recently, German archaeologists excavating the capital of the Hittite kingdom have discovered a comparable document on a sheet of bronze; this deals with a treaty between the High King and a distant relative. Recording the text of laws on sheets of metal or engraving them on stelae was quite usual in early historical times, the best-known example being the stela carrying the Code of Hammurabi. Aristotle himself records that such columns often consisted of orichalcum. Plato could hardly have invented either the metal or its application.

What was actually hidden behind the term orichalcum, where it was found, and how it was worked, is revealed by the Greek geographer, Strabo:

> Near to Andeira, there is a stone that becomes iron when burned, and then, if it is heated with a certain earth in a furnace, zinc separates out, and this, when copper is added, give the 'mixture', which many call orichalcum.

Strabo describes an alloy of zinc and copper – in other words, the preparation of brass. Orichalcum is thus nothing more than brass, and in modern Greek the term is still used for this alloy. The mineral in which zinc and copper are found in association is still known internationally today as 'aurichalcite'.

Obviously the preparation of orichalcum was restricted to the area of which Strabo speaks, and this is located, as expected, in the immediate vicinity of Troy. Andeira lay approximately eighty kilometres southeast of Troy. Recently, it has also been found that brass artefacts were not first produced in Roman times, as had been thought previously, but some 2000 years earlier. Chemical analyses revealed the origin of the ore used: naturally, it was from the Troad.

Finally, let us consider yet another example of the correspondence between Atlantis and Troy. In Atlantis there was a primitive ritual sacrifice of bulls, which the kings carried out every five or six years. It is described as follows:

> There were bulls who had the range of the temple of Poseidon; and the ten kings, being left alone in the temple, after they had offered prayers to the god that they might capture the victim which was acceptable to him, hunted the bulls, without weapons, but with staves and nooses; and the bull which they caught they led up to the pillar and cut its throat over the top of it so that the blood fell upon the sacred inscription. Now on the pillar, besides the laws, there was inscribed an oath invoking mighty curses

The Minoan site of Monstiraki lies in the Amari Valley, west of the Psiloritis Massif. The roof over the excavations may be made out, right of centre

The Late Bronze Age city of Tiryns that, according to its excavator, suffered a severe earthquake about 1200 BC

In the Minoan site at Apodoulou, rubble walls, more than two metres high, have remained undamaged to the present day

The remains of Nestor's Palace lie in the group of trees to the left of the centre of the picture. From their residence, the kings had a fantastic view over the Gulf of Navarino

When Roman control of Tunisia collapsed, this mausoleum was buried under five-metre-thick wadi deposits

Hydraulic engineering reached a high point in Roman times. This aqueduct supplied Carthage with water from the mountains

The pottery fragments found during excavations here at Akrotiri, may often be reassembled into whole containers

In archaeological surveys – such as here at Skourta – the pottery fragments found are not normally spectacular

The *terra-rossa* soils that occur in the Mediterranean region above limestone rock are fertile. To be used for agriculture, however, they require artificial irrigation

Whenever *terra-rossa* soils are retained, they enable a dense growth of vegetation

Nowadays, over wide areas of Greece the topsoil has been completely washed away. No plant cover can grow on the bare limestone

Terraces may be used to stabilise those remnants of soil that still exist

This false-colour satellite image shows (shaded area, centre) the luxuriant vegetation on the Argive Plain

Computer processing of the same image reveals additional properties of the countryside. These include areas where sediment is entering the sea, and different zones in the coastal region

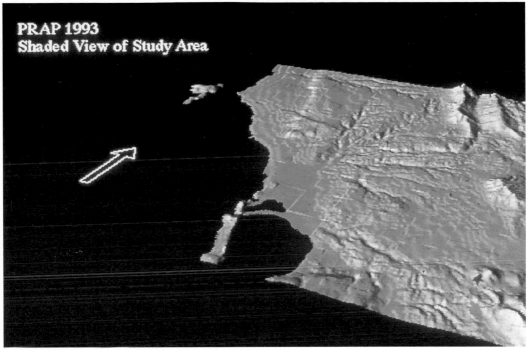

PRAP 1993
Shaded View of Study Area

Topographical data relating to a study area may be entered into the Geographical Information System.
This example shows the area around Nestor's Palace

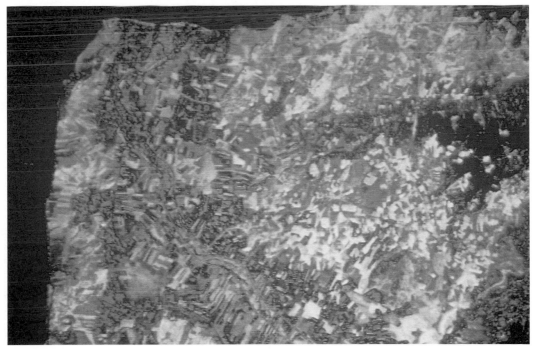

This computer-processed Landsat image of the Trojan Plain shows the marshy areas (heavily shaded) on the
coastal strip

The dried-up harbour basin at Pylos shows clearly as a rectangular field, seen here to the right of the building

The artificial dam near Tiryns directs the river, which originally flowed from the lower left to the upper right, into the channel on the left-hand side of the picture

A restored section of the wall at Apollonia. The fields in the distance are still worked by hand

In the vicinity of Apollonia, wartime bunkers dominate the otherwise intact landscape

In Albania, agriculture is still carried out in a form similar to that used thousands of years ago

On Thera, building in the town has extended over the edge of the caldera

A wadi in northeast Tunisia

A coin minted at Troy, with a representation of the sacrifice of an ox, as described in the Atlantis story

Primitive labyrinths on a rock surface in northern England

An aerial photograph of the artificial cutting on the coast at Troy

Grooves caused by wear on the ship causeway across the Isthmus of Corinth, in a photograph taken by Walter Werner in September 1978

on the disobedient. When therefore, after slaying the bull in the accustomed manner, they had burnt its limbs, they filled a bowl of wine and cast in a clot of blood for each of them; the rest of the victim they put in the fire, after having purified the column all round. Then they drew from the bowl in golden cups, and pouring a libation on the fire, they swore that they would judge according to the laws on the pillar, and would punish him who in any point had already transgressed them, and that for the future they would not, if they could help, offend against the writing on the pillar, and would neither command others, nor obey any ruler who commanded them, to act otherwise than according to the laws of their father Poseidon. This was the prayer which each of them offered up for himself and for his descendants, at the same time drinking and dedicating the cup out of which he drank in the temple of the god

The mention of bulls in cult observances has often been interpreted as a sign of the similarities between Atlantis and Minoan Crete. In the palace at Knossos there are frescoes that show young men jumping over bulls. However, this sort of game or contest and the ritual described above are fundamentally different. Bulls were also venerated, not only in Crete, but also, much earlier, in Mesopotamia, Syria/Palestine, Egypt and Asia Minor. In Plato's account, the bulls protected the temple's holy enclave against any unauthorised access and desecration. As holy animals, they were allowed to roam freely around the temple. Their spiritual power was thus transmitted to the temple and its god, Poseidon. The ten kings of Atlantis, at regular intervals, took part in a ritual in which a bull was captured using staves and nooses. The simple weapons were to ensure that the skin of the animal was not damaged. None of its blood must escape, because the blood symbolised its mystical power, and this had to be conveyed in full to the pillar and the sacred laws. Finally, the king was also allowed to acquire some of the power, in that he drank some of the blood.

In a comprehensive work on the Greek religion, which appeared at the beginning of the twentieth century, Jane Harrison, a Cambridge scholar, called the ritual described by Plato 'purely magic'. Such a primitive ritual would hardly have been invented by Plato, because by his time it had become quite meaningless, so, she argued, it must be historical. Harrison was able to support her statement with archaeological findings. There are, for example, coins from the Roman period, on which the bizarre bull ritual described in the Atlantis account is depicted. One of these coins shows the goddess, *Athene Ilias*, in human form, as she stands before a pillar from which hangs a bull ready for sacrifice. It is obvious that the bull's throat will be slit, only not over the top of the pillar but against its side. Where does this coin come from? From Troy, of course. It was discovered there, long ago, in the excavations directed by Heinrich Schliemann. The German archaeologist Hans von Fritze, who was the first to describe the coins, wondered how the Trojans had come to depict such an unusual ritual. He suspected that an age-old local epic was the inspiration – an epic just such as that handed down in the Atlantis story.

At the end of his story, Plato suddenly seems to have noticed what his account was really about. After he recognised the similarities between Atlantis and Troy, in the last section of the *Critias* he suddenly introduces moral standards, which Atlantis had allegedly failed to uphold – a common cliché in antiquity for the relationship between Hellas and Troy. For hundreds of years, the Greeks had admired their eastern neighbours in Troy, and had obviously peacefully cooperated with them, until eventually 'human nature got the upper hand, they then, being unable to bear their fortune, behaved unseemly, and . . . grew visibly debased'. In the very last full sentence, Plato even uses Homer's device, and summons the council of the gods with which the *Iliad* begins. But the attempt to rescue the trilogy fails. The great thinker, for the first and only time, breaks off a book – in the middle of a sentence. How could a work, aimed at the progressive west, have as its central argument the glorification of an eastern metropolis in the dim and distant past? Experienced and vain enough never to destroy something in which he had put so much work, Plato simply laid the manuscript aside.

An Independent Opinion

Although almost all of the features of Atlantis that have been mentioned seem to be unique – the war against Greece, the location on the narrow straits to the *Pontos*, the 1200 ships, the name, the twin springs, the north winds, the political system, the palace, the mysterious material orichalcum, the bull cult – it is possible to find *individual* attributes elsewhere. Persia also waged war against Greece, Byzantium lay on a narrow strait leading to the *Pontos*, Xerxes led 1207 ships against Greece, the name 'Atlas' occurs again in North Africa, and so on. Such individual characteristics may be identified all over the world and at many different epochs. However, to claim identification with Atlantis they must be present at *one* location and at *one* time. *All* fifteen typical features of Atlantis are fulfilled at Troy – thirteen through archaeological findings and two from Homer's descriptions. So how much of

Plato's story remains 'in the realm of fantasy'? Basically, none of it.

Despite this, there is no absolutely *objective* method of judging the validity of a theory. As a first step, one can ask various experts for their opinion, but even they often have difficulty in recognising the worth of revolutionary innovations, especially when these diametrically oppose the prevailing interpretation. There are innumerable examples of this. For example, it was known 1800 years before Copernicus that the Earth revolves around the Sun, and not the other way round. Aristarchos of Samos discovered this, but none of the great astronomers, in particular Hipparchos, wanted to endorse it, and so it sank into oblivion, until Nicolaus Copernicus rediscovered it centuries later. Even more amusing are some more recent mistaken opinions. When Louis Pasteur stated that bacteria could cause disease, colleagues treated the idea as 'an absurd fantasy'! Lord Kelvin, President of the Royal Society, remarked, only eight years before Orville and Wilbur Wright left the ground in an aeroplane: 'Machines that are heavier than air will never be able to fly!' And when, in 1927, sound film was introduced, Harry Warner, one of the founders of the Warner Brothers film studios remarked: 'Who the hell wants to hear actors *speak?*'

The more categorical such opinions are, the less likely they are, in general, to be correct – and vice versa. Perhaps in time we may be able to obtain a totally impartial opinion from a machine – provided it is 'correctly' informed. In fact, mathematics has a procedure, the 'Monte-Carlo Method' for this, a method of successive approximations that should help to compare one unknown against other unknowns. It is nowadays employed, among other applications, in decision analysis. In this method, one first breaks a complicated problem down into easily comprehensible sections, each of which is then individually processed. Subsequently, the individual partial results are related in a structured manner, and then combined.

The United States military use this procedure to determine the most favourable locations for mobile rocket-launchers – a problem that does not differ fundamentally from the question of determining the most likely location for lost Atlantis. I have obtained this program, and fed it with over one thousand details concerning Atlantis. The principal thought behind this was to determine mathematically the validity of various Atlantis theories. To do this, I took the 36 most important features of the city, as described by Plato, and compared them with 26 different suggestions for Atlantis locations. However, the idea that Plato had merely invented Atlantis, or that Atlantis was simply an abstract representation of contemporary Athens, was also included in the analysis. I first divided the 36 features of the city into six

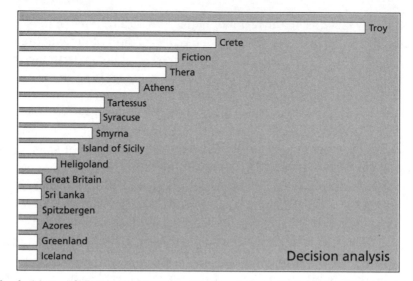

The decision analysis process determines that Troy is the most likely site of Plato's Atlantis

groups, namely: the main features of the story; a description of the natural catastrophe; geography; city layout; cultural achievements; and special features.

In the 'geography' group, for example, there were eight features: size, position on a strait, Pillars of Heracles, island nature, landscape, springs, wind, and woods. If a feature is present at any particular place, then it is assigned a value of 100, for full agreement. If a feature is not present, then it is given a value of 0; otherwise some value in between, although this has to be assigned by the user, and is thus subjective. Thus Troy was assigned a value of 0 for 'size', and Heligoland a value of 100, for 'island nature'.

Finally, the program produced a listing of the different places where Atlantis might have been. The result was expressed as a so-called 'probability', which again lay between 0 and 100. At the lower end of the scale lay the Yucatan, with a 'probability' of 2. Most suggestions for a location outside the Mediterranean for Atlantis reached values less than 7. Exceptions were Heligoland (10) and the Scilly Isles off southwest England (16). The suggestion that Atlantis represented ancient Athens was surprisingly good (32), but so was the idea that Plato had invented it (42). The best values for a historical Atlantis were obtained by Thera (39) and Crete (52). Troy, however, put all other theories and suggested locations in the shade, with a value of 91! The concept that *Atlantis = Troy* may therefore be demonstrated mathematically, with a result that is beyond any doubt.

Chapter 8

Troy: The Circle-girt City

Anyone who wants to understand what is happening in science, needs to find a carefully balanced passage that threads its way between the Scylla of dry rationalism and the Charybdis of enthusiastic mysticism.

ERNST PETER FISCHER (1998)

Back into the Labyrinth

'If Troy really is Atlantis, so what?' That is a question many archaeologists have frequently asked me. Well, the significance of the identification naturally lies in providing a new stimulus and perspective for future research programmes, and thus in expanding our knowledge of Aegean prehistory. This stimulus impacts on various issues: first, research into the countryside around Troy; second, the significance of the Late Bronze Age cultures in the vicinity of Troy; and, third, our understanding of events after the Trojan War. This chapter deals with each of these topics.

First comes research into Troy itself. It is time to make optimum use of the information handed down to us by Plato in the Atlantis story for the benefit of archaeology. To do this, we can turn the procedure round and apply the description of Atlantis to Troy, so as to find out more about the Late Bronze Age city. The Atlantis tale provides us with valuable indications of how the outer regions of the city, now no longer preserved, or still unknown, may have looked. These allusions may be used, in line with technical-reconstruction procedures, as the basis of new working hypotheses for specifically directed searches of the countryside for features of the reconstructed picture of the city that may have been preserved. If these are discovered where predictions suggest they should be, then the theory that Atlantis is actually Troy is confirmed.

An extremely important allusion that arises from this conception con-

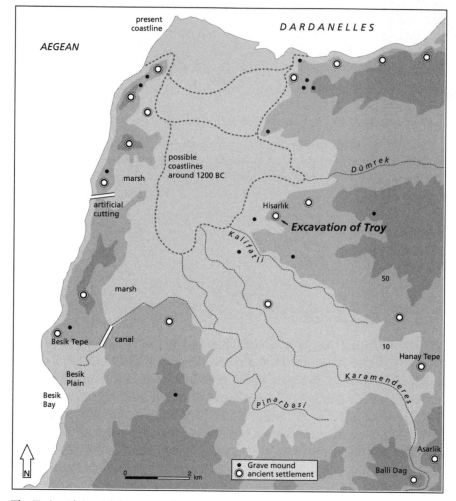

The Trojan Plain with its two artificial cuttings and an indication of the probable coastline around 1200 BC

cerns the size of the Bronze Age city. Ever since the first excavations by Heinrich Schliemann in the 1870s, Troy has been seen as an insignificant, isolated outpost in western Asia Minor. The British archaeologist, John Bintliff, maintained, in the 1990s, that it was a fishing village, with one hundred inhabitants at the most. Other Aegean prehistorians have described it as a 'pirates' stronghold'. The known area of the Bronze Age city was, until recently, restricted to 15,000 square metres – which corresponds approximately to the size of a football pitch.

Here the former conception of prehistoric Troy is in complete contrast to the minutely detailed picture that Plato gives of the glories of Atlantis. If the identification of the two cities as one and the same is really correct, then 'Troy must arise as a magnificent ancient Venice' as *Der Spiegel* wrote in 1992. In fact, our picture of Troy has changed from one extreme to the other in recent years: The known area of the Bronze Age city has increased *twentyfold*! And there are, as yet, no obvious limits to this 'growth'. Already Troy may no longer be considered as just an oriental trade centre, but instead as one of the greatest cities of the period. It is thus starting to assume the stature that Plato ascribed to Atlantis.

An additional stimulus arising from the identification of Troy with Atlantis concerns the arrangement of the buildings and the layout of the city. One of the principal features of Atlantis is the fact that it was constructed as a series of circular zones. The city was laid out in concentric rings around the central palace and temple precincts. Even the hierarchy among the soldiers was circular in nature, corresponding to their status and reliability – just like the structure of the Hittite forces of the period, as it has been handed down to us. Albrecht Mann, an Aachen-based expert on the history of building, maintains that 'the circular form of city, particularly one built in a series of rings' arose in the Mediterranean cultures of the 3rd and 4th millennia BC and, above all, served 'the new purpose in society of raising the prestige and the accommodation of the monarchs'. So we may suspect that the circular form is not simply an expression of defensive techniques but may also be a reflection of a basic ideology and of the theocratic structure of the society. Albrecht Mann sees it as a 'stamp of the divine, god-bestowed and hence absolute, kingly rule'. In Plato's account, we find the following:

> and in the centre of the larger of the two there was set apart a race-course of a stadium in width, and in length allowed to extend all round the island, for horses to race in. Around the race-course were the guard-houses for most members of the bodyguard. The most reliable of them were posted on the smaller, earth wall, lying closer to the citadel, but those who were to be completely trusted lived on the citadel itself, in the immediate vicinity of the palace.

We have already seen, in discussing the labyrinth, that the inner area of Troy was similarly built in rings. The king's residences in the sixth city – belonging to *many* members of the nobility – were built on ring-like terraces. At present, archaeological findings are unable to provide us with any more information.

Nevertheless, in Atlantis the water-engineering works below the city were also supposed to have been circular in nature. The inhabitants of Atlantis had surrounded their city with canals and artificial harbours, so that rings of land and water alternated. A radial cross-canal linked the water-filled excavations together and led out to the sea.

'Atlantologists' have symbolically represented the layout of canals

The 'Atlantean Cross'

described by Plato as the so-called 'Atlantean Cross'. This symbol may portray the main layout of the city, but it by no means correctly represents Plato's description. Above all, in the Atlantis tale only one cross-canal is mentioned, not four as shown in the 'Atlantean Cross'. If we correct the symbol appropriately, what we obtain is a figure that corresponds to the 'primitive labyrinth': a series of zones, with a single, radial cross-canal. This symbol does actually occur: it has been confirmed archaeologically dating back to at least 2000 BC.

So, gradually we begin to close the circle. The Atlantis story obviously describes a simplified form of the labyrinth – a figure associated with Troy for thousands of years. Either the layout of the city followed the form of the 'primitive labyrinth' or it even had the shape of the classical labyrinth. That would only have been visible from a bird's-eye view. From any other viewpoint, the city would have appeared as a series of concentric rings, just as described in the Atlantis story.

After the collapse of the Late Bronze Age states, the majority of political leaders had neither the power nor the means to lay out cities from the ground upwards – as had happened at Troy several times. As a result, the settlements were largely left to their own devices and developed according to their own individual sets of rules. Eventually the labyrinth could no longer be employed as a plan for a city. It was, however, retained in the more compact, symbolic form as a dance floor, which corresponded to a model of the city.

In a still smaller form, the labyrinth also appears as rock carvings, which are generally found on islands or uninhabited coasts, and again exposed on open stone surfaces. In the northwest of Spain and in Cornwall these labyrinth carvings have a definite association with deposits of tin. To all appearances, prospectors and miners employed the sign as a cult symbol. The association with tin deposits corresponds to one of the main characteristics of Troy. Many of the labyrinths in Spain were carved in the period after 1200 BC. Could they perhaps have been carved by scattered seafarers from western Asia Minor, seeking new sources of raw material or a new home?

The Harbour at Troy

The most important suggestion that may be drawn from the Atlantis account relevant to the investigation of the countryside around Troy concerns the position of the harbour. In fact, despite intensive searches, the harbour at Troy could not be found until now. Many even suggested that Troy had no harbour and that the ships were simply pulled out on to a sandy beach on the Aegean coast. However, if we apply the description of Atlantis to Troy, various artificial harbour basins must have lain in the coastal plain. Hollow depressions are still readily recognisable in the ground there, just as at Nestor's harbour. In fact, I first appreciated the full significance of the latter because I had seen the characteristic basins a few days earlier at Troy.

Subsequent research with borings at Troy has shown that many of the depressions actually represent silted-up basins. Thus far, a reconstruction on the basis of the Atlantis story is fully confirmed. Nevertheless, without further research we cannot say whether these basins are of natural or artificial origin. In this respect the observations hardly take us any farther forward.

In Atlantis, however, there were other components of the artificial port installation, which must also be detectable in the modern-day landscape. One construction was mentioned specifically: the artificial junction canal, which was dug through the solid rock as an entrance for ships:

And beginning from the sea they bored a canal of three hundred feet in width and one hundred feet in depth and fifty stadia in length, which they carried through to the outermost zone, making a passage from the sea up to this, which became a harbour, and leaving an opening sufficient to enable the largest vessels to find ingress ... and they covered over the channels so as to leave a way underneath for the ships; for the banks were raised considerably above the water.

This artificial cutting was thus about one hundred metres wide, thirty metres deep, and should have reached several kilometres from the coast towards the citadel. Any construction of this size must still be recognisable in the landscape even more than 3000 years later. And indeed, it is present at Troy. West of the citadel, there lies an artificial cutting through the steep coast on the Aegean – just as described in the Atlantis story – and this cutting has precisely the sizes mentioned in the account: it is one hundred metres wide, thirty metres deep, and lies some kilometres away from the citadel, right on the sea. But, above all, it runs directly towards one of the silted-up basins!

But that is not enough. There is yet a second canal, somewhat farther south, that also cuts through the coastal hills. And yet again, on the land-ward side of this cutting, there is an extensive, sharply defined, marshy area, which looks like a former basin. So the channels give the impression of being artificial entrances to harbour basins in the Trojan plain that have subsequently silted up. Nevertheless, the southern cutting is far too narrow to have allowed ships to pass, and the northern was never deep enough to have normally carried water. So the purpose of these impressive con-structions escapes us, in the absence of further knowledge.

The same applies to the age of the constructions. The narrow southern channel carried water from the plain out to the Aegean as late as the nineteenth century, driving a mill as it did so. One might assume, therefore, that the channel was constructed for this purpose and is thus no older than the mill – around two hundred years old. Use as a channel for a water mill, however, bears no relation to the size of the work. For this reason, the geographer Peter Wilhelm Forchhammer from Kiel, who saw the mill and channel when still in operation in the nineteenth century, hoped that 'no one would get the idea of thinking that this canal was the work of a Turk, who had built it to feed the wheel of a humble water mill'.

Forchhammer was of the opinion that the artificial canal must have been constructed very much earlier, that it had filled with sediment over the centuries, and had finally been used once more but this time to drive a mill. The canal is undoubtedly much older than the mill because, as early as the eighteenth century, experts were arguing about its age. A Swedish engineer, who reported on the installation in 1790, came to the conclusion that 'anyone who understands the slightest thing about engineering, must conclude that this canal is an ancient construction'. The engineer dated it to the time of the Trojan War.

Unfortunately, such impressions cannot be confirmed by measurements – a fact which is probably the greatest problem in general when it comes to the geoarchaeological reconstruction of past landscapes. On the one hand, research into human impact on the landscape requires a lot of experience and understanding to be able to read the 'handwriting' of former engineers and fit this into the correct time-frame. On the other hand, in many cases geoarchaeological knowledge remains, in the end, on a subjective level, depending as much on persuasion as on concrete proof. From a patient's walk, a doctor can form a diagnosis, and then express this in complex technical jargon – and we accept his opinion. An archaeologist can assign a pottery fragment to a particular period on the basis of the clay used, the way it is worked, the shape and the decoration – and again that opinion is accepted. Geoarchaeologists can assign a canal cutting to a particular period on the basis of the extent of the plan, the degree of erosion, and even from the growth of lichen on worked stone surfaces – but there is no guarantee that their opinions will be taken seriously. In science, the first thing one sees is what one likes to see – and the discipline of 'geoarchaeology' is too young for its opinions to have obtained the necessary authority.

So, one can interpret the artificial cuttings at Troy as 'purely whims of nature' (as the theatre academic Birgit Brandau maintains) or as elements of an ingenious water supply system (as in the work of the best-selling author, Gisbert Haefs). The latter has used the history of the Trojan War as background for a historical novel, in which the silted-up harbour at Troy is mentioned. In the novel, a young Caucasian inventor called Tsanghar discovers several places in the countryside that appear strangely regular, like filled-in basins, and he recognises these as being the remains of a network of canals and inner harbour basins that were linked to the sea through artificial cuttings through the chain of hills. Thereupon, the Greek hero Odysseus scrutinises Tsanghar 'as if he suspects he had other mysterious senses that ordinary mortals do not possess'.

On Transporting Ships

Troy was frequently destroyed, and each time the city was rebuilt, care must have been taken to ensure that its most important asset, namely its water supply and harbour installations, functioned as well as possible so that the maximum profit was achieved from trade. In this respect, the Trojan plain serves as the perfect example of hydraulic engineering. Even the famous river Scamander, which crosses the plain, indicates, by its very name, human influence on the natural hydrological features. 'Scamander' in effect means 'man-made foam'. And the Roman geographer Pliny mentions an 'old Scamander', indicating that even 2000 years ago, the river bed was not the original one.

If people did artificially alter the watercourses on the Trojan plain, then basically the information that we have acquired in the meantime should suffice for us to carry out a technical reconstruction of these water-engineering works. After all, we have at our disposal the indications from the Atlantis story; a series of observations in the field; the results of test borings; our existing knowledge about the way in which Late Bronze Age hydraulic works functioned; and, in particular, the experience gained at the harbour of Nestor.

The two cuttings through the coastal hills suggest the presence of a complicated layout. But how could they have functioned, when one of the two linking channels was too narrow for ships to pass and the other was too high? The shape of the two cuttings is highly significant. One is narrow and deep, the other is wide and shallow. The narrow, deep channel must have carried water from the plain towards the sea; on that, all are agreed. The wide, shallow channel, on the other hand, must undoubtedly have had some other function. Its dimensions indicate that it served to help in the transport of very large objects – objects as large as ships – through the hills. If the bottom of this cutting was never below water level, then it indicates that its builders never *wanted* it to be below water level. We must discard the idea that people in the past put a great deal of effort into digging deep holes, without the slightest notion of why they were doing it. The skills of the Late Bronze Age engineers were very considerable; presumably in some respects their achievements exceeded our own imagination. In any case, they knew how to exploit the technical possibilities of their own time to the utmost.

Anyone who can lay out a 500-metre long, 30-metre deep cutting just above water level could also have dug a bit deeper to produce a proper link with the sea. Obviously, however, they did not want to do this. Why? Because with an open connection, salt water would flow into the plain and ruin the fertile agricultural land. Also, because, within a year, the cutting would have filled up with the sediment that the current flowing parallel with the coast constantly carries past the entrance. Finally, because the basins in the plain behind the hills needed to be full of fresh water to keep the wooden ships' hulls free from worms and weed. There are, then, any number of reasons why the cutting should not have been deeper.

If this cutting did not contain any water but yet served for the transport of ships, then this can only mean that the ships must have been hauled overland. Most prehistorians, until the discovery of the harbour of Nestor, assumed anyway that this was the only method employed at that period. With larger ships, however, this could not be managed without something more. They required artificial cuttings, along which the ships could be drawn. A certain engineer and major named Müller has more detailed information to report. During his investigation of the Trojan plain in 1798, he remarked:

> With steep, even if not very high coastlines, it was, on the one hand, impossible to draw ships of even moderate size directly out of the water on to the strand, and on the other hand, they would have been damaged in doing so. It was therefore necessary to have devices that made the former easier, and which prevented the latter. This was done by trenches, which were actually cuttings made in the shore, which gradually (*en pente douce*) ran down into the water, and by means of which the ships could easily, and without damage, be drawn out.

That overland transport of ships was already being carried out in the Late Bronze Age, we know from the saga of the Argonauts handed down by Apollonius of Rhodes. The Greek heroes had to haul their boat across considerable distances. In classical times, the Isthmus of Corinth even had a 'slipway' that was a staggering twelve kilometres long. The cutting at Troy, in contrast, was only 500 metres long. Loaded on to wagons with several axles, the ships could have been hauled this distance without any problems.

This idea explains the purpose of the wide, shallow cutting, but what was the second artificial channel used for? To prevent the harbour basin from silting up! Artificial harbours on coastal plains inevitably become silted up, not because of the sea's currents but through river sediments. How could this be prevented? We already know the solution to this problem

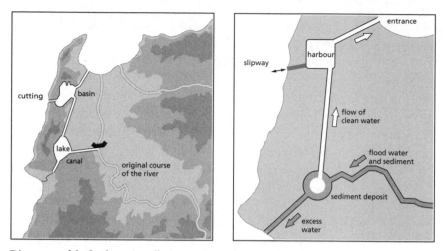

Diagrams of the harbour installations at Troy, showing the possible way in which they were used

from the harbour of Nestor, which was built in the same period and in an almost identical sediment-rich environment as the harbour works at Troy. To remain free from sediment, the harbour basin at Troy also needed a 'clean-water flush'. To this end, the two rivers that flowed out from the plain were combined and artificially dammed so that the transported sediment was deposited in the settlement lake. Then the clean water was taken from the lake and led into the artificial harbour basin. So the latter remained full of fresh water, even though it had a direct connection in the north to the sea, because the flow of fresh water prevented the salt water from entering and depositing sediments. All that remained was to lead any excess, sediment-rich river water into the sea. This was the task of the narrow, deep channel.

The artificial harbour installations offered Troy invaluable advantages. The ships lay within the plain, well sheltered from the wind, from sight and from attackers – and could, in case of emergency, be defended. The entrances to the harbour could be supervised in the best possible manner and, on top of everything, it was possible to demand an extra obolus for the special service of overland transport. The Trojans probably also used the northern coast on the Dardanelles as a harbour – perhaps for ships from the east that passed through the Dardanelles. The ship trackway would then have been an additional entrance and exit, which could be used depending on the wind direction and intended course, and which, in the case of war, could serve as an emergency exit, to evade a blockade of the northern coastline. If the northern shore were used for eastern trade, and the artificial basin for western, it would have been possible to make a profit on the goods in transit from one harbour to the other.

'The Myth of Troy'

Probably the most important consequence of identifying Atlantis with Troy is a reassessment of Troy itself – a reassessment that was, in fact, long overdue. Throughout the whole of western cultural history, a period of thousands of years, Troy has been seen as the very symbol and prototype of a magnificent city *per se*. Frithjof Hallman, who has written a book on *Das Rätsel der Labyrinthe* (*The Riddle of the Labyrinth*), lists all the places where, at the end of the Trojan War, refugees may have founded new settlements on the Trojan model. Among these there is, of course, Rome, in which most influential families, including those of Caesar and Augustus, traced their ancestry back to Troy. According to Hallman, London, Bonn and many other cities in Italy, France, Germany, Austria, Belgium and Scandinavia are offshoots of Troy. Even Paris may have been founded by scattered Trojans, later being given the name of a Trojan prince as a result.

For centuries in the Middle Ages, too, Troy was a central topic of interest in society. This 'Myth of Troy' was, until now, completely incomprehensible. Why should the Greeks have waged war for ten years against an insignificant and isolated den of pirates? Why should their siege have been such a outstanding achievement? Why should the *losers* of the Trojan War, of all people, be revered for thousands of years? Until now, archaeological investigations in the field have been unable to explain the Myth of Troy. The identification with Atlantis, however, has forced us to view Troy through different eyes. Does the myth perhaps have some legitimacy? Does our image of the Late Bronze Age perhaps deviate from the facts? Is it possible that, now the Atlantis story has been resolved, other major riddles of Mediterranean archaeology may also be solved?

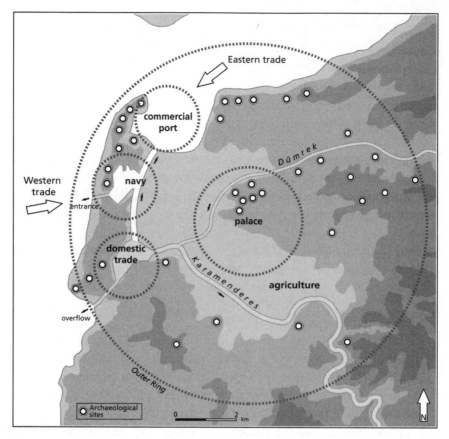

Technical reconstruction of the city of Troy and its outlying area

Chapter 9

Western Asia Minor:
The Gordian Knot

The time will come when our successors will wonder why we knew nothing about such obvious matters.

SENECA

A Caravan Crosses Central Asia Minor

In the year 1800, Great Britain was establishing its constitution; Friedrich Schiller wrote *Maria Stuart*; Goya painted the group portrait *La Familia de Carlos IV* (*The Family of Charles IV*); Beethoven composed his third Piano Concerto; and the Italian physicist Alessandro Volta discovered the laws of alternating current. Napoleon had not been First Consul for a full year, but had considerably strengthened his position; in Italy and the Rhine valley his forces were pushing back the Austrian army. In the same year, a caravan with five Tartar emissaries was trekking through the Phrygian highlands in the heart of Asia Minor. Accompanying the noblemen, who were obviously travelling on the orders of the Sultan, there were messengers, envoys and servants. The whole column included thirty-five horses and pack animals. Hidden beneath the clothes of the Turkish Tartars, however, were some English officers, who, during the Napoleonic War, were travelling the entire breadth of Asia Minor, from Istanbul to Egypt. One of the military attachés, Captain William Martin Leake, recorded his impressions of this journey in a travel diary. He was particularly interested in archaeological monuments.

On the way from Scyit Gazi to Hürevpasa Han, the caravan crossed a valley called Doganlu, where the travellers came across chamber tombs and reliefs carved in the rock. A particularly imposing relief on a vertical cliff-face looked like the representation of the facade of a building, and was covered all over with geometrical patterns. Leake made a drawing of this and copied the inscriptions on it. In his diary he noted:

> Of all the words, the second and fourth of the above inscription are the most remarkable. Written in Greek, they run 'MIDAI FANAKTEI' or 'for King Midas'. They give the impression that the entire monument was erected to honour a Phrygian king of the house of Midas.

Before this discovery, the stories about the realm of the legendary King Midas were regarded as pure fairy stories. Greek mythology recounts how King Midas was given the gift of turning whatever he touched into gold. Granting this wish nearly caused him to die of starvation, because even his food turned to gold. Only bathing in the River Paktolos cured him, and ever since the Paktolos has run with gold.

Leake's find and many other inscriptions, discovered later, established that there really was a ruler with this name. According to ancient sources, in the second half of the 8th century BC he influenced wide areas of Asia Minor outside Phrygia. At that period, Greece first began to develop its own identity, Homer's epics came to be widely known, the Olympic Games were established, and Greek sailors started to explore and colonise the coasts of the Mediterranean and the Black Sea. In the course of this expansion the Greeks came into contact with many foreign peoples. The most lasting impression made upon them was left by their immediate neighbours in western Asia Minor. It was from there that the saga of King Midas and his immeasurable wealth reached Greece. Midas was the first king of Phrygia to be known by name to the Greeks – and also the last. It is said that he killed himself when hordes from the northeast overran his country and the kingdom collapsed.

The father of Midas, Gordius, is also a famous historical personage. According to the story, he lashed the pole and yoke of his chariot together with a highly complicated knot, and let it be known that whoever could untie the knot would become ruler of all Asia. Five hundred years after his death, the knot had still not been untied. At the time, Alexander the Great, who was attacking the Persian hordes with his army, passed through the former capital of Phrygia, which had become known as Gordion, on his campaign. The Macedonian general took the task of solving the Gordian Knot on himself – it is said that he sliced it in two with his sword.

A few generations later, another ruler in western Asia Minor managed to amass so much wealth that his name is still synonymous today with untold riches. He was called Croesus, and was the last independent ruler in western Asia Minor. After him, the region fell to the Persians.

Leake's discovery confronted archaeological research with a contradiction, which received little attention: how could these unimaginably rich leaders have marked the *end* of centuries throughout which culture flourished, when classical antiquity only *began* much later?

The Peculiarities of Asia Minor

Asia Minor lies at the intersection of three continents and four seas. For thousands of years the subcontinent has therefore served as a bridge between Europe and Central Asia, as well as a region through which numerous different populations have passed. In peaceful times, the region experienced innumerable impulses and stimuli from outside; in times of crisis, however, the tides of war from both east and west met there. From one side, the Indo-Europeans, Assyrians, Persians, Christianity, and the Seleucids flowed across the country, while from the other came the Greek forces, the Romans and the Crusaders.

The complex topography of this land-bridge encouraged a multifarious cultural development. With a length of about two thousand kilometres, ranges of mountains reaching as high as two or three thousand metres, deeply incised river valleys, and limitless plateaux, the subcontinent constitutes one of the most varied regions of the Earth. In the interior, between the bordering ranges of mountains in the north and south, there extends a broad, largely riverless, high plateau with innumerable salt lakes. The swelteringly hot summers have given rise to a monotonous, treeless semi-desert with naked, scorched mountains. The bordering mountains in the north and south divide this high plateau from the seas. The coastlines are correspondingly steep and, because of the relief, only short stretches of the rivers are navigable. However, on the Aegean coast to the west there extend ideal areas for settlement. The complicated structure of the landscape has led to the formation of numerous natural harbours, fertile plains and rivers that are navigable well into the interior. In addition, the strip of land on the Aegean coast has an especially pleasant climate. The Greek historian, Herodotus, who came from this region himself, maintained that the climate was the best in the world.

The complicated geography of the Anatolian subcontinent necessitated the formation of small, independent societies, in which the population was organised into communities, city-states and principalities. The resulting political fragmentation shaped the region for a long time – until the Greek colonisation and the Persian campaigns of conquest in the middle of the first millennium BC. Later, attempts to found states comprising the whole of Anatolia failed until the late Middle Ages. Apart from a few exceptions, the cultures of Asia Minor cannot be regarded as national units, such as archaeology tends to identify. This has encouraged the impression that Asia Minor was potentially a fertile ground for culture, where farming and herding folk eked out a simple existence until outsiders encouraged them to higher achievements.

In fact, waves of immigrants repeatedly ensured a degree of homogeneity in the indigenous mixed culture, and thus first revealed the extraordinarily high level of the ancient civilisation in Asia Minor. Even if the newly arrived groups and the native population had initially fought one another, the various cultures combined over the course of time, and from the mixture new forms of states generally arose.

Only when the small states voluntarily combined into political alliances, they became easier to define archaeologically. This happened quite frequently and generally as the result of pressure from external enemies. The known cultures of Asia Minor in the Late Bronze Age and the Early Iron Age generally formed such alliances. From the moment of their emergence, the alliances possessed an extraordinarily high technical and cultural level, and often fabulous riches, as the examples of the kingdoms of Phrygia and Lydia demonstrate.

Progress in the Stone Age

According to our current state of knowledge, the transition from nomadic to settled hunter-gatherer communities first occurred in southeastern Turkey. There, on the banks of the Euphrates, lies Nevali Cori. Emerging about 10,000 years ago, it is the oldest permanent settlement in the world. Excavations there in the 1980s, under the direction of the German prehistorian Harald Hauptmann, brought to light, amongst other things, a 15 by 15 metre temple with a mosaic floor. The site must have been a centre for religious ceremonies, but also served as a store for foodstuffs.

In recent years, various other Neolithic settlements have been excavated. Among these is Çayönü, a site that was occupied in the 7th millennium BC, when people were unable to produce pottery but were beginning to experiment with metals. However, the best-known site in Turkey remains, as previously, Çatal Hüyük, which has been excavated for some years under the direction of Ian Hodder from Cambridge. Çatal Hüyük forms an extensive mound near the southern border of the central Anatolian lowland plain. The whole mound, consisting solely of settlement layers, is bisected by a river, which flows down from the Taurus Mountains in the south on to the salt flats in the north; one of the two halves of the mound alone measures as much as 500 by 500 metres. To begin with, this settlement had no name. Because it lies near a road junction, the inhabitants simply called it 'hill at the crossroads' or, in Turkish, just 'Çatal Hüyük'.

Çatal Hüyük was inhabited from the middle of the 8th to the middle of the 7th millennium BC, and is one of the oldest cities in the world. The houses consisted of air-dried mud bricks and formed enclosed spaces like a honeycomb. The inhabitants did not gain access to their living rooms through doors, but through openings in the roof. Some of the inner walls had paintings, which look similar to Palaeolithic cave paintings. The population obtained its food supplies through agriculture. Wheat and barley grew in the fields, and cattle, goats and sheep grazed the meadows. The bones of deer and wild boar have been found in the excavations, showing that the surroundings of the settlement were then thickly wooded. Mussels, from the sea, and metals indicate that, even at this early period – nearly 10,000 years ago – far-reaching trade networks existed.

We also know about the Late Neolithic culture that succeeded Çatal Hüyük; from places like Hacilar, for example. When this settlement was inhabited about 5700 BC, pottery – which first appeared about 6500 BC - was already widespread. Peas and lentils were now grown, in addition to wheat and barley. Artificial irrigation made agriculture easier, while the extent of hunting for deer, aurochs and wild sheep slowly declined.

In the 6th millennium BC, the first fortifications appeared. The carefully planned and constructed fort at Mersin in Cilicia dates from about 5200 BC. It had a continuous protective wall with slit-like window openings and strategically located accommodation for soldiers. Stone walls also protected the city of Poliochni on the island of Lemnos, while villages such as Demir-chihüyük cut themselves off from the outside by a circle-like arrangement of their houses.

It appears that there were no great upheavals or migrations in the Neolithic. Up to 3000 BC, culture seems to have developed continuously, without any obvious, more fundamental interruptions in the history of settlement.

The Age of Metals and Fortifications

In the 3rd millennium BC, a new wave of immigrants reached Asia Minor. They spread rapidly and settled large areas of the country. From their fusion with the original inhabitants of Asia Minor, a complex culture arose with a common language, having several different dialects, that was spoken across almost the whole of Asia Minor between the 2nd millennium and the 7th century BC. This language is known today as 'Luwian'. Even one hundred years ago, it was realised that the names of Greek cities that end in -nthos (for example Korinthos (Corinth)) or -ssos (for example, Knossos), are not of Greek origin, but arose at an earlier period when Greek was not yet spoken in the southern Balkans. We know now that these names are of Luwian origin. Many of the places with Luwian names were already important settlements by the Early Bronze Age. From this, many experts conclude that, in the 3rd millennium BC, a proto-Luwian people may have settled around the Aegean, including Greece. According to this view, Greek was not the first Indo-European language to be spoken in Greece. In any case, the Luwian culture in Asia Minor is the oldest Indo-European literate culture, although it is also, unfortunately, one that has been little researched.

The transition to the Early Bronze Age about 3000 BC was accompanied by crucial technical changes. The introduction of the plough ensured an accelerated growth of agriculture. Sailing ships facilitated foreign trade and increased the speed of communications. The wheel helped transport, and also in the production of pottery. Grapes and wine enriched the sources of food. The rapid technical advances changed the way and manner in which people lived together and communicated with one another – as a result of this process, the first urbanised city-states arose.

The trigger for the technical changes about 3000 BC may have been dramatic advances in metalworking. The first bronze tools appear at that time; they were much harder and more durable than their copper precursors. Apart from copper and tin, the components of bronze, the miners also extracted silver, gold, electrum, lead, iron, and semi-precious stones such as carnelian, jasper and nephrite. Rock formations in which these ores and minerals occur are widely present in Asia Minor – at the same time, however, they are rare in countries both to the east and to the west of Asia Minor. The introduction of bronze and the increasing dependence on ore deposits meant that many countries were no longer able to supply their own needs. A demand for raw materials and manufactured metal products thus arose, which acted as a further stimulus to mining.

To connect the mines efficiently with the refining centres, port cities and consumer markets, trade routes had to be established. Long-distance trade achieved the status of a hallmark in Bronze Age culture – above all, because the tin required for the bronze had to be obtained from considerable distances. The tin probably came from Central Asia. Lapis lazuli from Afghanistan, found at Troy, reveals how far the trading networks reached.

Trade was totally under the control of the local rulers. Over the course of a few generations, these princely families were able to amass amazing riches. Discovered hoards, such as the so-called 'Priam's Treasure' from Troy, bear testimony to the affluence of the upper classes in society. To safeguard this prosperity and, at the same time, intensify exchanges with foreign countries, the ruling elite felt themselves obliged to erect well-organised and, above all, well-protected cities. Their administrative and temple areas were normally placed on a central hill, often in the form of a citadel. In Troy, for example, massive stone walls with additional mud-brick structures protected the acropolis and its royal dwellings. The access to the central area of the city was by means of well-protected gates, flanked by watchtowers. At one time, additional walls protected the lower city beneath the citadel. The number and diverse types of weapons (daggers, swords, spears and battle-axes) generally indicate that the Bronze Age cultures had a penchant for displaying weaponry and waging war.

Many settlements in western Asia Minor took a lively interest in east–west trade. Unfortunately, only a few of them so far have been investigated archaeologically. One of these, excavated by the British prehistorian James Mellaart, is the city of Beycesultan on the central Anatolian plateau on a tributary of the Meander [Büyük Menderes] about two hundred kilometres inland from the Aegean coast. The city existed from the 5th to the 1st millennium BC, and was protected in the Early Bronze Age by a massive wall. The houses in Beycesultan had large courtyards with verandas on both end walls. Round hearths and clay representations of horns, which call Cretan cults to mind, were found there, although much earlier than on Crete.

In the vicinity of Izmir, an excavation is currently under way of the Early Bronze Age port of Limantepe, which was occupied from the 4th millennium BC until the 14th century BC. The site lies on a rise that runs out into the sea. In classical times this peninsula was part of the Greek trading colony of Klazomenai. It has been established from the excavations that thousands of years earlier there was a large city here with its own port. The central portion of this Early Bronze Age settlement was surrounded by a massive defensive wall in the form of ramparts. Parts of this structure even reach down into the water, where they form a breakwater, enclosing a harbour. An extensive lower town lay outside the acropolis.

About 2300 BC, most of the cities in Asia Minor fell victim to major destruction. Radical changes also took place in central Greece and in the Peloponnese. Many cities were abandoned following the destruction. Subsequently, about 1900 BC, there was a new surge of settlement and development. There was an increase in the foundation of new cities, and there were closer ties between the individual regions around the Aegean than previously. Innovations and the spread of new goods accelerated, to an extent that had never happened before.

Assyrian traders, who primarily wanted to acquire metals and minerals, opened up a trade route that ran from Assur in Mesopotamia to the central Anatolian plateau. The political division of Anatolia into many small states facilitated the establishment of this trade route. The local rulers in Asia Minor allowed the Assyrian traders to set up their depots on the outskirts of existing cities. Naturally, they demanded a portion of the profits, and so the wealth and importance of cities along the trade routes increased rapidly.

By far the most important trading colony was called Karum. It lay near the former city of Nesa, the modern-day Kültepe, and thrived between 1920 and 1780 BC. During the course of the archaeological excavations, more than 15,000 documents in Akkadian cuneiform were discovered. These texts inform us of the Assyrian interest in silver, gold and copper. They also illuminate the relationship between the foreign traders and the local inhabitants. The scribes in the trading cities also used cylinder seals, which they decorated with local, Anatolian motifs. The use of seals had been introduced by the Sumerians in Mesopotamia in the 4th millennium BC. In the period between 2000 and 1500 BC, such seals were actively used along the trade routes, and later in Crete as well.

At the end of the 18th century BC, a newly strengthened Mitanni, a state in the eastern Anatolian mountains, severed Assyrian trade with central Asia Minor. The breakdown of foreign trade weakened Assyria so much that it was soon incorporated into Babylonia. Within Asia Minor itself, the breakdown in foreign trade also caused an economic crisis. The dynasty of rulers of the city-state of Kussara in central Asia Minor used this crisis to their advantage and expanded their kingdom. A few generations later, a king named Tabarna assumed the throne in Kussara. He decided that the capital was too far to the east, and thus too close to the powerful Mitanni. As a result, about 1600 BC he moved his residence – and consequently his sphere of influence – to Hattusa, an abandoned city on the Kizil Irmak river, adopting the name 'Man of Hattusa' ('Hattusili'). He is now known as the founder of the Hittite empire.

The Hittite Empire

The Hittite kingdom thus arose from an ancient Anatolian culture, and does not simply represent the reign of an Indo-European ruling caste, as was previously assumed. In fact, the immigrant Indo-European stock and the original Anatolian population had become integrated over thousands of years.

The Hittite capital was located in one of the few regions of central Asia Minor where water is present in significant quantities. The city lay on a northward-facing slope and was centrally and conveniently placed, so long as the Hittite interests primarily extended over the region on the Black Sea. Later, however, a new (and hostile) state arose in the north: Kaska. The Kaskans consisted of a loose confederation of semi-nomadic tribes of horsemen, who according to the Hittite high-king Mursili II, did not recognise the rule of any individual – obviously meaning that they had no overall leader. They laid claim to an area that had previously been controlled by the Hittites. As a result, the Hittites had to direct their territorial interests towards the south and the southeast, in the direction of Palestine and Babylonia. Under these circumstances, Hattusa was less favourably placed, because many mountain ridges lay across the complicated route towards the south.

Access to the markets on the Danube and on the Black Sea was also extensively blocked. On the Aegean coast in western Asia Minor there lay Arzawa, a state that existed long before the Hittite one, being mentioned in ancient Assyrian texts. Arzawa consisted of a form of federal amalgamation of small states and city-states with poorly defined borders. Many of the federated states were part of Arzawa itself, but others – so-called Arzawa countries – belonged only in a wider sense. What is certain is that, via the Dardanelles, the Bosphorus and the Danube, Arzawa was able to establish contact with Europe.

The Hittite rulers tried specifically, primarily with military pressure, to turn the smaller states around their kingdom into vassal states, so as to interpose them as buffers against larger, more distant opponents. Even the very first high-king of the Hittites led his forces against western Asia Minor. 'The political activity of the Hittites was, however, primarily directed

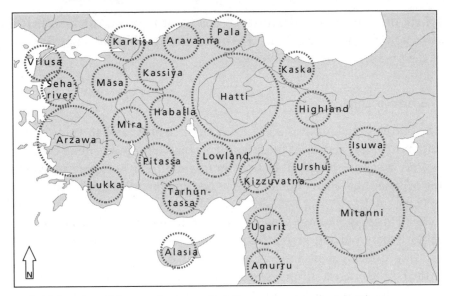

Probable location of the most important Late Bronze Age states in Asia Minor

towards the east', according to the German-American Hittite specialist, Albrecht Goetze. 'In the west they largely restricted themselves to keeping the existing peoples within reasonable limits.'

The strategic efforts of the Hittites were not always crowned with success. In the 14th century BC, Arzawa and Kaska were able to wrest control of Asia Minor from the Hittite kingdom, and to condemn it to temporary insignificance. Subsequently, Arzawa was regarded for a while by Egypt as its main contact in Asia Minor. The Arzawa rulers regarded themselves as of equal rank to the Egyptian royal house, and even a provincial prince, such as that of Mira, an Arzawa country, allowed himself to correspond directly with the Egyptian pharaoh.

It is evident from the information found at Hattusa regarding prisoners of war that from a demographic point of view the Arzawa states must have been of considerable size. In one case, the high king of the Hittites claims that his forces had conquered 91 cities in Arzawa and captured 166,000 soldiers. From the descriptions of the campaigns, we also know the names of rivers, cities and states in Asia Minor, which enables us approximately to reconstruct the Late Bronze Age political geography in the region. According to this, the heart of the Hittite culture appears to have become restricted to the area within the bend on the Kizil Irmak river, which was known as the Halys in antiquity. In any case, the collective term 'Hittite', used for Middle and Late Bronze Age pottery in central Asia Minor, should not, under any circumstances, be extended beyond country or linguistic borders – as the American prehistorian, Machteld Mellink, emphasised some forty years ago. Around the Hittites, particularly in the west and southeast, there remained several dozen small- and medium-sized kingdoms under the control of Luwian rulers.

Within the Hittite kingdom itself, the original ancient Anatolian population affiliations also seem to have been preserved. Only the organisation of administration, industry, trade and military matters took place centrally, through the aristocracy in Hattusa. The centres for handcrafts, religion and foreign trade, as well as the libraries, remained close to the palace. At the same time, though, the rulers tried hard to adopt many elements of the ancient culture of Asia Minor, among them being, above all, the names of places, persons and gods, as well as other aspects of the religion. Also the fact that the scribes were not only masters of the related languages Hittite and Luwian, but of six others as well, indicates that ancient Anatolian elements persisted in the unified state. Presumably, therefore, the centralised organisation of the Hittite kingdom was only a veneer over the diversity of the unified tribes within it. The situation may perhaps be compared with multi-ethnic states like the former Yugoslavia or Georgia, where ethnic complexity likewise temporarily disappeared beneath a centralised political system.

Fundamentally, the Old (1640–1450 BC) and New (1380–1200 BC) Hittite Kingdoms thus formed relatively short and regionally restricted interludes in the history of Asia Minor during the 2nd millennium BC. Before, during, between and after the Hittite Kingdoms, the original Luwian population with their complex culture prevailed over the major portion of Asia Minor. However, because of the political divisions, the Luwian culture is hardly detectable archaeologically.

It is quite the opposite with the Hittite culture. For one hundred years, excavations have been carried out at Hattusa, which, from the very beginning, have revealed text documents, and which have therefore acquired a very high standing in archaeological research. Over that period more than ten thousand texts and fragments have been found, which provide us with a deep insight into the society of the time. The great importance that we currently accord to the Hittite kingdom in comparison to their Luwian neighbours must therefore be partly caused by the course of research in the region.

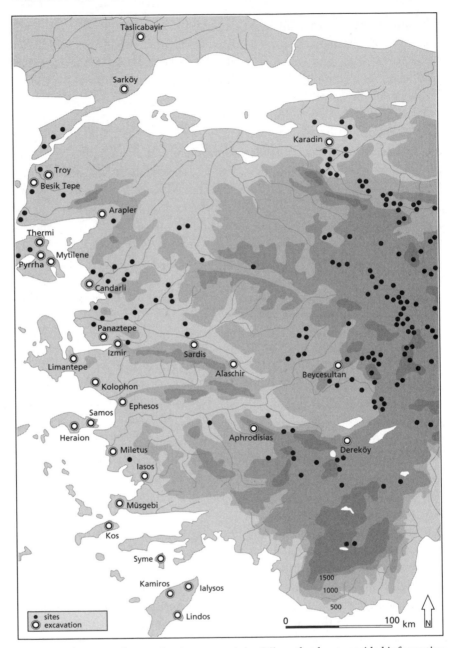

Known settlement and grave sites in western Asian Minor that have provided information about Late Bronze Age cultures

World War Zero

The final destruction of the Hittite empire occurred in precisely the same manner as the temporary interruption in its dominance in the 14th century BC. About 1200 BC, almost the whole of the eastern Mediterranean region experienced international tensions and, finally, wars and destruction. The Hittites appear to have been deeply involved in these conflicts from the very beginning, because the central authority had to request support from its vassal states in the form of all available land forces and ships. What is probably the last official inscription from a Hittite great king describes how the country fought its first and last sea battle, in which it lost control of the previously annexed island of Cyprus. Eventually, the enemy confronted the Hittite units on the mainland as well. Finally, however, a wave of destruction rolled across the country from the northeast – not from Cyprus in the south – and reached the capital.

Around 1190 BC, enemy forces broke into Hattusa, looted the palace complex, destroyed all official buildings, and finally set them on fire. It is not known with certainty who was responsible for this destruction. Internal dissension between various family members of the royal house has been confirmed, but the desecration of all religious and political symbols that is evident in the deliberate destruction instead indicates an external enemy. Many experts assume, therefore, that an already weakened Hattusa fell victim a second time to an attack by the enemies in the north, the Kaskans. Along with the capital and many other centres, the empire itself came to an end. It is true that the rural population was obviously relatively unaffected by the war's upheavals, but the break-up of the aristocratic ruling class and the destruction of the central infrastructure sufficed to ruin the political and economic organisation of the state for ever. For more than three thousand years the Hittite interlude, which lasted five hundred years, remained completely forgotten.

The collapse of the Hittite empire about 1200 BC was no isolated incident. All the states around the eastern Mediterranean suffered a major cultural collapse, which was one of the most critical in the history of the human race. It was then that Troy went up in flames and subsequently sank into obscurity. In Greece, the Mycenaean palace culture collapsed, the port of Ugarit fell to an attack, and numerous other trading centres in Syria, Palestine, Cyprus and Asia Minor suffered the same fate. The collapse of the political centres and trading cities naturally also caused foreign trade relations and economic structures to break down completely. A crisis affected the whole eastern Mediterranean, which makes it difficult to determine today whether the economic breakdown was the result of the chaos of war or its very cause.

The novelty of trade monopolies had proved too much for society. The cultures of the previous millennia had involved agrarian states. They were self-sufficient and long-lived, and waged what were purely local wars. The Late Bronze Age, by contrast, was the first major era of foreign trade and of influential trading powers. Trade led, on the one hand, to competitive advantages and, on the other, to controls, monopolies and mutual dependence. These, in turn, caused tensions, disputes and far-reaching armed conflicts. So there came about a sort of 'World War Zero', such as may only be conducted between economic powers.

Various, independent texts from Asia Minor, Syria and Egypt, written in the crisis period, speak of an acute danger from external enemies, or even of battles that had already taken place. According to these documents, certain smaller peoples had combined and, having done so, began to attack the Near East and Egypt from the sea. These attackers are now known as the 'Sea People'. They appeared for the first time in 1208 BC. Egyptian forces were then fighting against the Libyans, the latter being supported by the 'Sea People' from the north – most of whom obviously came from the Aegean.

Some years later, the Sea People returned. Their ships assembled at the southwestern corner of Asia Minor and thence assaulted the coasts of southeastern Asia Minor, Cyprus, Syria and Palestine. In doing so, they reached the borders of Egypt. Pharaoh Rameses III, on whose mortuary temple inscriptions and depictions of the battles against the Sea People may still be seen, claimed to have overcome the attackers, and subsequently to have conceded them the right to peacefully settle on Egyptian territory.

The invasions of the Sea People accompanied an unparalleled decline from the cultural achievements of the 'Golden Age' to the level of simpler farming and herding folk. The population returned to their original, independent and decentralised mode of living, or else they left their original homeland and tried to find new regions to develop. In the course of time, new immigrants filled the vacant spaces, which created a far-reaching and mutually beneficial intermingling of many different kinds of peoples that eventually led to the formation of completely new centres and cultures. From these migrations arose (among others) the Philistines, Israelites, Phoenicians and Etruscans.

For this reason, the transition between the Bronze and Iron Ages should not be seen as *just* a cultural collapse. The political systems of the Late Bronze Age were extremely simple, not to say primitive, the political map being determined by rival city-states and minor states, which both kept a check on and also fought one another. The main cornerstone of commerce was agriculture, and international trade was largely limited to luxury goods. Wealth was limited to just the actual rulers, who, when all was said and done, took advantage of tributes from the rural population. The cultural advance, too, benefited only this uppermost stratum of the hierarchically structured society. The writing systems, above all the Linear B that was used in the Greek palaces, were highly complicated and virtually incomprehensible to the uninitiated. Almost one hundred syllabic symbols, and numerous additional symbols and ideograms, prevented its use as an everyday script. A more comprehensive cultural development, the spread of popular education, and the creation of true literature would have been hardly possible within the structure of Bronze Age states.

Under these circumstances, the Mediterranean cultures of the 13th century BC had probably reached the peak of their cultural development. Any further advance required the destruction of the existing culture and a completely new beginning. The crisis years of the 12th century BC were thus – even though they may well have been violent – like a thunderstorm that clears the air, and they laid the foundations for a fundamental political and economic renaissance. In many regions around the Mediterranean, such as on Rhodes, Euboea and Cyprus, and in Palestine, the succeeding 'Dark Age' was, anyway, restricted to a few decades at the most. These areas, as well as Sicily, Sardinia and large parts of Italy soon profited from the collapse of the Bronze Age superpowers. So it was not just the invasions and destruction of the crisis years that were critical for cultural development, but equally the events that followed them.

Many cultural developments, which are still of fundamental importance for our society today, were introduced shortly after the crisis years. Among them are the concept of a single God, the minting of coins, the most practical system of writing yet seen, as well as the oldest significant texts in western culture, including the Old Testament and the Homeric epics. It is not surprising that the far-reaching, drastic, political, economic and cultural changes at the transition from the Bronze Age to the Iron Age were also partially recorded in these writings.

According to this view, the so-called 'Dark Age' in the centuries after 1200 BC was, in reality, a time of new departures: new raw materials were discovered, new methods of production invented, and new markets developed; new links with distant countries were also forged, and curiosity and receptiveness to different ideas and philosophies held sway. Why, then, was this dawn of western culture described as a 'Dark Age'? Applied to Greece, and to Greece alone, this description might be correct, because cultural and technical advances were reduced there to a minimum during the period between 1200 and 800 BC. When applied to Asia Minor, Cyprus or Palestine, however, it is misleading.

Where is the Problem?

The current state of knowledge concerning the development of culture, from the beginning of settlement until the appearance of classical antiquity, appears unbroken and conclusive. Archaeological field studies in the past thirty years have established that the most significant cultural stimuli came to Greece from Asia Minor. It was from there that, at the beginning of the Early Stone Age, the first settled cultures reached the west. They brought the knowledge of agriculture, herding, and the practice of living in fixed houses and village societies, which have remained part of our own culture to the present day. The next stimulus to cultural development at the beginning of the Bronze Age also arrived in the west from the east. It was then, and again from Asia Minor, that the plough, bronze-working, a hierarchical society, and foreign trade arrived. Later, this trend continued: at the beginning of the Iron Age there were yet more introductions from the east. This time they brought the political concept of the city-state, the alphabet, religion, art, coinage, astronomy, and the concept of a system of weights to Europe. Everything indicates that the principal flow of cultural and technical innovations continued in the same direction, until the Persian conquest of the 6th century BC.

According to our present understanding, however, a significant interruption in this flow of knowledge must have occurred – just at the time when the Minoan culture on Crete, the Mycenaean culture on the Greek mainland, and the Hittite culture in central Asia Minor were at their peak. In the 2nd millennium BC, western Asia Minor appears to have been insignificant as an intermediary between Asia and Europe or, at the very least, the region does not appear in our reconstructions of the past. The latest textbook on the corresponding period, entitled *The Aegean Bronze Age*, written by the British prehistorian Oliver Dickinson, hardly devotes a single word to the Aegean coast of Asia Minor.

Yet western Asia Minor is the region with the greatest continuous usable area for agriculture in the whole of the eastern Mediterranean, with the most natural harbours, and with the best access to trade routes. Above all, western Asia Minor has mineral resources like those found nowhere else – and it was trading in metals that determined the fate of nations in Minoan and Mycenaean times. So why, of all regions, would it have remained sparsely populated?

In fact, the documents found in the Hittite capital of Hattusa indicate that there were at least two dozen states in western Asia Minor, and that, for at least some of the time, these were politically and militarily significant, which is why securing the western borders made more military demands on the high-king in Hattusa than any other border. The correspondence from Egypt also confirms that there were states in western Asia Minor that – again, at least some of the time – were more important than the Hittite empire. A pharaoh once even asked for the hand of the daughter of the king of Arzawa (in western Asia Minor) in marriage whereas the Hittites were dismissed, or, as the Egyptians put it, 'The land of Hattusa is destroyed'.

So, in accordance with the general view of the Aegean Bronze Age today, after the suppression of Minoan Crete, about 1450 BC, Mycenaean Greece must have possessed sole control of the Aegean. So, when near-eastern documents mention mysterious peoples from the west, for lack of any alternatives we are forced to assume that this means the Mycenaeans. We therefore ascribe control of sea trade in the Late Bronze Age to Mycenae; assume that it is Mycenae that is hidden behind the mysterious country termed 'Ahhiyawa' in Hittite documents; and see the Mycenaeans as the 'Sea People', forefathers of the Philistines and also – together with the Caananites – of the Phoenicians.

Both archaeological findings and the information provided by ancient texts argue, however, against Late Bronze Age Greece having such major significance. Our picture of the Mycenaean culture is largely shaped by the cyclopean fortifications, but these were created in an extremely short time and were obviously the result of large-scale community action. The normal architecture of the Mycenaean Palace Period is unspectacular. If we leave the cyclopean fortifications aside, very little remains of the Mycenaean culture that is particularly impressive, despite exhaustive research efforts. The sum total amount of gold recovered from the 'Golden Age' of Mycenae weighs only about seventeen kilogrammes. Similar amounts of gold, worked to a comparably high degree of craftsmanship, are known from Troy, a thousand years earlier; from Georgia, two thousand years earlier; and from Bulgaria, as much as three thousand years earlier. Even the wide distribution of Mycenaean pottery is largely restricted to the short time-span between about 1325 and 1250 BC, and it merely confirms that Greek products were also included in foreign trade. Its subsidiary importance may be seen from the freight found in Late Bronze Age wrecks, because these were primarily laden with metal, with very little fine ceramic ware. In addition, petrographic analyses undertaken in recent years have shown that much of the alleged 'Mycenaean' pottery was actually produced on the spot in foreign countries, and merely followed a Mycenaean fashion.

An important argument against an all-powerful Mycenaean Greece is also given by Greek historical writings. The historian Thucydides recounts what was thought about Mycenaean Greece:

> Before the Trojan war there is no indication of any common action in Hellas, nor indeed of the universal prevalence of the name ... It appears therefore that the several Hellenic communities, comprising not only those who first acquired the name, city by city, as they came to understand each other, but also those who assumed it afterwards as the name of the whole people, were before the Trojan war prevented by their want of strength and the absence of mutual intercourse from displaying any collective action.

Even among Greek historians, the individual Mycenaean states were thus considered to have been 'wanting in strength'. Any contact and exchanges between them were limited, and there is nothing to indicate that Mycenae exerted any form of national sovereignty or control. The Greek geographer, Strabo, even states that not one of the highly characteristic cyclopean fortifications was erected by Greeks: engineers from Asia Minor must have supervised the construction. This statement is confirmed by the archi-tecture itself: the 'cyclopean' style of construction is primarily found in Asia Minor, and the bas-relief above the Lion Gate in Mycenae is the sole one of its type in prehistoric Europe, whereas in Asia Minor there are hundreds of them.

How, then, did our obviously exaggerated picture of Mycenaean Greece arise? When Heinrich Schliemann indicated, with the first prehistoric excavations around the Aegean, that high cultures had existed long before classical antiquity, it was a source of embarrassment to the established studies of prehistory, which did not allow for non-European and pre-classical cultures. There were, therefore, neither any schools of thought, nor any experts, and certainly no training available in setting up a new discipline. So the principles of classical archaeology were simply applied to early Aegean history: according to this, Greece did not first set the pace for cultural advance in classical antiquity but had already done so in the Bronze Age. Just as before, European culture had its origins in Greece, but now it dated back to Minoan and Mycenaean times. Seen from this perspective, the discovery of prehistoric cultures even supported the current school of thought.

Nevertheless, what people overlooked was the fact that a far-reaching change had occurred between the Mycenaean and the classical periods. Shortly after the collapse of the last independent states in Asia Minor and the capture of Lydia by the Persians, the eastern Mediterranean was shaped *Hellenistically* – that is to say, the flow of culture from east to west, which had lasted for ten thousand years, suddenly reversed. The relationships that prevailed from the 6th century BC, however, *cannot* be applied to earlier periods.

Even today, Aegean prehistory is full of major puzzles, and the question cannot be avoided as to whether many of these puzzles are not being solved because the research that is taking place is based on a false premise. The unsolved problems include, among other things the question of the source of the Minoan and Mycenaean, or the Phoenician and Etruscan cultures following the collapse of the Late Bronze Age states, as well as the origin and the whereabouts of the so-called 'Sea People'. Attempts to find an answer to these questions are generally initially based on the idea that radical cultural changes were initiated by influences from Central Europe that spread to the south and east. So the home of Indo-European societies was assumed to be in northern Germany; the 'Sea People' must have been of central and southeastern European origin; the 'Dorian migration' took place from north to south; and the origins of the Etruscan culture were even traced back to Central Europe. None of these ideas, however, can be supported by any archaeological findings. With the recognition that these influences probably originated in the Near East, interest in the major questions of Mediterranean prehistory died out. Might it be that many of these questions could be solved if the west of Turkey were to be given more attention?

Even if this is only conceptually correct, the impetus given by the notion that Atlantis equals Troy should have an effect, not only on the reconstruction of the Trojan landscape but also on our whole understanding of the Aegean Bronze Age, because it helps us to recognise that there is a gap in our knowledge arising from the way in which research has developed, and one which possibly has serious consequences. We know far too little about the situation in western Asia Minor during the 3rd and 2nd centuries BC, and cannot, therefore, account for the indigenous cultures in our current models. Was the 'Myth of Troy' perhaps fully justified? Is it possible that Troy and Greece, in reality, were evenly matched opponents? Was there, perhaps, some justification for the respect that Troy was accorded in the Roman Empire? Did the 'Sea People' perhaps originate in western Asia Minor? Or the Etruscans? Or the Phoenicians? At present, we can ask ourselves these questions, but not answer them.

Chapter 10

The Dark Age: Where the Bull
Came from that Bore Europa Away

An idea that is not dangerous is unworthy of being called an idea at all.

OSCAR WILDE ('Intentions')

The States of Asia Minor

Could western Asia Minor have been the great unknown power that left behind so many puzzles of Mediterranean archaeology that remain unsolved to this very day? Was it the centre of a 'superpower', equal in strength and influence to Egypt itself, that has remained unknown until now? The German linguist Helmut Bossert supported this view with research into the origin of the name *Asia*. Originally, this name was applied solely to Lydia; later it came to designate a whole continent. Bossert put this down to the fact that, among the inhabitants of western Asia Minor, the memory persisted of a former larger *Asia*, a country that, at one time, included the whole western coast of Asia Minor:

It was a state that was, so to speak, a superpower, which maintained active trade links with distant Egypt, and which did not shy away from armed encounters with the Hittites . . . The Mycenaean Greeks, whose migrations into western Asia Minor began about 1500 BC, heard the name 'Asia' at a time when it still applied to a large kingdom, whose extent towards the east, the Greeks – who settled near the sea – were unable to estimate. After the collapse of *Asia* as a result of the population movements of the early 12th century BC, the term *Asia* was inevitably restricted to what was later known as Lydia, the core of the former Greater *Asia*. To assume that the knowledge of a once far greater Asia was lost, and the Ionian geographers

213

Early Iron Age cultures in Asia Minor

derived the name for an enormous portion of the Earth from a relatively insignificant strip of land called *Asia*, appears, however, to contradict all logic and experience.

That western Asia Minor was neither completely uninhabited nor part of Mycenaean Greece or of the Hittite Empire is indisputable. However, a 'superpower', as Bossert calls it, could hardly have arisen there. The Hittite documents indicate that, during the Late Bronze Age, western Asia Minor consisted of small political units. These small nations and city-states lay outside the region controlled by the centralised Hittite Empire. Over the course of the centuries, there must have been times when these splintered states were on good terms with one another, as well as times when they were at loggerheads and fought one another. Whenever there was a massive threat from outside, however, they would have been well advised to overcome their fragmentation, so as to be able to engage the dangerous enemy with unified forces.

In principle, therefore, in the Late Bronze Age, western Asia Minor had a very similar structure to the Mycenaean and Minoan states. For us, the region is not of importance because it was an outstanding political power but, quite simply, because until now this piece has been missing from our historical jigsaw. The third leg of a stool is no more important than the other two, but it is absolutely essential for stability. The steering wheel in a car is not more important than the engine or the wheels, but one would not be able fully to comprehend the way in which a car works if one had no idea of the steering wheel's existence.

Because of the absence of any published excavations, we know next to nothing about the cultures of ancient Asia Minor in the Late Bronze Age, in what is the western region of modern-day Turkey. We know even less about the period in the centuries that followed! Only from the 8th century BC does the situation become clearer. Over the area covered by the former Hittite Empire, various culturally distinct regions had formed. These included Urartu, which lay east of the upper Euphrates in the area of Lake Van; the former Phrygia in western Asia Minor; the so-called 'minor Hittite states' in the southeast towards Syria; and a state called Tabal in the south.

The Urartu culture, which has been well researched, provides a striking example of how the ethnological and political situation may have appeared during the obscure centuries. In the 13th century BC, and thus during the height of the Hittite Empire, an Assyrian army advanced on eastern Anatolia, to capture important copper mines from the Hittites. In the description of this campaign, its leader mentioned a region called 'Uruatri', in which he had attacked eight countries and fifty-one cities. He used this name for the region that is also known by the designation of Mount Ararat, on which, according to the story of the Creation, Noah's Ark grounded after the Flood. When arranging the Hebrew biblical text, Jewish scholars translated the proper name (which had been written with just consonants as 'rrt), as 'Ararat', because normally, where a vowel was missing, the letter 'A' was inserted. We now know from Assyrian cuneiform documents that the Hebrew 'rrt actually corresponded to the Assyrian term 'Urartu', which was used over the whole of the Near East. It represented a mountainous region occupied by small states and city-states, in which yet another Assyrian king was to do battle against sixty local rulers. Obviously as a reaction to such attacks, the beleaguered mountain folk joined together in an alliance. They called themselves the 'Biani'. For about sixty years, from about 810 to 740 BC, this alliance was the most influential power in the Near East.

The centre of the kingdom lay about 1300 to 1700 metres above sea level in the border area between the modern states of Turkey, Armenia, Iran and Iraq. The upland basins in this region are marked by internal drainage to salt-water Lakes Van and Urmia, and to freshwater Lake Sevan. The mighty Euphrates and Tigris rise there, together with several of their tributaries. The alliance of states forming Urartu consisted of many cities, protected by impressive walls. Castles and forts were partly hewn out of the rock, and partly multistorey constructions of ashlar blocks. Extensive, artificial irrigation systems and canals assisted agriculture and horticulture. The fertile upland pastures offered plenty of space and feed for cattle, sheep, goats, pigs and horses. Wheat, barley, rye, millet, sesame, flax and grapes were grown in the fields. The ground was also rich in minerals, including copper, iron and lead. The volume of bronze products is remarkable, amounting to thousands of kilogrammes in weight. It is uncertain where Urartu obtained the tin required in the manufacture of bronze.

By the end of the 9th century BC, through a consistent policy of expansion, the allied states of Urartu had assumed political leadership of the Near East, severely restricting Assyria's interests. The Urartian kings have left behind accounts of successful attacks on southern Georgia, Azerbaijan, and Aleppo in northern Syria. As proof of their territorial gains, they displayed cuneiform inscriptions and relief sculptures in their characteristic style at the entrances to their palaces. The strategic aim of the expansion consisted of obtaining control of economically important areas, such as fertile plains and mineral-rich mountain regions; in contrast, Urartu never sought access to the sea.

Developments in Phrygia and Lydia

According to our current state of knowledge, western Asia Minor appears to have been practically depopulated following the end of the Bronze Age. This situation enabled groups of people, who had lived outside Asia Minor, to migrate into the mineral-rich region. The Phrygians were one of the many immigrant peoples. As the site of their capital, they chose a city, later to become known as Gordium, that lay on one of the most important east–west routes, already heavily used in the Late Bronze Age. The city of Gordium, named after its founder, is the only thoroughly investigated, influential city dating from this period. Excavations revealed three layers, with differing pottery styles. The lowest contained typical pottery from the Hittite period. It passes, without any obvious signs of catastrophic destruction, into a layer with hand-thrown pottery, which is itself replaced by the uppermost layer, in which were found wheel-thrown vessels of an early Phrygian type. The pottery made by hand – that is, without the use of a potter's wheel – is normally ascribed to the immigrants, but is present in contemporary layers in Greece and at Troy.

The immigrants did not completely displace the original inhabitants, but simply swelled their numbers. It is also obvious that the immigrant Phrygians maintained contact with their land of origin in the Balkans, which may have contributed to the kingdom's considerable economic success. The Phrygian kingdom appears to have consisted, like Urartu, of a coalition or confederation of various principalities. The American prehistorian, Machteld Mellnik, describes the western Phrygian culture as 'fabulously powerful' and upholds the view that many of their successful achievements may be traced back to the preceding – and essentially unknown – culture in the Late Bronze Age.

New, radical changes occurred at the end of the 8th century BC. About 714 BC, the Scythians swept into southern Russia, driving out the nomadic people, the Cimmerians, who had previously lived there. The latter subsequently crossed over the Caucasus to the south, where they weakened Urartu, and then moved west, conquering the Phrygian kingdom and driving the last king, Midas, to his death. After the collapse of Phrygia, the neighbouring country, Lydia – another of the states in western Asia Minor, and rich in tradition – used the newly created power vacuum to increase its influence as the intermediary between the Asiatic east and the European west. The historian Herodotus stated that the Lydian dynasties had ruled for more than twenty-two generations over a period of 505 years, when the last ruler – the ill-fated Croesus – assumed the throne. The beginning of these dynasties would therefore have fallen in the period around 1200 BC. However the genealogy described by Herodotus depends more on epic stories than on historical facts.

The capital of the Lydian kingdom was Sardis in the valley of the river Hermos. It also lay on an important east–west link, one indeed that stretched from Ephesus on the Aegean coast as far as Susa on the Persian Gulf, 2500 kilometres way. Not only goods but also important ideas flowed along this route from Babylon to western Asia Minor, and from there on again to the coastal cities of the Aegean. The architectural monuments and rock facades that have been preserved also show a mixture of oriental and Aegean traditions. Although Lydia's extraordinary wealth primarily rested on the flourishing east–west trade and its rich mineral deposits, it also arose from highly skilled handcrafts, the production of fine cloth, and on large amounts of livestock.

Excavations at Sardis by American archaeologists have established that a settlement had existed on this site from at least as early as the 3rd millennium BC, and that Late Bronze Age traditions were maintained throughout the so-called dark centuries of the Early Iron Age. The names of the

Lydian kings (Sadyattes, Alyattes) belong to the same linguistic family as those of the western Asia Minor dynasties (Maduwattas) from the time of the last Hittite kings. This again gives the impression that the Early Iron Age states in western Asia Minor adopted Late Bronze Age traditions.

The main concern of Lydian king Alyattes was to defend himself against the Medes in the east. These were a western Iranian people, who had already conquered Assur and Nineveh, and who had thus brought the Assyrian kingdom to an end. The Medes controlled the eastern half of Asia Minor, and confronted the Lydian forces along the river Halys. The battle between the two armies took place on 28 May 585 BC and was inconclusive. Subsequently the Lydians and Medes agreed on peace, where Nebuchadrezzar II of Babylon acted as intermediary, because he had an interest in putting a stop to further expansion by the Medes. About 600 BC, Babylon was therefore actively involved in the fate of western Asia Minor.

The successor to Alyattes was Croesus, the last king of the Lydians. Croesus took away the independence of the Greek cities that had been established in the meantime on the western coast of Asia Minor, binding them to Lydia with treaties. In addition, he concluded treaties with the Greek mainland, as well as with Babylon and Egypt, hoping that these international links would enable him to mount a decisive strike against his enemies in the east. There, Persian tribes had risen against the Medes and, within an extremely short time, had conquered the whole of the Median kingdom, including the capital, Ecbatana. Now their king, Cyrus II, and his forces were in central Asia Minor at the border of the Lydian kingdom. In the decisive battle, the Lydian king was separated from his troops, trapped in Sardis following a defeat, and finally captured when the city was taken. Lydia became a Persian province. When the Persians also threatened the coastal cities, vast numbers of the Greek population fled from their colonies into Thrace, Sardinia and Sicily, as well as back to their motherland.

Caria: A Rendezvous

The Aegean coast of Asia Minor was the actual point of contact between the Greeks and Asia Minor. The region south of the Meander, at the mouth of which lies Miletus, is known as Caria. The mountainous nature of the landscape along this coast provided an abundance of natural harbours, but meant that it did not have particularly favourable links with the interior. Except for the Xanthos and the Indos, most of the rivers flowed into the Meander and not out to the coast, so only a few fertile valleys and coastal plains were accessible. Despite this, in ancient times Caria was the hub of important trade routes. The sea route from the East to the Aegean, which had been of strategic importance not just in later years but for many thousands of years previously, passed this southwestern corner of Asia Minor. At Miletus, this sea route and the end of an important land link to and from Persia came together.

Both Herodotus and Strabo state that the Carians were once known as the Leleges, although Homer differentiates between the Carians and the Leleges, both of whom fought on Troy's side. According to Homer, the Leleges originally settled in the southern Troad, where apparently their capital was Pedasos. After the Asia Minor alliance had lost the Trojan War, the Leleges migrated southwards, and finally settled in the Carian region around Halicarnassus. According to Strabo, they founded eight cities there, the ruins of which exhibit a characteristic form of masonry, these still remaining partially visible today. One of these settlements was called Pedasa, obviously named after the old capital, Pedasos. In the 6th and 5th centuries BC, Pedasa was even more important than its neighbouring city, Halicarnassus, the probable birthplace of Herodotus.

The Carians were frequently associated with the Phoenicians. 'Carian' and 'Phoenician' seem, in Homer and Herodotus, to be synonymous with 'foreign' and 'oriental'. The Carians were considered to be enterprising, courageous and sea-wise. Their seafaring achievements were so renowned that they were described as being 'Sea People' – exactly the same term as that found in the inscriptions on Egyptian temples. The Greek ecclesiastical historian, Eusebius of Caesarea, even mentioned a 'Carian thalassocracy' – that is, a Carian dominance of the sea – during the late 8th century BC, without, however, giving any further details of this power's achievements.

The great metropolis of Caria was Miletus, which, in the supposed 'Dark Age', must have been one of the most flourishing cities in the eastern Mediterranean. Excavations in recent decades have revealed the existence of an extensive Late Bronze Age and Early Iron Age city. In the 13th century BC, Miletus had fortifications with walls several metres thick. Numerous settlement horizons confirm that the fortifications and harbour installations were used continuously and extended over a period of several generations.

According to the Greek historian, Herodotus, when the Greek colonies in western Asia Minor were founded, no women from Greece were involved; only men took part, and they married Carian women. Famous Greek citizens of Carian cities, such as Thales and Herodotus, were half-Carian, and had Carian ancestors. So it is not at all surprising that Herodotus should regard the Carian people as 'by far the most highly respected in the whole world'. Although the Carian coastal cities of his time were ruled by Greeks, a large part of the population was of old Asia Minor stock and continued to use their own language. At the time of Solon's visit to Saïs, Carian mercenaries were serving in Egypt. Their graffiti, written in the Carian script and language, have been preserved to the present day, including some on the legs of the giant statues of Rameses at the enormous temple, hewn out of the cliffs, at Abu Simbel.

The Situation in Greece

In Greece itself, settlement ceased at many sites with the destruction that occurred at the end of the Late Bronze Age, while at others, including Mycenae, Tiryns, Athens, Thebes, Delphi and Iolkos, reconstruction took place. In these cities, the Mycenaean culture persisted into the 12th century BC, but the overall number of settlements shrank in such a drastic manner that it probably indicates a general decline in population. Nevertheless, in many areas on the edges of the Mycenaean sphere of influence, the population density rose. This was the case, for example, on the east coast of Attica, on Euboea, Chios, Crete and Cyprus.

In the 11th century BC, the so-called 'Ionian migration' began, during the course of which Greek communities occupied and settled the islands of the Aegean and the western coast of Asia Minor. These were obviously individual, autonomous communities, which were sometimes led by individual rulers, who went down in history as the founding fathers of the Ionian cities. The early Anatolian names of most of these cities indicate, however, that they existed before the Greek colonisation. Although settlers came from every Greek stock and region, Thucydides states that most of them came from Athens, led by the Athenian royal family. Athens was, in fact, a busy, active city, even during the darkest years between 1200 and 1000 BC.

In the 10th century BC, exchanges between the individual settlements in Greece increased perceptibly. Pottery became more unified, and ironworking techniques became more widely practised. Until the first half of the 9th century BC, however, it is obvious that distinct poverty still prevailed on the Greek mainland. Houses were simply constructed, and neither the architecture nor grave-goods indicate any marked social distinctions. It is not until about 850 BC that richer graves occur at Lefkandi on Euboea and in Attica. Golden jewellery, amber beads, faïence and bronze vessels, as well as a battle-axe from Cyprus, indicate increasing maritime trade. At about the same time, farming must have shifted from cattle breeding to agriculture. The population density initially rose slowly, but then, in the 8th century BC, increased dramatically.

About the middle of the 8th century BC, Corinth and Sparta arose as new powers in Greece. More and more traders and would-be settlers left there for the colonies in Asia Minor. Because the Lydian king conducted strict policies against the coastal settlements set up by the Greeks, they initially had no chance to expand into the interior, and thus repeatedly had to establish new colonies. So they spread from the coast of Asia Minor to Thrace, the Dardanelles, the Bosphorus, and all round the coast of the Black Sea. Eventually Croesus established peace with the Greek cities on the coast, and their trade could spread farther east as far as Sardis. In doing so, they gained access to Mesopotamian goods and ideas. It was at this time that the Greek school of philosophy arose in Miletus, represented by Thales, Anaximander and Anaximenes.

Influences from the East

For Greece, western Asia Minor was a major market and the link with the East. Innumerable discoveries and stimuli – ranging from art, architecture, military science and religion to literature – came by this route from the East or Asia Minor to Europe, where these fused to form what we call Greek culture. The German archaeologist Georg Karo states that 'one of the most important and, at the same time, the most difficult of the tasks facing the history of ancient culture and art, is to track down the oldest influences of the East on Greece'. The task was, however, one to which he devoted only his early years as a researcher.

The concept, so characteristic in classical antiquity, of the city-state, the *polis*, is primarily derived from the regional politics of ancient Asia Minor in the Late Bronze Age and Early Iron Age. The Berlin author, Helmut Uhlig, who has investigated the significance of the cultures in ancient Asia Minor, maintains:

> Here we have one of the reasons why the idea of a state was never developed in Greece. Isolated Greek cities, such as those that arose between 1000 and 800 BC on the coast of Asia Minor, and which also conformed to an Anatolian lifestyle, were not an appropriate environment

for the idea of a state to arise, nor indeed for any form of state to be created.

He also refers to the work of the Mannheim scholar, Hans Erich Stier, who, in 1950, compiled a list of elements that Greek art had acquired solely from the East:

Almost all decorative ornamentation that replaced and eventually drove out geometric forms: palmettes, volutes, plaits, the lotus, and so on; figurative, rather than mathematical or abstract depictions; metal bowls and bronze shields; helmet plumes; insignia on shields, and shield grips; in painting: animal friezes, animal fighting scenes, contrasting figure compositions, heroes fighting from chariots or on foot, pictorial subjects like those on the Arcesilas kalyx and the Busiris vase, archaic dress, the differentiation of faces through the use of light and dark shading; sculpture and its basic themes since the old style of portrayal with left leg advanced was supplanted by the three-dimensional style, the colossal form of the oldest statues; standing and seated figures; animal sculpture; types of lions, where the Near-Eastern fearsome type, with open jaws, is in contrast to the majestic Egyptian type; figures ... oriental fabulous creatures like the Sphinx, among others; the caryatid motif; figured stone basins, and such like; the lamps; the elongated necks of the oldest figures from the Mantiklos Apollo to the standing Attic goddess, which resemble the Tell-Halaf sculptures; the position of the arms and legs; the representation of the musculature, which resembles Assyrian practice (for example, as in the bas-relief representation of sports on a monument in the Athens Museum) ... the motif of the lion conqueror and similar representations; gravestones, and so forth; temple architecture and, in particular, columns – and indeed not just the Ionian and its variants – and finally, musical instruments such as the lyre and the aulos; the origin from the East of important singers like Alcman (from Sardis) and others – these are all things the eastern origin of which is partly proven and is partly substantiated on the basis of considerable investigation, and which gain in probability in the light of conclusions about the helmet-plume.

Following this impressive list, Stier continues: 'In view of this state of affairs, it could not be said to be inappropriate, if one were to ask what concepts in ancient Hellas did not derive from the East.'

Regarding weaponry, Herodotus states that the Greeks adopted the idea of displaying coats of arms on their shields, together with the use of helmet plumes and shield-grips, from western Asia Minor; previously shields were carried on straps over the shoulder. As for the acquisition of religion, one hundred years ago the German prehistorian Julius Beloch stated:

> Foreign cults naturally found their way into the Greek colonies on the coasts of the barbarian lands at a very early stage. In the 5th century BC, the trading and business cities of the Greek motherland also began to fill with Orientals; there were numerous Lydian, Phrygian, Syrian and Egyptian businessmen, and the masses of slaves, which were continually increasing, in all their multitudes, mainly originated from countries in the east or from Thrace. All these barbarians tenaciously remained loyal to their native cults; the individual groups of countrymen banded together into associations to carry out their religious offices in the house of one of the members. The foreign nature of these ceremonies, and the secrecy with which most were surrounded, could not fail to create a great impression on the Greek population; pious people, who gained no satisfaction from the state religion, thought that here they had found the way to salvation. So the foreign religions made many converts, and it was, as always in such cases, women, in particular, who flocked to take part.

Another clear example of how the achievements of the flourishing cultures in western Asia Minor were taken up and spread by the Greeks, thus becoming part of our own culture today, is the development of coinage. In the Late Bronze Age and the Early Iron Age, trade was primarily based on barter, in which precious metals in any shape, but mainly in the form of bars or bean-shaped pellets, served as a substitute for currency. Coins developed from these pellets in three stages. Initially, the pellets were struck with a metal bar, causing a deep notch, which showed whether they consisted of pure metal or not. Later the pellets were marked with thin scored marks so that wear could more easily be detected. Finally, the pellets were marked with an emblem, which guaranteed its value and origin – this was how the first coins arose. This development took place in the 7th century BC in Lydia. The basic cause was probably the widespread presence of electrum, a mixture of gold and silver, in northwestern Asia Minor. Because the proportions of gold and silver in the pellets varied, a centralised form of control needed to be introduced, to guarantee the value of the currency. King Gyges therefore standardised electrum coins and guaranteed their value. From 650 BC, higher values were stamped with a lion's head, while lower ones had a lion's paw. About 625 BC, the minting of coins was adopted by the Greek cities of Miletus and Ephesus, introduced to the European mainland, and there spread widely. Croesus eventually developed the idea further, in that he had coins minted from pure silver and pure gold.

In the colonised areas on the west coast of Asia Minor, the communities of Greek origin thus came upon a higher, more multi-faceted culture than they had been used to in their parent country. In the 7th century BC, some Greek manufactured products were still quite rudimentary when compared with those of the east. Only in the 6th century BC – after the old kingdoms in Asia Minor had fallen to the Persian forces – did Greece free itself from dependence on the east. The Greeks of the subsequent period of classical antiquity were fully aware that their culture was based on foreign influences and components. Plato (*Epinomis*, 917 D) remarked rather laconically: 'Whatever the Greeks have taken from the barbarian, they have turned into something of greater beauty and perfection.'

The State of Science

The 6th century BC ambivalence is also clear in the state of science. Thales of Miletus, with whom the beginnings of Greek cosmology, geometry and philosophy are generally associated, was a contemporary of Croesus, but also of Solon and, like the latter, he was considered one of the Seven Wise Men. His outstanding practical skills were based on a fertile amalgamation (so typical of Asia Minor) between knowledge handed down from earlier times and new discoveries from Egypt and Babylonia. In the case of Thales, just as with Solon, we cannot prove that he actually visited Egypt. It is, however, extremely likely, because Naukratis, the most important trading settlement in Egypt, was founded from its parent city of Miletus.

The work of enlightenment carried out by Thales makes us recall the content of the discussion between Solon and the priests at Saïs. Before his time, natural events, such as earthquakes, had been ascribed by the Greeks to the wrath of Poseidon, the 'earthshaker', whereas Thales tried to find a rational explanation for them. He believed that the Earth floated on water, and that earthquakes occurred because of turbulence in this medium.

During the war between the Lydians and the Persians, Thales predicted an eclipse of the Sun which actually occurred on 28 May 585 BC, putting a stop to the indecisive battle on the Halys. It was forty years later before Lydia was finally conquered. With the fall of the last of the old states of Asia Minor, the sequence of the celebrated kings Gordios, Midas and Croesus came to an end – there were no kingdoms for any successors. The conditions for the arts and sciences, though, remained generally favourable, because contact with Babylonia and Egypt were closer than ever before. So it is not surprising to find that practically all the authorities in the natural sciences and philosophy (Thales, Anaximander, Anaximenes, Xenophanes, Heraclitus, Eudoxus, Anaxagoras and Empedocles), in poetry, from Homer to Sappho (Semonides, Hipponax, Callinus, Mimnermus and Alcaius), together with historians such as Herodotus and geographers such as Hecataius, had eastern roots. It was only with Socrates and Plato that the school of philosophy shifted to Athens.

The conquest of the Lydian kingdom by the Persians in 546 BC also led to the subjection of the Greek coastal cities. Hordes of Greek communities left their colonies there, to build a new life for themselves in the west; in Sicily and southern Italy. This is why the cradle of Greek arts and sciences is actually to be found in two different places, namely in Sicily and western Asia Minor, but not on the Greek mainland.

Pythagoras also came from Samos, an island off the coast of Asia Minor, where he was born in 570 BC. At the age of 28, he left his home as a protest against the tyranny that then ruled it, and moved to southern Italy. The famous theorem, that is still ascribed to him, did not originate with him at all, because it had been in practical use in Babylon for hundreds of years. Pythagoras made a significant advance, however, by proving that the theorem applied to every conceivable right-angle triangle.

The most outstanding Greek philosopher of the closing years of the 5th century – judged on the extent and diversity of his work – was Democritus, from Thrace. Werner Ekschmitt, in his book *Weltmodelle* (*World Models*), significantly wrote:

> Democritus wrote a remarkable book *About the Planets* that was astonishingly original. Where did a Greek get the material for such a book? If Democritus was the first to produce such a monograph, then this actually presupposes that the findings of Babylonian astronomy, in their very broadest extent, were known in Greece at that time.

Probably the most important cultural achievement that Greece obtained from the East was writing. It is well known that the Greek alphabet developed from Phoenician script. It is another question whether it came directly from Phoenicia to Greece. At the time when the Greek alphabet arose, the knowledge of writing had been continuously present in Asia Minor –

Greece's principal contact point for the East – for over 1000 years. At present, the earliest script discovered in Asia Minor is Babylonian-Akkadian cuneiform. It was brought to Asia Minor along with the ancient Assyrian trade colonies about 1870 BC. In the Hittite capital it was used for records in eight different languages, but mainly for Hittite and Luwian texts. Apart from cuneiform, the Hittites also used the so-called Hieroglyphic Luwian script, which arose in Anatolia and was possibly in use there shortly before cuneiform – therefore in the 3rd millennium BC. This is a script with clearly pictorial symbols, in which the direction of writing – like the earliest Greek script – alternates from line to line. It was employed particularly on stone monuments and seals, and, even after the upheavals of the crisis years, it still remained in use for centuries.

Between the 16th and 14th centuries BC, the first truly alphabetic script came into common use at various places in Syria and Palestine. Its symbols were partly derived from Egyptian hieroglyphs, but were assigned to individual sounds. The so-called 'Phoenician Script' thus existed before any actual Phoenician culture. The Ugaritic script, which was abandoned when Ugarit fell about 1200 BC, had many similarities with the later Phoenician script. In the 11th and 10th centuries BC, similar scripts were already being used in Syria and Palestine, but it was not until the 9th century that a form of standardisation took place. In eastern Asia Minor, this Phoenician alphabetic script occurred alongside Hieroglyphic Luwian after 900 BC.

In western Asia Minor, the Phoenician alphabet developed into the Phrygian, which corresponded to Greek in style, but which had additional signs at its disposal – which seems to point to an early form rather than a late one. At nearly the same time, the very earliest Greek script occurred on Crete and on geometric vases from Attica. Seen purely from a geographical point of view, it seems more probable that the script spread from Phoenicia, via Asia Minor, to Greece, than that it should have made a dogleg via Europe and then back to Asia Minor. It is true that the knowledge of writing did not *have* to reach Greece through intermediaries in Asia Minor – it is, however, surprising that no one has yet taken a critical look at other possibilities.

The Rise of Etruscan Culture

If, in the 12th and 11th centuries BC, western Asia Minor was more or less depopulated, naturally the question arises: where had the population gone? The simple weapons of the Late Bronze Age hardly enabled whole popu-

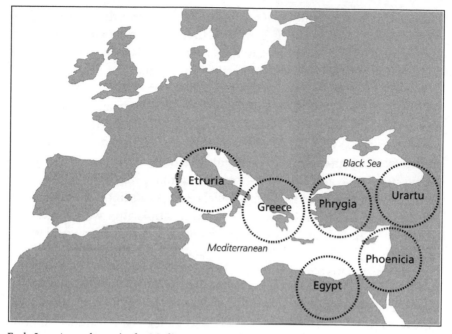

Early Iron Age cultures in the Mediterranean region

lations to be wiped out; so the inhabitants must have left their homes – but where did the people go? If they went west, to Italy, they may have co-founded the Etruscan culture; if to Syria, the Phoenician; in Palestine they became the Philistines, and in Egypt the 'Sea People'. All these are roles that hardly anyone at present ascribes to groups that migrated from Anatolia. Archaeologists in the field tend, as a rule, to emphasise the significance of the indigenous culture rather than that of immigrants, and European experts still tend to favour Greek influences.

Yet there are various indications that stock from western Asia Minor were involved in many mass migrations. Herodotus, for example, claims that the later Etruscan settlements in central Italy were founded by emigrants from Lydia, who took the knowledge of seafaring, trade and handcrafts with them, and thus formed the basis for the Etruscan and the later Roman cultures.

In fact, on the island of Lemnos, which lies offshore from Troy, a number of inscribed pottery fragments and a gravestone from the 6th century BC have been found, the inscriptions on which indicate that the language spoken there largely corresponds to Etruscan, both as regards grammatical structure and vocabulary. The widespread belief in ancient Greece that the

227

Etruscans originally came from northwest Asia Minor is thus supported by archaeological findings. It is true that the Etruscan language does not appear to be related to the Luwian–Anatolian, but it is highly probable that various languages were spoken in northwestern Asia Minor.

Not just the Etruscan language but also their artistic legacy indicates that they differ from all the other groups in Italy. The German, but Helsinki-based, language researcher, Harald Haarmann, has compiled a whole catalogue of features, with a total of 36 components, which are found in both the Etruscan culture and in 'Aegean' cultures. With the monumental grave architecture and grave goods – traditions that were abandoned only extremely slowly – there are close parallels with Asia Minor; the enormous grave mounds in central Italy show striking similarities with the extensive fields of tumuli in the area around the ancient Phrygian and Lydian capitals.

Further elements of Etruscan culture similarly resemble those of the Late Bronze Age civilisations of the Aegean. For example, sites for the newly founded cities of the 9th century were chosen to be strategically beneficial, mostly a few kilometres inland on a raised plateau or a rounded hilltop, just as at Troy, Pylos, Mycenae and Knossos before them. The individual Etruscan cities, just like their Late Bronze Age forerunners, did not form a single community, but remained as independent city-states, which, however, could combine in a loose city federation if the need arose.

Etruscan engineering knowledge also corresponds with the achievements of the Late Bronze Age. In Italy, whole schools were devoted to instruction in water management. The graduates were so skilful that, even after the fall of Etruria, they were consulted by the Romans regarding technically difficult engineering works. Their main task consisted of draining marshy areas in valleys and on the coastal plain, and leading the excess water away through a complicated system of canals to where there was a lack of water. Near Orbetello, a unique coastal control system was constructed, which functions to this day. Ingenious artificial canals and tunnels carry currents and counter-currents alternately, in such a way as to prevent the installation from silting up. Another impressive water-management scheme was at Porto San Clementino. It consisted of a canal, spanned by a ten-metre-high barrel vault, built from stone blocks. Only in the Second World War was this construction destroyed.

Intermediaries in Time and Space

According to various Greek and Roman historians, the Phoenician culture, which spread following the crisis years, had itself also originated from immigration, although it was based on structures that were already present in the city-states in Canaan in the Late Bronze Age. The cities on the Palestinian coast, including Byblos, Tyre, Sidon and Berua (the modern-day Beirut) were already trading with Egypt, Cyprus, the countries around the Aegean, and the Land of the Two Rivers.

The migrations following the crisis years must, however, have provided the critical impetus for the formation of the true Phoenician culture. One of the most important movements of people in Syria/Palestine at the time was the immigration of nomadic tribes from Sinai. For this reason, one historian concluded that the Phoenicians may have arisen from an amalgamation of the nomads and the Canaanite residents in the coastal cities. This explanation is not convincing, however, because the presence of wood for ship-building does not turn nomads into seafaring pioneers. More popular, and more plausible, is the idea that part of the sinister 'Sea People' merged with the Canaanite population, giving rise to the great Phoenician seafaring culture. As the pictures on the walls of the Egyptian mortuary temple in Medinet Habu show, and as is stated in numerous documents, the Sea People actually settled in Canaan. They were acknowledged experts in navigation and ship-building, and the combination of nautical expertise and adventurousness on the part of the Sea People and solid craftsmanship and an aptitude for trade on the Canaanite side, might well have been predestined to produce a nation like the Phoenicians. But where did the Sea People originate?

As so often, people sought to find the solution to this riddle in turning to the Greeks. One of the groups among the Sea People, the Peleset, settled in Palestine – they later became the Philistines; because of this, Palestine was also known as the 'Land of the Philistines (*Philistia*, in Greek). Now, for one thing, the pottery of the Philistines is very similar to contemporary Greek pottery, and second, the Old Testament states that the Philistines originated in Crete. Because Mycenaean Greece is seen as ruling over the Late Bronze Age Aegean, this seems to fit perfectly: the Sea People must, at least partially, have been Mycenaean Greeks.

What people fail to consider in this scenario is that the Peleset must have settled in the most fertile and valuable areas of Palestine, which, up to that time, had been under Egyptian control. Egypt did not simply allow the

Peleset to settle, but gave them responsibilities and rights. It is absolutely unthinkable that the great power on the Nile would have made such concessions to a barbarian people, which had treacherously attacked it only a short time before. A Greek involvement in the Sea People's invasions is simply not consistent with the generally friendly relations between the Egyptian New Kingdom and Mycenae. How events really occurred at that time, it is impossible for anyone today to say, yet no one seems to be considering possible new solutions.

The Phoenician culture is notable, among other things, for the almost complete absence of any specific territorial kingdom. A narrow strip of the Mediterranean coast of Syria, Lebanon and Israel, interrupted by deeply incised river valleys, is all that they had in the way of a motherland. Bordered by the sea in the west and the mountains of Lebanon in the east, the Phoenician powerbase stretched from Arwad in southern Syria to somewhere near Akko in modern-day Israel. Nevertheless, what we call Phoenicia today was not a political unity – and was not known as Phoenicia. The inhabitants of this region regarded themselves primarily as citizens of their individual cities. They called their homeland 'Canaan'. Their cities had a unique, specifically maritime character. Some of them lay on cliff-lined peninsulas, which not only offered protection but also provided two natural harbours: one south of the peninsula and the other on the north. Small islands off the coast were also chosen as settlement sites, obviously because they were easy to defend.

John Manuel Cook, a British archaeologist and expert in ancient geography, noted that the coast of Lebanon and the position of the ports exhibited great similarities with the coast of western Asia Minor. In both cases, the city settlements are relatively isolated, not just from the interior but also from one another.

As a rule, past cultures leave their archaeological mark through architectural remains and contemporary written documents, but, when it comes to the Phoenicians, neither the one nor the other has been preserved to any great extent. Although numerous archaeological excavations have been carried out in the neighbouring state of Israel, so far none of the Phoenicians' home cities in the Lebanon have been exposed. The reason for this lies in the fact that these cities were destroyed in antiquity and their remains subsequently largely used for building materials. The remnants are buried beneath metre-thick layers of later debris or are covered by modern buildings. Our current knowledge of the Phoenician people from archaeological findings comes from excavations in foreign countries, where they set up trading posts.

The later development of western civilisations would be largely unthinkable without the Phoenicians, yet, despite this, their immensely important history and role probably first became possible and, above all, visible, through the failure of militarily superior superpowers. During a period, such as the Late Bronze Age, when cultural development was at its peak and when many superpowers rivalled one another for supremacy, a culture like the Phoenician was forced into the background to such an extent that it left hardly any archaeological traces. On the other hand, even strong, major powers would probably not have stood idly by and watched the development of a nation that was extraordinarily rich in goods and influence, but poorly equipped militarily. It was precisely for this reason that, until now, the Late Bronze Age cultures in western Asia Minor have been overlooked. According to our current state of knowledge, it would have been perfectly possible for a power that was territorially insignificant, but which was highly influential in international trade – like the Phoenician culture in the Early Iron Age – to have remained unknown until now.

After the destruction and reforms of the crisis years around 1200 BC, the Phoenicians first of all used the few raw materials at their disposal for trade. The forests of Lebanon produced valuable and desirable timber, iron ore and marble were found in the mountains, and fish, crustaceans and the marine snail that provided royal Tyrian purple came from the seas. The Phoenicians soon recognised that particularly high profits could be obtained from turning the raw materials into products of the various arts and crafts. This gave rise to Phoenician textiles, furniture, ivory carvings, glass and metalwork, which were highly esteemed all over the Near East and around the Mediterranean. Even well away from the large cities, far-reaching technical changes were taking place. New achievements, such as agricultural terracing and plaster-lined cisterns and storage pits carved out of solid rock, enabled a far greater usage of agricultural land than previously.

Obviously, metals were of great significance, whether they were precious, semi-precious or base. Together with luxury items and spices, they were transported over great distances. In the 12th and 11th centuries BC, iron gradually replaced bronze as the main metal in use. Initially, the probable reason for this was because the tin required for making bronze was no longer available. Iron did, incidentally, offer numerous advantages over bronze: it was more plentiful, cheaper and harder. On the other hand, there were many disadvantages: up to five times as much charcoal was required to smelt it, which made working with it more expensive. In addition, iron is not so easy to work and corrodes very much faster.

The Phoenician craftsmen also set new standards in working precious metals. They perfected already known techniques, and created valuable objects that were prized all round the Mediterranean. Another technique that the Phoenicians advanced was that of glass-working. In this case, too, they did not discover the production process, but they contributed greatly to its spread. Glass had already been produced in considerable quantities by the middle of the 2nd millennium BC. For the Phoenicians, glass production was that much easier, because the silicates required were available on the coast of Lebanon in vast quantities.

However, the principal activity that this culturally influential people developed was not the production of goods but trade in them. For example, Phoenicia provided Greece with papyrus, which was produced in Egypt, and transported from that country to Gebal, for onward sale. Not for nothing did Byblos, the Greek name for this Phoenician city, become the synonym for paper. Even today 'book' in Greek is *biblio*, and the Book of books is called the 'Bible' worldwide.

The location of the Phoenician cities was also well-chosen with regard to international trade routes. Both the land route from north to south, and the sea route from west to east, were interrupted in the coastal region of Lebanon. For a long time, numerous mountain spurs prevented the creation of routes along the coast. People and goods that were on their way from the Nile oases to Asia Minor, or that were travelling in the opposite direction, were forced to continue their journey aboard ship. In addition, the transport by ship from countries bordering on the Mediterranean to the Euphrates, and thence downstream to Babylon, was interrupted by a broad stretch of land in Syria, so that goods on this trade route similarly had to be transferred to another means of transport. Even during the 2nd millennium BC, the coastal and trading cities in Syria and Palestine profited from the key position in which they were located. In the Early Iron Age, however, when the trade routes stretched as far as Spain and India, the Near East was able to exploit its geographically and politically advantageous position as never before.

To exert the greatest possible control over these trade routes, and to have reliable ports of call, the Phoenician cities established maritime bases, which eventually developed into manufacturing and trading centres. In contrast to the Greek colonies that were set up in the 7th century BC in increasing competition with the Phoenician trade centres, the Phoenician settlements were not, as a rule, small bridgeheads intended to serve for conquest and the acquisition of land. Instead, they tended to occupy the spaces that were outside the spheres of influence of the land-based powers.

Phoenician sea trade followed routes that had already been established in the Late Bronze Age. Its principal concern was with the ore deposits in Cyprus, Sicily, Sardinia, Etruria and southern Spain, as well as those on various islands in the Aegean. The Phoenician trades benefited from the transport of goods at least as much as the states whose goods and information they were handling. Established purely with the aim of facilitating foreign trade, the Phoenician settlements had their own maritime character, reflecting the interests of the businessmen and sailors. The Hamburg expert on the Phoenicians, Hans Georg Niemeyer, identified the following criteria for the choice of site for Phoenician settlements. In politically weak regions, but in the neighbourhood of important ore deposits and other sources of raw materials, they sought out limited, relatively small areas for settlement, which, when feasible, had no access to the hinterland. Alternatively, they chose offshore islands or easily defended tongues of land. Also desirable was a harbour, protected from the wind, where ships could be beached or lie in the roadstead.

The Phoenicians were also outstanding water engineers. At Dor, one can still find quays built of sawn natural stone and paved platforms, dating from the period between the 13th and 11th centuries BC. In the port city of Achsiv, north of Haifa, they chiselled semicircular basins out of the wave-cut platform that extends far out to sea, to obtain artificial harbours. And at Sidon, they developed an ingenious hydraulic system of basins and canals, in which the wind largely determined the flow of water. It served to supply sediment-free water to the basins, to prevent the harbours from silting up.

Written information about the Phoenicians has mainly reached us via other cultures, with the Old Testament being the most informative source. When the description of a nation rests exclusively on foreign sources, then it is only too easy for contemporary prejudices to creep in and be handed down to the present day. Even the *Iliad* and the *Odyssey* have been instrumental in producing such clichés. In the *Iliad*, the Phoenicians are said to be a wealthy, skilful people that produced bold and experienced seafarers, as well as craftsmen who created artistically decorated vessels from precious metals. In the *Odyssey*, on the other hand, they are essentially portrayed as crafty slave traders and rogues.

Europe, the name of our continent, derives from Europa, a Phoenician princess, with whom Zeus fell in love when he saw her and her friends playing on a beach. He approached her in the form of a white bull, lay down, and let himself be stroked. Europa bedecked him with her companions' garlands, and swung herself on to his back, upon which the bull plunged into the sea and carried her to Crete, where they made love, and she subsequently brought three sons into the world, one of whom was the legendary King Minos. Greek mythology and the name of the continent have thus preserved a remembrance of where the critical impulses originated that have shaped our culture.

Part Four

The Future of the Past

Chapter 11

Archaeology Yesterday, Today and Tomorrow

> But [just as] it is of not much use if a sack gets fuller and fuller, but then no one
> is around from time to time to 'tie it up', so therefore, from time to time – and also
> with considerable intellectual audacity – [someone] needs to tot up the total . . .
> and makes his discoveries accessible to members of other disciplines.
>
> ROMAN HERZOG (1993)

The Philhellenes' View of the World

Archaeology today stands at a crossroads. The shrinking budgets of the 1980s
and 1990s had particularly disastrous effects in the cultural field, because, for
one thing, it lacks an influential lobby able to press forceful demands, and
also because the practical benefits of grants become obvious only in the very
long term. In economically difficult times, jobs are cut and risks avoided. The
fewer the number of available positions, the sooner they are given to those
who have satisfied the current system as closely as possible. High unemploy-
ment rates of necessity promote Political Correctness. Only those who do
not raise any objections, or about whom no objections are raised, can
survive. This is accompanied by an inevitable loss of individuality. The deci-
sion-making elite, who, on the one hand, demand conformity, on the other
hand simultaneously regret this loss of individuality, and paradoxically, in
doing so, regret that everyone conforms. This phenomenon is particularly
prevalent in the higher education sector, but may also be observed in politics,
business and sport. The former trainer of the German national football team
is just one example among many. He treated all nonconformists with con-
tempt, and handled the rest – all world stars – as if they were prepubescent
Boy Scouts, only finally to complain that there were no sporting personalities
any more! The problem lies in the fact that, at present, individual personalities are not encouraged – little in sport, hardly at all in politics, rarely
in business, and certainly not at all in culture and science.

Research, however, is one of those fields that depends on dissidents and troublemakers. Excess conformity makes it lifeless and boring – and causes it quickly to fall behind in the international stakes. This is precisely where the problem lies: although every individual aspect and the system as a whole act absolutely correctly, the latter doesn't keep moving. It lacks controversy and tension, which start by prompting ideas and thus setting a process of development in motion. In the end, any synthesis always presupposes an existing thesis *and* an antithesis. *Where is the antithesis?* Without it, both science and culture flag, and thus become less productive than they were previously and even less worthy of support. It sets up a vicious, never-ending, downward spiral.

Archaeology is more strongly affected by this syndrome than almost any other discipline. There are a number of reasons for this. First, archaeology is seen as of national importance, and is therefore firmly managed. The Deutsche Archäologische Institut (German Archaeological Institute), for instance – without support from which hardly any German archaeologist working overseas during the last hundred years would have had a career – comes directly under the Foreign Minister! Second, the power of decision in archaeology, unlike almost any other discipline, is in the hands of a small conservative elite. The latter determines the allocation of research funds, work permits and academic chairs, as well as salaries, honours, publication in specialised journals and invitations to speak at conferences. Differences of opinion are therefore stifled. The consequences of this are well defined by the German *Brockhaus* dictionary (under 'Utopia'):

> A system, where a small elite is entitled to the monopoly of truth and political power, is unable to react in an innovative way to new challenges. In fact, new insights are always held only by minorities outside the current apparatus of power. Anyone who holds them back kills innovative ideas and, in doing so, any further development.

The third reason why archaeology is under exceptional strain from the ever more rapid changes that are the spirit of the times, lies with its history. The study of antiquity arose at the end of the 18th century as a concomitant of a new European way of thought. The trigger for its development at the time was the national conflicts between France and the German-speaking countries on the one hand, and between Europe and the Turkish Empire on the other. Until about 1700, the Ottoman Empire had stretched right through North Africa from Gibraltar to Egypt, and through southeastern

Europe from Vienna, across the whole of the Balkans to the Caspian Sea, as well as down into the Arabian peninsula. Archaeology's original task consisted of providing nascent Europe with a historical identity, which would help it to face this omnipotent Ottoman Empire as an equal power.

The range of interests of archaeology in those days was restricted, by definition, to research into Graeco-Roman cultures. According to contemporary understanding, the origin of western culture must have lain in ancient Greece and Rome. Phrygia, Lydia and Phoenicia, and the kings Gordios, Midas and Croesus, had all existed before classical antiquity, and not only that, in Asia – they were thus outside the 'civilised' world in both time and place. The supposed 'Dark Age' therefore remained dark for the very reason that it lay before the hellenistic world and was thus, in traditional archaeology's view, insignificant. By adopting this attitude, archaeology accepted the prevailing contrasts between Europe and Asia, and accentuated them. The Canadian historian, Bruce Trigger, has defined the aims of this original archaeology more precisely in his highly praised textbook *A History of Archaeological Thought*:

1 Colonial Archaeology: It should strengthen the unity of the modern state, by finding past cultures on its own soil, and emphasising their achievements.
2 National Archaeology: It should support territorial claims, by establishing the historical unimportance of foreign cultures.
3 Imperial Archaeology: It should strengthen the ambitions of the leading powers, by devaluing regional history and marginal groups.

The philhellenic archaeology of the 19th century concentrated on the first aim, and varied it slightly, because it strove to obtain not a national but a European conception of the past. It aimed at glorifying ancient Greece and ascribing to it unique, almost supernatural, qualities. The development of Europe in the 18th and 19th centuries was a success story, which, according to archaeology, had its origin in ancient Greece. 'The history of mankind stood at a turning-point in the 5th century BC', wrote Peter Levin in the first sentence of his book of popular archaeology about *Greece*, which appeared in 1980. 'It was then that the light was lit, that illuminates everything to this very day. Europe is the result, and the key to its existence lies in Greece.'

Oriental cultures provided an appropriate counterpart. The sphere of influence of the Ottoman Empire visibly dwindled in the 18th and 19th centuries, and the culture of the Orient was correspondingly depicted as underdeveloped and degenerate. Some experts even maintained that the Central European states, which, in the 19th century, were determining the fate of the world, must have enjoyed a corresponding role in prehistory. In their view, it was unimaginable that nations of such importance in the modern world should have played subordinate roles in the past. Ian Morris, Professor of Classical Archaeology at Stanford University in California, states that even someone who asserted the influence of the 'Orient' on Greece, was still choosing a language that characterised the East as wrong and unchanging; as the receptacle for useless wisdom that required the youthful spirit of Greece to become European. As the Tübingen pre-historian, Manfred Korfmann explains, even archaeological investigations hardly crossed the border between Greece and Turkey, because 'the political differences in the 19th and 20th centuries together with the deeply rooted philhellenism' of research, predetermined narrowly defined 'guidelines'. Cultures such as the Phoenician-Punic one, according to Hans Georg Nie-meyer, were 'only too readily classified by the Eurocentric, and particularly philhellenic, archaeological sciences as "peripheral" '.

Naturally, modern archaeology has long since overcome the phil-hellenism of the time of Winckelmann. But it has neither been able to bring itself to a critical reappraisal of the principles of philhellenic archaeology, nor rid itself of the structures of the past one hundred years. For this reason, the preliminary work by the philhellenes still forms the basis today on which archaeological research – for lack of any alternative – must rely. How western oriented our outlook still remains today is seen, for example, from the *Handbuch der Altertumswissenschaften* (*Handbook of Archaeological Sciences*), which consists of numerous volumes and takes up 280 centi-metres on a bookshelf. Most of this is concerned with Greek grammar, Roman civil law, and similar topics, and just two centimetres – a selection by Albrecht Goetze, written in 1957 – is devoted to Asia Minor.

In the 20th century, the reverence for ancient Greece and Rome and their cultural legacy also formed the main framework of archaeological teaching: ancient philology, the history of art and architecture, were, and still are, the cornerstones on which the whole construction rests. Any change to this structure threatens the stability of the whole edifice, and could thus cause it to collapse.

Another reason why archaeology today is at a crossroads relates to its methodology. While the state of knowledge in many scientific disciplines has doubled in just a few years, archaeology still employs methods that were established a hundred years ago. The first scientific excavation – at Olympia – defined the standard: the larger the excavation, the better. Large excavations produced a large number of sculptures but also generated innumerable small finds. Examination of the small finds required a lot of attention and, by doing so, helped to substantiate the claim for scientific rigour. Coping with the material pushed all other tasks into the background. There remained hardly any strength and energy, over and above cataloguing the finds, to consider the true sense and purpose of the work. In addition, the vast amount of data has meant that archaeologists have increasingly been forced to specialise. But what happens when the solutions to their problems are to be found outside their narrowly defined range of vision?

Traditional archaeology's approach to research is in direct contrast to what science, in its true sense, strives to achieve. This may be illustrated by a model. If we imagine that available knowledge is a sphere, then the exact sciences attempt to expand its surface area, in that they add new knowledge to what is already known. Because scientific advance occurs at different rates in different fields of a discipline, the surface of the sphere is uneven. The ideal goal, predetermined by nature itself – namely, to discover every-thing about it and thus attain the absolute truth – may be envisaged as a second spherical shell far outside our existing knowledge. Any expansion in knowledge would, however, also cause the area of the boundary between knowledge and ignorance to increase. This means that, the more we know, the more we appreciate how little we really know. The principle of research is obviously to increase the volume of the inner sphere, so that we may come as close as possible to the hypothetical outer sphere.

Because archaeology is based on a specific world-view, it followed utterly different rules. In the spherical-shell model, archaeology behaves in the opposite manner to the natural sciences. It postulates that it has absolute knowledge, the outermost shell, from the very beginning. Philhellenism expressed the wishful notions of contemporary middle-class intellectuals, as dictated by the times and partially reflecting political motivation. All subsequent 'research' was directed solely to providing additional support to this picture. After reaching the outer shell, however, no further progress is possible. Any movement takes place either within the actual surface itself, which signifies neither a gain nor a loss of knowledge, or else is directed inwards towards a lower level. To avoid this retrograde step, archaeology must proceed extremely cautiously. One step too many, or one step too far, could jeopardise the existing dogmas.

With his excavations at Troy, Heinrich Schliemann breached archaeology's self-imposed restrictions with respect to both geography and time. For one thing, he turned up on the wrong coast of the Aegean; for another, he – like Arthur Evans at Knossos – ruthlessly removed the existing classical ruins to discover the foundations from prehistoric times that lay beneath them. After Schliemann's death, no one ever again actually doubted the existence of prehistoric civilisations. However, to prevent archaeology's view of the world from having to be completely redefined, scholars unceremoniously declared that only the prehistoric sites on *European* soil were authentic testimony to earlier high cultures. Knossos was thus the centre of the Minoan culture, and Mycenae that of the Mycenaean. Troy was left in the cold. Although the memory of Troy – and not of Knossos or Mycenae – was omnipresent in western cultural history for thousands of years, the archaeologists regarded the site as an insignificant Greek colony on the other side of the Aegean.

When Aegean prehistory merged with archaeology, naturally other rules had to apply besides the basic philhellenic principles – but where should these concepts come from? There was little option but to raise the views of the pioneers to the status of dogma. They would, in future, define the outermost shell – absolute truth – in our model. In general, no doubt was ever cast on these propositions, and they were replaced only when new discoveries were definitely confirmed and could no longer be shown to be wrong. This meant that new ideas and discoveries were forced to compete with completely different claims and expectations, in comparison with the pioneers' attempts at interpretation (shaped by wishful thinking). These attempts are still partially accepted today as expert opinion, despite their never having been proved, doubted or even carefully examined. An example may make this clearer. In excavating royal graves at Ur, Sir Leonard Woolley wanted to reach the prehistoric layers, but first encountered a layer of clay, more than two metres thick, without any artefacts. The excavators had their own idea as to how this discovery should be interpreted, but left it to a neutral person to express their suspicion. When Lady Catherine Woolley was looking at the stratigraphy, they asked her how the layer of clay could be explained. She turned round, and casually remarked in leaving: 'It was obviously the Deluge!' This remark came to be accorded the status of an expert opinion, and ever since then, the Deluge mentioned in the Bible has been accepted as a historical event: a flood at the head of the Persian Gulf.

The spherical-shell model also explains why archaeology, despite being what is, in comparison with other sciences, a harmless field of work, advances in a uniquely slow manner. Slowness supposedly equates, in archaeology, with the expression of scientific carefulness. However, the longer a works lasts, the closer it also gets to the ultimate goal, that of making *no* progress at all, and thus of not endangering the level already attained in the outermost spherical shell.

Whereas scientific discoveries are generally welcomed, or are at least the subject of lively discussion because they go beyond the boundaries of previous knowledge and open up new intellectual fields, archaeology has always denigrated its discoverers, because they jeopardise the already established view of the world. The decipherment of Egyptian hieroglyphics by Jean François Champollion in 1822 was still rejected by archaeologists twenty years after his death. They were afraid that knowledge of hieroglyphs might increase the interest in a non-Greek, and thus 'barbaric', people. And when the headteacher, Johann Karl Fuhlrott, discovered the bones of a Neanderthal in a cave near Düsseldorf in 1856, the opponents of the theory of evolution made use of some remarkable arguments in their attempts to refute the significance of the discovery. Rudolf Virchow, President of the Deutsche Gesellschaft für Anthropologie (German Society of Anthropology) – who personally promoted the principle 'always practise honesty and stand by the facts whatever happens' – endorsed the interpretation that the Neaderthal was a bow-legged, Mongolian Cossack with rickets, who had been lucky enough to survive multiple head injuries, but who, during a campaign by Russian forces against France in 1814, had been wounded, and (stark naked) had crawled into a cave, where he had died. Thirty years passed before the specialists recognised their mistake. Again, when the Spanish nobleman de Sautola discovered the Late Ice Age painted cave at Altamira, 'critical' scientists described him as a forger and a cheat – and their error was only recognised 22 years later. As is well known, the same thing happened to Heinrich Schliemann over his excavations at Troy, Mycenae and Tiryns. Even just before his death, the London *Times* wrote that the ruins at Mycenae and Tiryns were the work of 'some obscure barbarian tribe' from the Byzantine period. In particular, the so-called prehistoric palace at Tiryns was the 'most remarkable hallucination of an unscientific enthusiast that has ever appeared in the literature'.

Because university archaeology was not receptive to progress, the greatest discoveries were reserved for initiatives by private individuals. Schliemann is the best example, but he is only one among many. Arthur Evans, the excavator of Knossos, as well as Howard Carter, the discoverer of the tomb of Tutankhamun, worked on their own account, and even the last great success in Aegean prehistory, the decipherment of Linear B, was the work of a non-specialist, the young architect, Michael Ventris.

In any criticism, the achievements of traditional archaeology are not, of course, condemned wholesale, but it must be made clear that its principles are primarily valid for the period after 600 BC. For earlier epochs we require new approaches to solutions and another intellectual framework.

New Methods of Archaeological Research

The symbiosis between the then current Central-European world-view and the definition of classical archaeology functioned smoothly until about 1960. Triggered by the political breakdown at the end of the Second World War, which also brought ideological disintegration, the post-war years saw the spread of a realistic attitude towards antiquity. The neoclassical view of the world and the classical school rapidly lost popularity, which robbed archaeology of its original socio-political relevance. Since then it has been seeking a new identity. Recently, Ian Morris remarked, in an impressive treatise on the current state of Greek archaeology, that the noticeable loss of confidence in the ideals of classical antiquity since the 1960s has gradually led classical archaeologists to examine the general direction of their discipline. Morris continues:

> Since then [the 1960s], a general loss of faith in Hellenism has led some archaeologists working on classical Greece to question the direction the field has taken, but there has been no attempt to understand why archaeologists of different schools have such trouble communicating. I do not argue that 'traditional' archaeologists of Greece are stick-in-the-mud reactionaries, evil geniuses scheming to preserve white male supremacy, or victims of false consciousness; I simply assert the historical specificity of our archaeological practices and the need to face the changes taking place within the groups which pay for, produce and consume the results of our research. The kind of archaeology which has dominated classical Greece for a century has been extremely successful, but its audience is shrinking as part of a much wider set of changes. Fields of inquiry which are perceived, rightly or wrongly, to do little more than create a foundation myth for Western supremacy cease to be relevant within a new episteme which has no room in its regime of truth for such ideas of supremacy.

Outside the sphere of classical archaeology, even thirty years ago many researchers had begun to question its particular methodology. They demanded that archaeological research should conform to the general advance in science. The 1970s saw the development in English-speaking countries, promoted by the American archaeologist Lewis Binford, of the so-called 'New Archaeology'. This requires that archaeological field studies, like investigations in the natural sciences, take a specific objective as their starting point, and that in the course of archaeological research not only should cultural development be determined but also the prevailing conditions that influenced it. This requires both the formulation of working hypotheses and a comprehensible, methodical discussion, from which it will emerge why certain explanatory models should be given precedence. Supporters of New Archaeology take as their starting point the fact that cultures consist of complex, interconnected subsystems – such as the state of technology, social structure, ideology, trade and demography – that may be understood and reconstructed individually, and the development of which obeys specific rules, similar to the laws of nature. From a knowledge of the various subsystems – at least according to the theory – models may be developed by which the development of a culture may be predicted on a theoretical basis.

This aspect of New Archaeology has since been refuted by Chaos Theory. The parameters involved in cultural evolution are so many and complex that accurate predictions are scarcely possible. This means that New Archaeology, in the narrower sense, is invalid, and that yet other new methods have to be found. This was how process-oriented archaeology (Processual Archaeology) came to be developed, in which the various processes that create societies are recorded and individually investigated. Among these processes, there are, to give some examples, food supply, agriculture, social structure, and the interaction between human settlement and the landscape. Because of the complexity of the systems, this approach functions only when applied to small, manageable societies, such as hunters and gatherers.

The newest trend in archaeological research may best be described as context-oriented archaeology (Post-processual/Contextual Archaeology). It has been promoted, in particular, by Ian Hodder at Cambridge. Contextual Archaeology is characterised by a renewed change of direction towards the use of historical accounts, chronology and material remains of past cultures, on the grounds that these are the primary objects available for research. Accompanying this change of direction is a critical detachment in comparison with abstract theories, as well as a marked interest in the environmentally related aspects of past cultures.

What Does the Future Hold for Archaeology?

What will archaeology be like in the twenty-first century? Predictions are, admittedly, rarely correct and generally surrounded with a cloud of wishful or worried ideas, depending on the view of the world held by the individual person who is doing the predicting. But a book with the subtitle *Archaeology in the 21st Century* cannot end without risking a preview of what may transpire.

There is, of course, the possibility that archaeology will hardly change at all in the future – after all, it has carried on for about 150 years in the same manner. This means, however, that, unlike practically any other form of expertise, it is experiencing long-overdue reform. The expected changes must therefore be all the more radical.

At present, research into the Aegean Bronze Age has also fallen behind on the international level as far as its methods are concerned. In Germany, in particular, this traditional field of research has practically died out. Aegean prehistory in general and German archaeologists in particular have, in any case, failed to follow the new trends in theoretical archaeology. As a result, Germany lacks anyone who is capable of providing instruction at the level of international conferences. Aegean prehistory is faced with a choice between fading away, carrying on gently, trailing along behind international standards, or else, by making a clear break with present tradition, risking a brave leap forward and establishing new standards. What is certain is that no new beginning based on the existing structures is possible. Any system is ultimately based on flesh-and-blood human beings, and their flexibility has limits.

If we compare the state of archaeology with that of biology, then present-day excavators resemble the entomologists of the nineteenth century, who, with tropical helmet and butterfly net, roamed exotic locations searching for new species of beetle. Both taxonomists and archaeologists were primarily interested in collecting as many objects as possible from as many localities as possible – in one case it was types of animals and, in the other, it was types of artefacts. These objects were subsequently identified, described, catalogued, preserved and stored away, with the aim of recording the distribution of a species in space and time.

Sciences such as zoology, botany, geology, physics and chemistry are completely different today from what they were one hundred years ago – archaeology, on the other hand, is not. The main focus of biological research nowadays is on the biochemical processes occurring within an organism, and the interaction between cells, whereas archaeology, as it has been doing since the year dot, carries on collecting and describing an endless succession of artefacts.

Naturally, it is not former naturalists who are now pursuing molecular biology and isotopic chemistry; it is instead a completely new generation of scientists. They are not *replacing* the former taxonomy, but instead they are *complementing* it. Luckily, despite the profound change of direction in biological research in the past two hundred years, it has actually been successful in preserving and maintaining the knowledge gained about plant and animal systematics in large research museums. When applied to archaeology, this means that, on the one hand, the current structure of archaeology cannot be *changed* and, on the other, that it also cannot be *replaced* without endangering the knowledge that has already been gained. It must, however, be *expanded*, sooner or later, by the use of alternative opportunities. Only when there is more than one way of carrying out archaeology, can a wide variety of opinions and discussions ensue.

What possible approaches, then, might archaeology adopt in future? Some answers have already been determined by changes in the structure of society, industry, and other research disciplines: the elimination of ideologies and independent national initiatives, of acceptance of authority, and of the practice of linking research personalities and their opinions – all this leading to a change towards a less hierarchical structure, interdisciplinary teams of experts, creativity, innovation and a multiplicity of ideas.

Until now, the main focus of archaeological research lay almost exclusively on the history of art and on the philological aspects of past cultures – in future, the situation regarding society as a whole, as well as technical and environmental aspects, must increasingly be included. Consequently, alternative training and career opportunities are required. It is not absolutely essential for prehistorians to have A-level Latin. If they are mainly concerned with dating techniques it is far more important to have an essential knowledge of the chemistry of radio isotopes. One possible way of achieving this might be for archaeology not to be a subject in conventional university courses but to be taught at polytechnic universities. It would also be sensible to introduce a form of combined studies, that would offer graduates in specific subjects (engineering, agronomy, navigation, and so forth) the chance to apply their knowledge to the investigation of past epochs.

Similarly, it is conceivable that archaeology as a subject could be divided into conservation and research. Correspondingly efficient teams of specialists would then be in a position to carry out rescue excavations rapidly, and thus preserve as many sites as possible from destruction, without tying up research capacity in doing so. The research specialists could subsequently become involved in the interpretation of finds that had already been recovered, and thus open up a greater extent of space and time than previously.

The fragmentation of the legacy from past cultures and its research is one of the greatest obstacles to archaeological research. Admittedly, study of cultural history in principle follows the same approach to a solution that we have already encountered in the interrelationship between human beings and the environment, and in decision analysis: namely, to reduce an extraordinarily complicated subject to comprehensible sub-topics so that these may be investigated individually. Archaeology, however, in contrast to both of the fields mentioned, has not carried out the final and decisive step: that of combining the results of the specialised investigations. About thirty years ago, it was still considered good form among experts in Aegean prehistory that they should be able to give a comprehensive summary of the overall field of interest. Kurt Bittel, Carl Blegen, John Chadwick, Albrecht Goetze, Nicholas Hammond, Vasos Karageorghis, James Macqueen, James Mellaart, Nancy Sandars, Anthony Snodgrass, William Taylour, Emily Vermeule – they, and many others, all wrote readily comprehensible books on Aegean prehistory and early history. Nowadays, there seems to be no one among the experts who is either in a position to do that, or who has any interest in doing so. Because an overall view seemed in danger of being lost in an ever-greater number of detailed studies, the American Journal of Archaeology has commissioned summaries of the archaeology of Greece – what has emerged from this, however, rather than the anticipated overall view of the cultural development, has been a catalogue of catalogues.

The mere accumulation of catalogue knowledge is neither sensible nor scientific. To satisfy the demand for both meaning and scientific rigour, specialised investigations need to be brought together. This means that 'generalists' are required, who are in a position to discuss and agree on the cooperation between the experts, and also able to evaluate the results and present them in an understandable manner. Formerly, the excavation director undertook this task. But nowadays?

Today, many field projects in Aegean prehistory are *multidisciplinary*, but they must also be *interdisciplinary*, which means that instead of individual isolated expert reports, comprehensive analyses embracing whole subjects and countries need to be attempted. Expert teams must investigate past cultures, free from any ideological baggage, and this work should no longer be carried out as a national affair but as international basic research. Correspondingly, education and career opportunities also need to be international in scope.

Finally, it would probably also do no harm if, instead of the innumerable villas and neoclassical temples of science in which so many of the archaeological institutes of Mediterranean countries and Central European countries are housed, an up-to-date communications and research centre, comparable with the Max-Planck Institutes, could be set up. This could be established far from existing centres on a green-field site or, even better, on a ship. The whole logistical operation, with its laboratories, storerooms, computer equipment, accommodation, and so forth, would then be permanently and most suitably housed, and could, moreover, be used in the most flexible manner.

Traditional archaeology and neoclassical thinking were largely moulded by German scholars. In the middle of the 18th century, Johann Joachim Winckelmann founded art history, about 1820 Wilhelm von Humboldt laid the basis for the reform of the university system, and it was after 1870 that Heinrich Schliemann expanded archaeology's range of ideas about Aegean prehistory. In the twentieth century, Germany has lost its leading role. With a little courage it could win it back in the twenty-first. This is, however, probably only possible if it discards nationally oriented concepts, creates international research institutes and employs foreign experts.

Adieu, Thera!

All in all, the eruption of Thera had lasting effects. At any rate, it prompted far-reaching considerations: about a geological super-catastrophe (which wasn't one at all!), cataclysmic earthquakes, climate change, ecological destruction in antiquity, the legendary Atlantis, and, finally, the rise of classical antiquity. In my search to find out how my colleagues would accept a 'reduced' conception of the Thera catastrophe, I received violent reactions. After three world congresses on the theme of Thera, it seemed utterly inconceivable that this was *not* the greatest catastrophe in the history of humanity. To reassure myself that my interpretation of the consequences of the eruption is not wrong, I went back to visit the island again.

It is seven o'clock in the morning, and I am at Zürich Kloten airport. The friendly person at the check-in desk asks me if I am travelling alone, and when I say 'Yes', replies 'The economy class is a bit full. I am giving you a seat in the business class, in the front row. Then you will be able to tell the captain where to go!'

The captain turns out to be an enthusiastic authority on Greece. So, even during the flight, we passengers are regaled with what is in store for us. As we cross Ithaca, he tells us about the travels of Odysseus and his return after many years full of adventures. Soon afterwards, the aircraft makes its approach over Thera, and the pilot positions it to give us a spectacular view on landing. He had not made an extravagant promise. The plane glides directly over the site at Akrotiri, which gives us a marvellous view of the Minoan settlement.

Once on the island, I hire a car, so that I can inspect every possible quarry in a few days. The deposits from the Minoan eruption are not so simple to find. The highest elevations of the island consist of limestone, and thus do not differ from the geological formations on the Greek mainland. The rest of the rock volume consists of basalt and other volcanic igneous rocks from earlier eruptions. The Minoan ash and pumice layers are, by comparison, decidedly thin, and, in addition, they do not by any means cover the whole of the island group. They may be recognised by the fact that they are bright, almost white in colour, and draped across older rocks like a damp cloth. From a distance, it is easier to see this white band on the surface than it is from nearby.

Quarries, from which the ash and pumice layers are extracted, have reduced the number of sites at which the Minoan layers are easily accessible. One can see everywhere the scars left by quarrying. Old equipment, conveyor belts and loading ramps, rusty and no longer working, stick up out of the landscape.

At the northern end of the island of Therasia, a large erosion gully runs beneath the Minoan ash layers down into the interior of the caldera. The masses of ejecta have filled up this hollow, and nowhere are the Minoan layers disturbed by faults. The collapse of the caldera must have occurred long before the Minoan eruption. The ash layers have covered the already-existing relief, like a dusting of castor sugar. At many points it is even possible to find ash layers from older eruptions, which hug the inner side of the caldera. Layers from the Minoan eruption are no longer found here. The pumice stone is so light (lighter than water), that it has been carried away by rain and erosion from the almost vertical walls.

I join a cruise around the islands. From the ship it is possible to see how the surface of the interior of the caldera has changed over time. The island of Nea Kameni in the centre of the caldera consists of basalt, and is less than five hundred years old. Its rocks give the impression of being fresh and unweathered. Alongside it lies Palaea Kameni, the rocks of which are up to 2000 years old, and which appear a bit rougher and more strongly weathered. But the sheer slopes on the inner side of the caldera on the main island must be significantly older. At present, the vulcanologists are still keeping the possibility open that at least a partial caldera collapse might have occurred in Minoan times at the northern end of the island group. But the erosion forms on the inner side of the caldera all appear of about the same age. The last great eruption took place 23,000 years ago; 100,000 years ago a gigantic eruption occurred, the ash layers from which are distributed over the whole of the central and eastern Mediterranean. On the latter occasion, the volcano ejected so much lava that it must almost certainly have produced a caldera collapse. This is probably how Thera was created, as we know it today – and as the Minoans knew it.

The Minoan layers, where they are present, are merely a few metres thick, which, by geological standards is fairly modest – as the American vulcanologist Floyd McCoy established almost twenty years ago. Nothing suggests that the greatest natural catastrophe in the history of humanity could ever have occurred here, of all places.

I visit the site at Akrotiri more than once. In doing so, what I find particularly interesting are the surroundings of the Minoan settlement. During an official guided tour I learn that only three per cent of it is known. What might the rest have been like? As always, I climb to the top of a hill, to obtain a view over the immediate surroundings. Slightly to the west of the site, a valley stretches into the interior. It is now covered in Minoan ash layers, a few metres thick, but before they were deposited it would have been suitable for a harbour. While, from the top of the hill, in the stifling heat, among the thyme and holm oaks, I ponder on the appearance of the Minoan landscape, the thought comes to me that on Thera two interest groups are getting in each other's way, although they actually complement one another. On the one hand there are the quarry owners, who, for the time being, are forbidden from carrying out any work, and on the other hand, there are the archaeologists, who, because of the thick layers of ash, can hardly make any headway with their excavations. Would it not be possible to let the quarry owners remove the ash layers, but as soon as any archaeological remains are found, hand work on the site over to the archaeologists?

In the afternoon I spend some time in the main town, Phira, one of the most picturesque places in Greece and one frequently depicted on postcards and calendars. Some of the cafés and hotels stick out over the edge of the cliff on the inner side of the caldera. At any time of day and under any lighting conditions, but particularly in the evening twilight, there is a fabulous view across the enormous collapsed centre of the ancient volcano.

Near the cliff, a businessman from Thera, Peter Nomikos, built a conference centre, in which the third Thera Conference was held in 1989. The new building stands on the site of a palatial building, which was irreparably damaged in the earthquake of 1956. However, the tunnels that belonged to the old building, and in which the owner formerly stored wine, have been preserved, and are now accessible from the conference centre. At the time of my visit, there is an exhibition of wall-paintings from Akrotiri in these passages. Using new archaeometric procedures, they have succeeded in reproducing the paintings, together with the texture of the surface, so not only was I able to see the originals in Athens, but also high-quality copies in this exhibition.

I am particularly interested in the depiction of a procession of ships at the West House – a grand building, which many suppose to be the home of an admiral. A fleet of magnificently decorated ships is setting sail from one port and sailing across the sea to another city. There has been a lot of puzzling over which two cities are depicted in the frieze. Marinatos maintained that the site of departure was somewhere in Libya; others have suggested an island in the immediate vicinity of Thera. My first thought is Crete. A city surrounded by rivers right on the coast of Crete? Perhaps Malia?

The place towards which the ships are heading, is, to all appearances, Akrotiri. Obviously the wall-painting depicts a feast-day that was particularly important for the city, or for the owner of the house. Could it have been a wedding party, accompanying the bride to Akrotiri? The harbour that they are entering is clearly recognisable. It is definitely similar to the buried valley immediately west of Akrotiri. From the wall-painting one can see where the main buildings in the city must have been sited: right beside the harbour.

After visiting the exhibition, I stroll along the edge of the caldera to the archaeological museum, which, according to a bronze plaque, is dedicated to the German 'Philhellene, Freiherr Hiller von Gaertringen'. At the very end of the 19th century, out of his own finances, he excavated ancient Thera at Messa Vouno, a high, windswept hill at the eastern tip of the island. Archaic sculptures and geometrically decorated vases are on display in the rooms.

There, amongst a large tour group at one end of the gallery, I catch a fleeting glimpse of a familiar silhouette. Can that really be my old geology teacher, Heinz Malz from the Senckenberg Museum in Frankfurt? Although

I find it hard to believe in such a coincidence, I find somewhere to stand where the members of the tour group will have to pass me in single file. And it really is him. What a surprise! Many years ago, I began my career in his micropalaeontology department, and subsequently we remained in contact. If I needed an expert in dealing with microfossils, there he was. We had written one or two papers together. In the meantime, he had retired, and now had the time and leisure for Mediterranean cruises.

Heinz Malz is as pleasantly surprised to meet me. 'We were just at Akrotiri,' he says, in a great hurry because he has to leave immediately so that he does not lose the group. 'The woman who guided us round the site said that the excavators used to believe that this was Atlantis. But, listen to this: in the meantime there has been a new theory, which, she said, is much more plausible, according to which Atlantis was really Troy.' Perhaps new discoveries are accepted faster than expected, I think to myself. But Heinz Malz continues: 'And this theory, so she said, had been proposed by a *Greek*. But I didn't say anything.'

When Heinz Malz had said goodbye, I recall some incidents from when I was a trainee. What a lot of practical science I had learnt in those six months! On one occasion, I proudly presented him with the drawing of a microfossil, on which I had worked for a whole day, and all he said was: 'Please don't expect me to praise your first attempt.' When I began to study geology some years later, another geology teacher gave me *Homo Faber*, by Max Frisch, with the dedication, the style of which I seemed to know: 'Don't just study – think about it as well!'

Bibliography

The information given in the individual chapters is primarily based on the following publications:

The Eruption of Thera

Buckland, Paul C., Dugmore, Andrew J., and Edwards, Kevin J. (1997), 'Bronze Age myths? Volcanic activity and human response in the Mediterranean and North Atlantic regions', *Antiquity*, 71, 581–93.

Driessen, Jan and Macdonald, Cohn F. (1997), *The Troubled Island – Minoan Crete Before and After the Santorini Eruption*, Aegaeum 17, Liege: R. Laffineur, 1–284.

Friedrich, Walter L. (1994), *Feuer im Meer – Vulkanismus und die Naturgeschichte der Insel Santorin*, Heidelberg: Spektrum Akademischer Verlag, 1–256.

Hardy, David A. (ed.) (1989), *Thera and the Aegean World III*, London: The Thera Foundation, 3 vols.

Lohmann, Hans (1998), 'Die Santorin-Katastrophe – ein archäologischer Mythos?', in Stuttgarter Kolloquium zur Historischen Geographie des Altertums 6 (1996), *Naturkatastrophen in der antiken Welt*, Olshausen, Eckart and Sonnabend, Holger (eds), Stuttgart: Franz Steiner Verlag, 337–63.

Marinatos, Spyridon (1939), 'The Volcanic Destruction of Minoan Crete', *Antiquity*, 13, 425–39.

Page, Denys L. (1970), *The Santorini Volcano and the Desolation of Minoan Crete*, London: The Society for the Promotion of Hellenic Studies, Supplement Paper 12, 1–45.

Zangger, Eberhard (1998), 'Naturkatastrophen in der ägäischen Bronzezeit. Forschungsgeschichte, Signifikanz und Beurteilungskriterien', in Stuttgarter Kolloquium zur Historischen Geographie des Altertums 6 (1996), *Naturkatastrophen in der antiken Welt*, Olshausen, Eckart and Sonnabend, Holger (eds), Stuttgart: Franz Steiner Verlag, 211–41.

Earthquake

Ambraseys, Nicolas N. (1973), 'Earth science in archaeology and history', *Antiquity*, 47, 227–9.

Evans, Arthur (1928), *The Palace of Minos at Knossos: Fresh Lights on Origins and*

External Relations: The Restoration in Town and Palace After Seismic Catastrophe Towards Close of M.M. III, and the Beginnings of the New Era, London: Macmillan, 1–390.

Soren, David (1988), 'The day the world ended at Kourion – Reconstructing an ancient earthquake', *National Geographic*, **174**, 30–53.

Stiros, Stathis and Jones, Richard E. (eds) (1996), *Archaeoseismology*, Athens: Fitch Laboratory Occasional Papers, 1–268.

Watrous, L. Vance (1994), 'Review of Aegean Prehistory III: Crete from earliest prehistory through the Protopalatial Period', *American Journal of Archaeology*, **98**, 695–753.

Climate

Carpenter, Rhys (1966), *Discontinuity in Greek Civilization*, Cambridge: Cambridge University Press, 1–80.

Davis, Jack (ed.) (1998), *From Homer's Sandy Pylos to the Battle of Navarino: An Archaeological Survey*, Austin: Texas University Press.

Drews, Robert (1993), *The End of the Bronze Age – Changes in Warfare and the Catastrophe ca. 1200 B.C.*, Princeton: Princeton University Press, 1–252.

McDonald, William A. and Rapp, George R. (1972), *The Minnesota Messenia Expedition – Reconstructing a Bronze Age Regional Environment*, Minneapolis: The University of Minnesota Press, 1–338.

Techniques

Noack, Wolfgang (1997), 'Geoarchäologie aus dem Weltraum – Wenn der Satellit den Spaten ersetzt', *Geospektrum*, **1**, 11–15.

Zangger, Eberhard (1993), *The Geoarchaeology of the Argolid*, Berlin: Gebrüder Mann Verlag, 1–149.

Zangger, Eberhard, Leiermann, Horst, Noack, Wolfgang and Kuhnke, Falko (1997), 'A 21st Century Approach to the Reconnaissance and Reconstruction of Archaeological Landscapes', in *Aegean Strategies: Studies of Culture and Environment on the European Fringe*, Kardulias, P. Nick and Shutes, Mark T. (eds), Maryland: Rowman and Littlefield, Savage, 9–32.

Zangger, Eberhard, Yazvenko, Sergei B., Timpson, Michael F., Kuhnke, Falko and Knauss, Jost (1997), 'The Pylos Regional Archaeological Project, Part 2: Landscape Evolution and Site Preservation', *Hesperia*, **66** (4), 549–641.

Humans and the Environment

Runnels, Curtis (1995), 'Umweltzerstörung im griechischen Altertum', *Spektrum der Wissenschaft* (May), 84–8.

Sieferle, Rolf Peter (1997), *Rückblick auf die Natur: Eine Geschichte des Menschen und seiner Umwelt*, München: Luchterhand, 1–233.

Zangger, Eberhard (1991), 'Prehistoric coastal environments in Greece: The vanished landscapes of Dimini Bay and Lake Lerna', *Journal of Field Archaeology*, 18 (1), 1–15.

Zangger, Eberhard (1992), 'Neolithic to present soil erosion in Greece', in *Past and Present Soil Erosion*, Bell, Martin and Boardman, John (eds), Oxford: Oxbow Books, 133–47.

Zangger, Eberhard (1995), 'Geology and the Development of the Cultural Landscapes in *Africa Proconsularis – Regional Studies in the Segermes Valley of Northern Tunisia*, Dietz, Søren, Sebai, Laila Ladjimi and Ben Hassen, Habib (eds), Copenhagen: The Carlsberg Foundation and The Danish Research Council for the Humanities, 57–83.

Engineering Knowledge

Haliman, Frithjof (1994), *Das Rätsel der Labyrinthe*, Ardagger, Austria: Michael Damböck, 1–188.

Kern, Hermann (1982), *Labyrinthe – Erscheinungsformen und Deutungen: 5000 Jahre Gegenwart eines Urbildes*, München: Prestel Verlag, 1–492.

Knauss, Jost (1996), *Argolische Studien: Alte Straßen – alte Wasserbauten*, Berichte der Versuchsanstalt Obernach und des Lehrstuhls für Wasserbau und Wassermengenwirtschaft der Technischen Universität München 77, München, 1–236.

Knauss, Jost (1997), 'Agamemnoneion phréar – Der Stausee der Mykener', *Antike Welt*, 381–95.

Knight, W.F. Jackson (1932), 'Maze symbolism and the Trojan game', *Antiquity*, 6, 445–58.

Leiermann, Horst (1994) *Technische Rekonstruktion der Planung alter Städte*, Stuttgart: Karl Krämer Verlag, 1–110.

Zangger, Eberhard (1994), 'Landscape changes around Tiryns during the Bronze Age', *American Journal of Archaeology*, 98 (2), 189–212.

Zangger, Eberhard (1995) 'Systematische Landschaftskontrolle im antiken Griechenland', *Spektrum der Wissenschaft*, (May), 88–91.

Atlantis

Brandenstein, Wilhelm (1951), *Atlantis: Größe und Untergang eines geheimnisvollen Inselreiches*, Wien: Gerold.

Mann, Albrecht (1983), *Ringwälle, Atlantis und Utopien*, Bau- und stadtgeschichtliche Lehrstoffe 2, Aachen: Fachgebiet Baugeschichte an der RWTH Aachen, 1–171.

Zangger, Eberhard (1992), *Atlantis – Eine Legende wird entziffert*, München: Droemer Verlag, 1–336.

Zangger, Eberhard (1993), 'Plato's Atlantis account: A distorted recollection of the Trojan War', *Oxford Journal of Archaeology*, **18** (1), 77–87.

Zangger, Eberhard (1998), 'Das Atlantis=Troja-Konzept. Auf den Spuren einer versunkenen Kultur in Westkleinasien', *Vierteljahrsschrift der Naturforschenden Gesellschaft in Zürich*, **143** (1), 13–23.

Troy

Raban, Avner (1997), 'Near Eastern Harbours: 13th–7th centuries B.C.E.', in *Mediterranean People in Transition – 13th to Early 10th centuries B.C.E.*, Gittin, S., Mazar, A and Stein, E. (eds), Jerusalem.

Werner, Walter (1993), 'Der Kanal von Korinth und seine Vorlaufer', *Das Logbuch*, Sonderheft, 1–71.

Zangger, Eberhard, Timpson, Michael, Yazvenko, Sergei and Leiermann, Horst (1998), 'Searching for the Ports of Troy', in *Environmental Reconstruction in Mediterrannean Landscape Archaeology*, Leveau, Philipp, Walsh, Kevin and Barker, Graeme (eds), Mediterranean Landscape Archaeology 2, Oxford: Oxbow.

Zick, Michael (1997), 'Troja – Neuer Streit um die Wiege unserer Kultur', *bild der wissenschaft*, (December), 50–58.

Western Asia Minor

Bossert, Helmut Theodor (1946), *Asia*, Literarische Fakultät der Universität Istanbul; Forschungsinstitut für altvorderasiatische Kulturen 323, Universite Matbaasi Komandit Sti., Beyoglu-Tilnelbasi, Istanbul, 1–184.

Joukowsky, Martha Sharp (1996), *Early Turkey – Anatolian Archaeology from Prehistory through the Lydian Period*, Dubuque, Iowa: Kendall Hunt, 1–455.

Zangger, Eberhard, (1994), *Ein neuer Kampf um Troia – Archäologie in der Krise*, München: Droemer Verlag, 1–352.

Zangger, Eberhard (1995), 'Who were the Sea People?', *Aramco World* (May/June), 21–31.

The Dark Age

Ekschmitt, Werner (1989), *Weltmodelle: Griechische Weltbilder von Thales bis Ptolemäus*, Mainz: Philipp von Zabern, 1–191.

Niemeyer, Hans Georg (1990), 'Die Phönizier im Mittelmeerraum', in *Die Phönizier im Zeitalter Homers*, Ulrich Gehrig and Hans Georg Niemeyer (eds), Mainz: Philipp von Zabern, 97–103.

Prayon, Friedhelm (1996), *Die Etrusker – Geschichte, Religion, Kunst*, München: C.H. Beck, 1–127.

Snodgrass, Anthony (1971), *The Dark Age of Greece – An Archaeological Survey of the Eleventh to the Eighth Centuries* B C, Edinburgh: Edinburgh University Press, 1–456.

Uhlig, Helmut (1991), *Die Mutter Europas – Ursprünge abendändischer Kultur in Alt-Anatolien*, Bergisch Gladbach: Gustav Lübbe Verlag, 1–287.

Archaeology Yesterday, Today and Tomorrow

Bernal, Martin (1987), *Black Athena*, New Brunswick; Rutgers University Press, 1–575.

Bernbeck, Reinhard (1997), *Theorien in der Archäologie*, Tübingen: A. Francke, 1–404.

Marchand, Suzanne L. (1996), *Down from Olympus – Archaeology and Philhellenism in Germany, 1750–1970*, Princeton: Princeton University Press, 1–400.

Morris, Ian (1994), 'Archaeologies of Greece', in *Classical Greece: Ancient Histories and Modern Analogies*, Ian Morris (ed.), Cambridge: Cambridge University Press, 8–47.

Trigger, Bruce G. (1989), *A History of Archaeological Thought*, Cambridge: Cambridge University Press, 1–500.

Index

Aegean prehistory
  Archaeology 22, 246
  chronology
    Evans 20–21
    Platon 21–2
aerial photographs 99
agriculture
  animal products 118
  deforestation 119
  'Fertile Crescent' 117–18
  migratory 118
  Neolithic 116–17
  ploughs, introduction 119, 198
  terracing 120
  water management
    irrigation 113, 126, 129–30, 197
    reclamation 130
Akkadian cuneiform 200, 226
Akrotiri
  ash deposits 251
  excavations 13, 251
  wall-paintings 251–2
Albania 121–3
alphabets see scripts
Amnisos
  destruction date 30
  excavations 29–30
  Thera eruption 30, 32
  'tsunmami damage' theory 24, 30–32
Anatolia see Asia Minor
Apodoulou 60–61
Apollonia, conservation 122–3
Ararat, Mount 215
archaeology
  see also geoarchaeology

absolute knowledge, claims 241
Aegean prehistory
  development 22
  future of 246
  conservation 247
  context-orientated 245
  crises, over-emphasis on 141
  discoveries, reception of 243
  as European identity search 15–16, 239–40
  evidence, adoption of 242
  extensive surveys 92
  field walking 75–6, 87–8, 92
  finds 145–6
  funding 237
  geology, relationship 22
  historical aims 239
  historical legacy 238–9
  individual initiatives 243–4
  information dissemination 248–9
  intensive surveys 92
  interdisciplinary approaches 73, 93, 247–8
  international co-operation 77–8
  methodologies
    archaic 241
    model 244–5
    non-scientific 241
    science comparison 246
  multidisciplinary approaches 73, 93, 248
  national policies 238–9
  permits 91
  philhellenic tradition 239–40
  post-processual 245

archaeology – *contd*
  processual 245
  research 247
  security issues 90
  site protection 89
  social context 90, 105
  as treasure hunting 89
  and unanswered questions 211–12
archaeometry 93
Asia, etymology 213–14
Asia Minor
  agriculture, ploughs introduced 198
  bronze 198–9
  city states
    allied 96, 198
    defences 199–200
    destruction 200
  coinage, development 223–4
  cultural renaissance 208
  cultures
    Early Iron Age 214
    Late Bronze Age 214–15
  earthquakes 63
  Greece
    city states 221–212
    influences on 222, 223
    trade 221
  immigration 196, 198
  intellectual developments 225
  language, common 198
  natural resources 208–9
  settlements, Late Bronze Age 204
  states 202
  topography 195–6
  trade
    metals 209
    minerals 198–9, 209
Assyrians 200
'Atlantean cross' 184, *184*
Atlanteans 169
Atlantis, Hellinikos of Lesbos 151
Atlantis
  as allegory 155
  bulls, sacrifice 176–8

canals 184–5
destruction
  Greek army 156
  sinking 156
  textual significance 167
Egyptian origins 28, 148, 150–51, 158, 160–61
etymology 169
Greece, contemporary 159–61
guardian, Poseidon 170
Hellinikos of Lesbos 151
historical veracity 152–3
hydraulic engineering 184–5
legend, transmission *152*
locations, supposed 148, 150, 151–2
mineral resources 173–4
as morality tale 153–4
orichalcum 174–6
Pillars of Heracles, location 164–7
Plato
  Critias 148–50, 168–9
  description 168–9
  destruction 167
  inconsistencies 154–5, 167
  knowledge base 155
  Minoan culture 28
  retelling 150–51
  scientific observations 155
  Timaeus 158–9
  unfinished manuscript 178
  as Utopia 153–4
royal succession 170–1
Solon 148, 150–51, *152*
theories
  Carthage 158
  Helike 158
  Minoan culture 28, 158
  Syracuse 158
  Thera 6, 28–9, 158
trade 172–3
translation errors 161
  dating 162–3
  island 163–4
  locations 162, 164–7, *165*
  size 167

Troy, correspondence 165–6, 168, 169–72, 173–4, 176–80, 211
'Atlantologists' 157, 159
Atlas, etymology 169

Beycesultan 199
Blegen, Carl, Troy, excavations 54, 72, 73
brass, orichalcum 174–6
bronze
  decline 231
  ores, trading 198–9
  Urartu culture 216
Bronze Age [Late]
  Asia Minor 214–15, 231
  eastern Mediterranean 8
bulls, sacrifice, Atlantis 176–8

calderas
  collapse 5
  formation, theories 23
  Thera, collapse 5, 13–14, 23, 37–8, 250
Canaan 230
canals
  Arcadia 130
  Atlantis 184–5
  Etruscan 228–9
  Tiryns 127, 128
  Troy 185–6, 187–9
Carians
  domicile 218–19
  Miletus 219, 221
  origins 219–20
  script 220
  'Sea People' 219
Carpenter, Rhys 72, 79–80
Carthage, Atlantis legend 158
Çatal Hüyük 197
catastrophe theory 53
causal relationships 44–5, 80–81
Çayönü 196
city states
  Asia Minor 96, 198, 199–200
  Greece 221–2

climate changes
  causes, volcanic eruptions 5
  and cultural changes 69–70, 79–80
  effects, vegetation 74–5
  evidence for 79–80
  geographic names 71–2
  mass extinctions 116
  pollen analysis 74–5, 76–7
coinage, development, Asia Minor 223–4
conservation 247
Creation, The 16, 17
Crete
  see also Minoan Culture
  earthquakes 47–9
  famines 70–71
  history 64
  Minoan sites 31
  tsunamis 35
Croesus 194–5, 217, 218
cultural changes
  Bronze/Iron Ages 206–7
  catastrophe theories 53–4
  climate changes
    evidence 79–80
    theories 69–70
  earthquakes
    evidence 56–7, 63, 64–5
    theories 49, 54–6
  invasions 65–6
  natural disasters, link proposed 14, 20
  post Dark Age 207–8
  simultaneous 66
  stimulus 208

dams, Tiryns 127–9, 128
Dark Age
  drought 70
  duration 207
  renaissance following 207–8
dating methods
  dendrochronology 44
  ice cores 43–4, 43

dating methods – *contd*
  radiocarbon 42–3
  volcanic gas composition 13, 42–3
deforestation 79, 119
  soil erosion 110–11, 119–20
Democritus 225
dendrochronology, volcanic eruption
    dating 44
discoveries, archaeological 243
droughts
  Dark Age 70
  famine, effects of 69–70

earthquakes
  Asia Minor, 1688 63
  Crete 47–9
  cultural changes
    evidence 56–7, 63, 64–5
    theories 49, 54–6
  effects
    buildings 54
    ground 52, 62
    localised 63
    societies 61–2, 63
  fault lines 63
  fires following 62
  Mycenae 55
  origins, Greek science 224
  seismic waves 61
ecological balance, loss of 120
Egypt
  Atlantis legend, source 28, 148, 150–
    51, 158, 160–61
  Greece, trade 130
  Peleset settlements 230
environment
  changes
    adaptation 114
    agricultural demands 117–18
  deforestation 110–11, 119–20
  ecological balance 120
  human demands 109–10
  human interaction 112, 247–8
  natural resources 108–9

protection 109
Etruscan culture
  language, origins 228
  origins 227–8
  pottery finds, Lemnos 228
  water management 228–9
Europe, etymology 234
Evans, Sir Arthur
  Aegean prehistory, chronology 20–21
  catastrophe theory 53–4
  earthquake, Crete 47
  Knossos excavations 20–21
evolution, human 114–15
excavations, selection 89
extinctions, mass 114, 116

famines
  Crete 70–71
  evidence lacking 79–80
  Lydia 71
  social effects of 70
'Fertile Crescent'
  agriculture, development 117
  early settlement 115–16
field walking, surface surveys 75–6, 87–
    8, 92
finds, assumptions about 145–6
forests
  felling, agriculture 119
  fires 119
Fouqué, Ferdinand
  Santorin et ses éruptions 9–10, 11
  Therasia, excavations 11–13, *12*
funding, archaeology 237

geoarchaeology
  evidence base 186
  foundation 16–17
  landscape reconstruction 111
  methodology
    proposition 93
    aims 93–4
    site choice 94
    documentary research 94–5

topography 95, 98–100
  site inspection 95
  specialists 95
  management structure 96
  working methods 96–7
  remote sensing 98–101
  field walking 101–2
  boreholes 101–2
  field magnetometry 102
  soil resistance 102–3, 104
  multinational teamwork 97
  research methods 58–9
  site surveys, aerial 98–9
  technology, limitations 103–5
  term introduced 73–4
Geographical Information Systems
  [GIS] 95, 98
geologists, international fraternity 27–8
geology, archaeology, relationship 22
glass working, Phoenician 232
Gordian knot 194
Gordium, excavations 216
Gordius 194
Gournia 33
grave goods, wealth indicators 221
Greece, working permits 91
Greece [ancient]
  Aegean influence 211
  alphabet, origins 225–6
  Asia Minor
    artistic influences 222
    city states in 221–2
    intellectual influences 225
    military influences 223
    trade 221
  Atlantis, contemporary 159–61
  Egypt, trade 130
  intellectual studies, origins 225
  philosophy schools, Miletus 221
  place names, derivations 170, 220

harbours
  artificial 133–5, 134, 135
    scouring 134, 188–9, 189, 228

Hattusa 203, 205
Helike 62–3
  as Atlantis 158
Hellespont, Atlantis legend 164–5
Hellinikos of Lesbos, Atlantis 151
Heraklion, earthquake, 1926 47–8
Herodotus
  Battle of Thermopylae 107
  Carians 219–20
  famines 70–71
  King Minos 22
Hittite empire
  army, defensive ring 139
  collapse
    parallels 205
    Thera eruption theory 41
    war 205–6
  extent 202–3
  Luwian culture 203
  Multi-ethnicity 203
  origins 200–1
  population 202
  subjugation by 201–2
  trade 201, 209–10
hunter-gatherers 116

ice core dating, volcanic eruptions 42–
  3
Individualism, suppression of 237–8
International Thera Conferences 29, 41,
  65–6, 249
invasions, cultural changes 65–6
Ionian migration 220
iron, rise of 231–2
Iron Age [Early]
  Asia Minor 214, 231
  Mediterranean 227

Karum 200
Knossos
  excavations, Evans 20–21
  'tsunmami damage' theory 24
Kopais 130
Kos, Andrew 25, 27

Krakatau, eruption 18–19, 38
Kussara 200–1

labyrinths
   'Atlantean cross' 184, *184*
   derivation 136–7
   form 137, *137*
   present day 140
   'Trojan Dance' 138–40
   urban planning 136–7
land reclamation 130
land-use, geological determination 112–13
languages
   common, unifying influence 198
   Etruscan 228
   Luwian 198
Leake, Capt William M. 193–4, 195
Leleges 219
Limantepe 199–200
Linear-B 72–3, 207
Luwian culture 203
   language 198
   script 226
Lydia
   famine 71
   origins 217
   Persians conquer 218
   Sardis 217–18

magnetic field, Earth's, variations 99
magnetometry
   aerial 99–100
   field 102
Malia
   destruction, war 32
   'tsunmami damage' theory 24, 32
Marinatos, Spiridion
   Amnisos, excavations 29–30
   Minoan culture, destruction
      theories 23–5, 28
Medes 218
Mersin 197
Messenia *see* Pylos

metals
   bronze 198–9, 216, 231
   coinage 223–4
   iron, early use 231–2
   orichalcum 174–6
   trade in 173, 209
Midas, King 194
Midea, destruction, earthquake theory
   56
migrations
   cultures, new 206
   mass 206, 227
Miletus 219, 221
minerals, trade 198–9, 209
Minoan culture
   see also Amnisos; Gournia; Malia;
      Mochlos; Niru Chani; Zakros
   Atlantis theory 28, 158
   chronology
      Evans 20–21
      Platon 21–2
   collapse 40–41
      Marinatos 23–5, 28, 40
      theories 20
      Thera eruption 40–41
      tsunami 24–5, 28, 37–8
   parallel developments 67
   sites, NE Crete *31*
Minos, King 22
Mochlos 33
Monaghan, Joseph J. 7, 34–5
Monastiriki
   agriculture 51, 58
   destruction, earthquake theory 52
   excavations 49–50
   irrigation 59–60
   layout 57–8
   purpose 56
   topography 50–51, 59–60
Mursili II, King 201
Mycenae
   defences 210
   earthquake damage 55
   food supplies 73
   trade, Hittite empire 209–10

Mycenaean culture
  see also Mycenae; Tiryns
  assessment of 210–11
  Atlantis legend 159–60
  collapse, theories 55–6
  contraction 220
  'golden age' 209–10
  Midea 56
  script, Linear-B 72–3
  'sea people' 229
  trade 132, 209
    pottery 210
  Trojan War 159–60
  water management 126–30

Nag Hammadi 85–6
natural disasters, cultural changes 14,
  54–6, 80–81
Nestor, King 72
Nevali Cori 196
Nile Valley, hilltop settlements 87–8
Niru Chani 24, 32
nuées ardentes 5
  modelling 34
  tsunamis 34–5

Olympia, excavations 17
orichalcum 174–6

palynology *see* pollen analysis
Peleset
  'sea people' 229
  settlements 230
Pellegino, Charles
  Thera eruption
    cultural changes 6
    Hittite empire collapse 41
  tsunami theory 30–31
philhellenic archaeology 239–40
Philistines, origins 229
Phoenician culture
  archaeological remains 230–31
  Canaan 230
  documentary sources 233–4

glass working 232
hydraulic engineering 233
maritime bases 232–3
origins 229
political organisation 230
script 226
settlement sites 233
trade 229, 231, 232
Phrygian culture
  conquest of 217
  Gordium 216
  migration 217
  pottery 216
Pillars of Heracles *165*
  Hellespont 165–6
  Straits of Gibraltar 164–5
place names
  Anatolian 220
  Greece, derivation 170
Plato
  Atlantis
    as allegory 155
    Critias 148–50, 168–9
    description 168–9
    destruction 167
    inconsistancies 154–5, 167
    knowledge base 155
    Minoan culture 28
    as morality tale 153–4
    retelling 150–51
    scientific observations 155
    Timaeus 158–9
    unfinished manuscript 178
    as Utopia 153–4
  use of simile 153
Platon, Nokolas
  Minoan culture
    chronology system 21–2
    tsunami theory 28, 33
ploughs, introduction 119
pollen analysis
  evidence
    agriculture 78–9
    climate changes 74–5, 76–7
  methodology 78

Pompeii, excavations 14
populations
    densities 220–21
    fluctuations 120
pre-classical cultures, discovery of 17–
        18, 210–11
pumice deposits
    Amnisos 30
    Thera 37–8
Pylos
    agriculture 78–9
    climate, pollen analysis 76–7
    deforestation 79
    harbour, artificial 133–5, *134, 135*
    Linear-B tablets 72–3
Pythagoras 225

radiocarbon dating, volcanic deposits
        42–3
reconstructions
    see also technical reconstructions
    erosion factors 107–8
    landscapes 111
research
    archaeology, future 247
    philosophy of dissent 238
Rhodes, volcanic ash deposits 38–9

Santorini *see* Thera
Sardis, excavation 217–18
satellite surveys
    European Remote Sensing satellites
        [ERS] 98–9
    Landsat 98
    SPOT 98
Schliemann, Heinrich
    methodology 241–2
    myths about 15
    Troy, search for 14–15
science, methodologies 246–7
scripts
    Akkadian cuneiform 200, 226
    alphabetic 226
    Carian 220

Greek alphabet 225–6
    Linear-B 72–3, 207
    Luwian 226
    Phoenician 226
    Ugaritic 226
sea levels
    interglacial 115
    Minoan era 36–7
'sea people'
    invasions 206
    origins 206, 211, 229
        Carians 219
        Mycenaeans 229
        Peleset 229
    Ugarit, destruction 54–5, 205
settlements
    agriculture, demands of 117–18
    environmental demands 109–11
    location 110
    vegetation, control 118
ships, overland transport 187–8
sites
    destruction 91
    discovery, field walking 75–6, 87–8
Skourta Plain 120–21, *121*
soil erosion
    deforestation 110–11, 119–20
    deposition 111
    dry areas 60
    prevention 120
    Zaghouan valley 132
soil formation 112–13
Solon, Atlantis legend 148, 150–51, *152*
stratigraphy, early theories 16
Suez Canal 10, 17
surface surveys
    extensive 92
    field walking 75–6, 87–8, 92
    intensive 92
Syracuse, Atlantis legend 158

technical reconstructions
    process 125–6
    Troy *191*

technology
  development 125
  geoarchaeology, limitations 103–5
Thales of Miletus 224–5
Thebes, harbour 133
Thera [island]
  famine 71
  geology 249–50
  volcanic eruptions
    ash deposits 38–9, *39*
    dating 42–4, *43*, 250
    effect 3–5
    Minoan collapse theory 39–41, 39–42
    pumice deposits 27–8
    records 9–11
    tsunamis 36
Thera [island group] *9*
  Atlantis, theories 6, 28–9, 158
  caldera
    collapse 5, 250
    dating 23, 37–8, 250
  emigration from 33
Therasia, excavations 11–13, *12*
Thermopylae
  Battle of 107
  Pass, erosion 107–8
Thucydides, on Mycenae 210
Tiryns
  canals 127, *128*
  dams 127–9, *128*
  destruction, earthquake theory 55
topography
  aerial photographs 99
  deposition 111
  erosion 60, 107–8, 110–11, 119–20
  initial surveys 95, 98–9
  magnetometry
    aerial 99–100
    field 102
  satellites
    ERS 98–9
    Landsat 98
    SPOT 98

soil resistance 102–3, *104*
'Trojan Dance', labyrinths 138–40
Troy
  Atlantis
    archaeological significance 181
    correspondence 165–6, 168, 169–72, 173–4, 176–80, 211
  canals 185–6, 187–8
  discovery of 14–15
  earthquakes 54
  excavations 54, 72
  extent 182–3
  foundation, mythical 169
  harbour 188–90, *189*
  labyrinths 136, 137–8, 138–40, 183–4
  legacy of 190
  mineral wealth 173–4
  plan 183
  reconstruction
    Atlantis model 181
    technical *191*
  Schliemann 14–15
  topography *182*
  trade 173, *174*
  wars, Mycenea 159–60
tsunamis
  causes
    nuées ardentes 34–5
    volcanic eruptions 5–6, 18–20
  computer modelling 7
  Crete, evidence 30, 32, 33–4, 35–6
  deposition by 26
  effects 19, 34
  evidence of 26–7, 36
  Krakatau eruption 38

Ubar, discovery of 99, 103
Ugarit
  destruction 54–5, 205
  script 226
Urartu culture
  agriculture 216
  location 215
  states 216

urban planning
    constraints 136
    labyrinths 136–7
    sewers 135–6
    water supply 135–6

vegetation
    historical determination 113
    pollen analysis 74–5, 76–7
volcanoes
    see also calderas
    eruptions
        ash deposits 38–9, *39*
        climate changes 5
        dating 42–4, *43*
        Krakatau 18–19
        towns 3–5
        tsunamis 5–6, 18–20
    gases, dating 13, 42–3

water management
    agriculture
        irrigation 59–60, 113, 126, 129–30, 197
        reclamation 130
    Atlantis 184–5
    canals 127, *128*, 130, 228–9
    dams 127–9, *128*
    Etruscan culture 228–9
    harbours, scouring 134, 188–9, *189*, 228
    land reclamation 130
    Mycenean culture 126–30
    sewers 136
writing *see* scripts

Zaghouan valley, land management 130–32
Zakros, tsunamis, evidence 33–4